HEALING HANDS

HEALING HANDS

J. Bernard Hutton
in collaboration with
George Chapman

Virgin

This edition first published in Great Britain in 1995 by
Virgin Books
an imprint of Virgin Publishing Ltd
332 Ladbroke Grove
London W10 5AH

First published in Great Britain in 1966 by
WH Allen & Company Ltd
Second impression 1966
Third impression 1967
Fourth impression 1969
Fifth impression 1971

Second (revised) edition 1978

A catalogue for this book is available from the British Library

ISBN 0 86369 893 X

Typeset by SX Composing Ltd, Rayleigh, Essex
Printed in Great Britain by
Cox & Wyman Ltd, Reading, Berks.

Contents

Dedication

I might have gone blind; I might have died. That neither happened is due to Pearl, my wife, who 'found' William Lang for me and to whom I dedicate this book in gratitude.

Foreword

Healing Hands was first published in May 1966 and revised in July 1978. Long before this book was written I was quite a well known healer and many articles had appeared in various national papers about Dr Lang and myself. But by writing this book, which was translated into several languages, J. Bernard Hutton spread the Chapman/Lang partnership across the globe.

Healing Hands was a great success and I know Joe, who passed into spirit some years ago, would be delighted to know that it has been re-published. Thanks must also be given to my son Michael, and to Virgin Publishing for making this possible.

George Chapman
1995

MIRACLE: a marvellous event occurring within human experience which cannot have been brought about by human power or by the operation of any natural agency, and must therefore be ascribed to the special intervention of the Deity or of some supernatural being; chiefly an act (e.g. of healing) exhibiting control over the laws of nature, and serving as evidence that the agent is either divine or is specially favoured by God.

The Oxford English Dictionary
(1961 reprinted edition)

Introduction

THIS IS a most unusual book written with the skill of an accomplished author about 'spirit healing', a subject which might be in danger of unenlightened dismissal without a preliminary introduction.

It is the true story of 'miracles' wrought by spirit healing through the devoted partnership of two men, a famous consultant surgeon William Lang, who lived in the nineteenth and early twentieth century, and who is known to a number of doctors living today, and his medium George Chapman, who is devoting his life to the mediumship by which Dr Lang, as he likes to be known, and his spirit colleagues are able to apply healing forces which are not within the range of ordinary treatment. Most doctors know only too well the limitation of their ability to relieve sickness and suffering, and this book should indeed help to convince them of the reality of spirit healing and its potentialities.

The scope of this book, however, is much wider and brings a message of hope to all who are stricken and are without relief, despite the dedicated care of doctors and nurses.

I cannot stress too much that this is not a book on Spiritualism; it is a very human and touching account of 'miracles of healing'. The author includes his own miracle and admits that like many people he had never heard of the spirit body, which is nevertheless an integral though unseen part of us all. To many such a proposition seems unnatural, but knowing this, Dr Lang conveys to all who visit him the simplicity of this idea, and the obvious reason why it is possible through the spirit body to receive treatment which helps the physical body.

There is nothing in this book which should offend any form of religious belief, or even the absence of it. Neither is there any intention of preying upon the emotions. All that is related is a presentation of *proven fact*.

I am convinced that the miracles described are not figments of the imagination. I know how hard it is for doctors to accept that which is not verifiable by the usual methods of assessment, but this book is one which should stimulate both doctors and patients to further unbiased enquiry. The greater the initial scepticism, the deeper will be the final conviction.

I have no hesitation in saying that from my own experience in my surgical career, I accept without question that 'miracles' can and do happen under the conditions so faithfully presented by Mr Hutton in this book which I believe will in due course be regarded as a pioneer reference to a hitherto little known 'Science of Healing'.

EDWARD TOWNLEY BAILEY,
M.B., B.S., F.R.C.S.(Eng.)
Consultant Orthopaedic Surgeon

Author's Note

WHEN I first came across George Chapman's name, and read that his spirit doctor control was the late William Lang, F.R.C.S., of the Middlesex and Moorfields Eye Hospital, I knew little or nothing about spirit healing. It was difficult for me to accept any statements that spirit 'operations' and similar treatment could cure incurable (or serious) diseases which had not responded to orthodox medical attention. I did not believe in miracles. It was not really surprising then that, having made an appointment with George Chapman for 6 January 1964, I went to Aylesbury with certain reservations. I was 'to meet the spirit doctor, Lang'.

The visit turned out to be gratifying. For after I'd received healing from Mr Lang, I was left in no doubt that his spirit operations had indeed brought about results which were not only stunning but convincing.

The more evident the improvement of my condition became, the stronger grew the desire in my mind to acquaint myself thoroughly with the intriguing subject of spirit healing. I made my first move and studied some of the available evidence about Mr Lang's and George Chapman's work. I discovered that my own experience was similar to many thousands of cases where the spirit doctor had succeeded in bringing about wonderful successes.

There was, however, much much more I needed to know if I was to present an unbiased and authentic account of Lang's and Chapman's work. Both Lang and Chapman said they would help me in any way they could. The scene was set and I was able to go ahead with the tedious, though satisfying, task I had set myself.

There were many tape-recorded interviews with Mr Lang while he was in control of his entranced medium. There were sessions with George Chapman during his waking state. These interviews frequently took the form of cross-examination, stubborn questioning, and requests for proof of any statement made. I travelled thousands of miles in Britain to interview those of Lang's patients I had picked out at random from Chapman's bulging case history files. As time went by, I had reel upon reel of tape-recorded statements from people who said that Lang had cured them. Some people claimed they had been cured completely by Lang from diseases which hospital doctors had said were incurable.

Apart from interviewing patients, I also checked their statements and medical histories. I wanted to be fully satisfied that I was in possession of *facts* and not highly coloured (and possibly inaccurate) emotional accounts.

Every patient's name and place of residence published in this book is authentic. I take this opportunity to thank each of them for their kind help and co-operation for, had these unselfish people not permitted me to record their individual cases and divulge their true identities, the authenticity and credibility of Lang's and Chapman's achievements would have been open to serious doubt.

I also want to thank William Lang and George Chapman for their untiring assistance, because without their invaluable help I would not have been able to write this book, and I acknowledge a special debt of gratitude to Liam Nolan for his advice and help with this book – travails which went far beyond the duties of a friend.

Being well aware that I have written an unusual book, I wish to make it abundantly clear that I have not the slightest intention of trying to influence or convert anyone to a new way of thinking. My task ends by having presented an objective account of the truth about the subject in question.

J. BERNARD HUTTON

Prologue

IT WAS an autumn day in 1963, and as the year died, the life seemed to be draining away from me too. The doctor standing by my bedside was quiet-voiced and serious. We were on friendly terms, and since I had never in my life felt as ill as I did now, I knew he would be honest with me when I asked him what was wrong with me.

'You've got a non-paralytic type of poliomyelitis,' he said. 'But I want some blood tests done.'

The words scared me. Poliomyelitis – could I really have it? The 'non-paralytic' part didn't ease my fear. I didn't know what to say. My head felt as if it was being split open. Aching pains throbbed in my legs and arms, and when I tried to stand up, dizziness engulfed me. Poliomyelitis. The word hammered and echoed in my brain. I went through a period then in which time and details fused. There was the hospital, blood tests, trolleys, sleep, weakness, confusion, pain. Antibiotics proved useless.

And then I began to go blind.

All my life I had suffered from poor eyesight, and from July 1958 onwards I had been under the care of a leading ophthalmic specialist, Mr Hudson. Mr Hudson had been perfectly frank with me from the beginning, and I had grown to accept the fact that there was precious little chance of my sight ever improving.

Now in 1963, having been diagnosed a polio case, I was also faced with the prospect of blindness. It became so bad that eventually all I could distinguish of a person standing ten yards from me was an indistinct outline. Finally, there were signs of double vision.

One morning, at a time when I was feeling utterly desolate, my wife, Pearl, shoved a copy of *Psychic News* into my hands. 'Read the story on that man at Aylesbury,' she said.

I was short tempered at this period, continually snapping at Pearl and the children. The idea of forcing my eyes to try to pick out the words of small newsprint was too much. 'Don't be ridiculous,' I said. 'You know how hard it is for me to read even a book with large type in it, let alone this silly nonsense.'

'No, please read it Joe, please,' Pearl insisted.

Grumbling, I lifted the paper to the tip of my nose to try and get the words in focus. I was painfully sensitive to the fact that anyone looking at me in this position must be tempted to laugh. This, as much as anything, had prompted me to give up reading altogether except when I was alone. Even then the effort and the pain from my eyes made it a trial.

I had to search the page for the story Pearl wanted me to read, and I was just about to throw the paper from me in frustrated anger when I picked out a fragment about some remarkable happenings in Aylesbury. It had to do with eye operations which, it was claimed, were being carried out by some spirit healer.

I went back to the beginning of the story and started to struggle through it. It told of a Dr Lang who had been a noted ophthalmic specialist in the latter half of the nineteenth and early half of the twentieth centuries. He died in 1937, but now, it was claimed, he was operating through a medium in Aylesbury.

I put the paper down with a derisive comment. Pearl, however, thought otherwise. 'Why don't you just give it a try, Joe?' she pleaded. 'We could drive up and at least *see*.' I was adamant at first in my refusal, but finally relented. I agreed to write for an appointment.

The medium was a man called George Chapman. Two days later I had a reply from him to the effect that Dr William Lang would see me at 2 p.m. on 6 January 1964.

Well, I thought, if it is a game, at least this Mr Chapman

is playing it elaborately. I looked at the letter again, *Dr Lang* would see me it said. Not Mr Chapman, but Dr Lang. I knew enough about Spiritualism to realise that this meant Mr Chapman would be in trance, controlled by the spirit doctor.

On 6 January we left our Worthing home early. Because of my eye condition, Pearl had long taken over the chauffeuring duties, and as it was going to be a long day out, the children had to come along too.

At about five minutes to two I knocked at the door of Mr Chapman's house. I think that at the back of my mind was the idea that even if the whole set-up turned out to be phoney, there might be a feature story for one of the Sunday papers.

I was shown into the waiting room, and a few minutes later the receptionist said: 'Mr Hutton, Dr Lang will see you now.' There it was again, *Dr Lang* would see me.

I peered through my thick lenses at the white-coated figure standing near the window in the consulting room. The face seemed lined and elderly, and the eyes were closed tightly. I just had time to feel surprised when, without opening his eyes, the man in the white coat said: 'Well, what troubles you, young man?'

I was surprised again. I was no young man; certainly not as young as the medium, Chapman, whose picture I had seen in *Psychic News*. Now that I was a couple of steps inside the room I could see the resemblance between the standing figure and the photograph of Chapman. But the face – it looked so much older. The wrinkles and lines were marks of true old age, but I knew Chapman was in his early forties.

The figure in the white coat moved towards me, eyes still shut.

'I am Mr Lang,' he said. Even the voice sounded old, I thought. 'You wanted to see me, didn't you?'

'Yes,' I said.

He held his right hand out towards me and I lifted my own hand towards his, but only halfway. I was watching his face. His eyes didn't open. But his hand, with no groping or feeling around, found mine.

'I am pleased to see you,' he said. 'Sit here, please.' He gestured to a chair facing the window. Outside the day was grey and cold, and the light, such as there was of it, fell on my face. 'Your eyes, young man, are giving you trouble,' he said.

'Yes,' I answered, 'and during the past two months they have been getting worse. I find it almost impossible to read now. I can't type. My work has come to a stop and——'

'May I see these please,' he cut in, and removed my glasses. He still hadn't opened his eyes. He held the glasses before his face as though he were looking at them. 'Oh, dear!' he exclaimed, shaking his head slowly. 'Minus eighteen.'

He was quite correct – my lenses *were* minus eighteen, but I hadn't told him anything about them.

He slipped the spectacles into his breast-pocket, then bent down closer to me and brought his thumbs up and felt my eyes. Not once did he open his own. After a minute or so he straightened up.

'You had a splint operation on both eyes when you were a child. A very nice job.'

I was astounded. How could he have known this? Not even Pearl, my wife, knew. I never spoke about it. In fact I hadn't even thought about it for years. It had happened a long time ago – when I was six years old. The surgeon who had performed the operation, Professor Elschnick of the Sanatorium Gottlieb in Prague, was dead.

He bent over me again, touching my eyes with his thumbs, and talking all the while. The stream of medical phrases and terms washed over me. '. . . and your sight is deteriorating all the time . . . lymph drainage system not functioning properly . . . diplopia. . . .' The words were only half caught, half heard. '. . . due to the derangement of the muscular balance of the two eyes . . . central scotoma. . . .'

I didn't know what to do or say or think. '. . . and some

lesion of the retina as well as swelling of the conjunctiva due to the presence of the fluid ... macula clouded over.. . .'

Finally, he straightened up once more. 'You are troubled with double vision too, young man, aren't you?'

By this time I could only nod.

'What is your profession?' he asked suddenly.

'I am a writer and a journalist,' I answered.

He pursed his lips and nodded three or four times. 'Well, you certainly depend on your eyes a great deal. I'll do my very best to help you.'

'Thank you, thank you very much,' I said. 'Anything at all that you might do would be most deeply——'

'That's quite all right, quite all right,' he said, dismissing my gratitude. 'Now there is something else – other than your eyes – troubling you. Let me give you a little examination.'

I expected him to ask me to take off my jacket and shirt, but he didn't. Seated where I was, he touched me gently with his hands. There was no sound in the room for what seemed like a couple of minutes. His eyes were closed the whole time. He hadn't opened them since I had come into his room.

'Now then,' he resumed eventually, 'the virus which brought about your illness, and which your doctor believed to be a non-paralytic type of poliomyelitis, has gone. But you have something which is very serious, a hepatitis virus which is upsetting your liver. Due to it, changes in your body temperature take place because the liver balance cannot be maintained. This hepatitis virus saps your strength.'

If I had been amazed before, I was speechless now. I had not told Chapman anything about my own doctor when I wrote to him, nor had I mentioned being ill. Yet here was the medium, telling me something that only my own doctor and my wife could possibly have known. And neither had been in touch with George Chapman. It was uncanny.

The temptation to accept totally everything claimed

about the dead surgeon now operating through his medium Chapman, was suddenly very strong. But the journalistic instinct reasserted itself. Words like telepathy, thought transference, clairvoyance, and all that they meant, flashed into my brain. Somewhere in these could be contained the answer to the mysterious knowledge of facts about me the medium was quoting. And yet, the medical terms, what of them? He certainly could not have got those from me. I had never heard most of them before.

He was talking again in that peculiar old-sounding, denture-clicking way of his, in a voice both thin and ancient. 'In order to help you, I shall have to perform an operation on your eyes. You needn't worry, young man, you see everyone has two bodies – a physical body and a spirit body. Now I shall operate on your *spirit* body and attempt to produce a corresponding effect on your physical body. You may hear me talking, calling out names and asking for instruments. Don't be alarmed. I shall be assisted at the operation by my son Basil and various other colleagues of mine you won't be able to see because they too have passed into spirit. But you won't feel any pain. Now I want you to lie there on that couch.'

My impressions of that last little spiel were, to say the least, amused. It was getting more and more like an elaborate charade, but I thought I might as well play along with it.

When the medium asked me to lie on the couch I expected him to ask me to undress. He didn't. I lay back, fully clothed, with my eyes wide open.

He came across to the edge of the couch and then lifted his hands and started to move them, and flick his fingers just above my eyes. His own eyes stayed tightly closed. The fingers of his hands opened and shut as though taking and using instruments. Suddenly I had an almost uncontrollable urge to burst out laughing. The mime seemed so funny. I had to bite hard on my lip to hold back the guffaw that was struggling to get out. Then I forced myself to listen to that old voice again.

'I have drawn away slightly your spirit body from your physical body, and am now operating on your spirit body. . . . I am making an opening through the supra tarsal fold and am attending to the fluids and parts behind the eyes . . . the crystalline lens, retina and so forth . . .' And so it went on.

The desire to laugh suddenly left me.

'. . . I have dealt with your eyeball now, and the muscles themselves because I found that the ciliary muscles were tightened up. . . .'

Then, incredible as it may seem, I began to experience the physical sensation of incisions being made. They were painless, but none the less capable of being felt. The man's eyes never opened, and he did not touch me. And yet, a little later I felt as though he were stitching up the wounds. It was all very far from being funny now.

As soon as my eyes were dealt with, I heard him pointing out to his unseen and unheard assistants that if the hepatitis virus was not attended to, the eye operations might not be of much use.

'Now I am going to perform an operation on your spirit body,' he said to me. 'I'll attempt to dispose of the virus.'

Again I watched his hands hovering above me. Again they looked as if they were handling invisible instruments, and again I had those strange painless sensations as though incisions were being made in anaesthetised flesh. And when it was over, there was the selfsame sensation of a needle being inserted, drawn through, reinserted.

When I was asked to sit up, I felt dizzy and dazed. And then a full and terrible alarm hit me, because I found I could not see at all! I could only barely distinguish between light and dark.

It suddenly came back to me that Mr Hudson, the eye specialist I had been attending since 1958, had once told me that the only remote possibility of an improvement in my eyesight lay in a complicated series of operations which might or might not succeed. He had stressed that if they were unsuccessful, I would be permanently blind. Other consultants had confirmed his opinion, and I had decided not to take the risk.

All this flashed into my mind as I sat sightless on that couch in Aylesbury. There was the frightful fear that the meddling of this so-called medium had resulted in what Mr Hudson had warned me about.

In a panic I began to shout. 'What's wrong now? I can't see anything. Do something for God's sake!'

The voice, unruffled, denture-clicking as before, came to me. 'Don't worry, young man, it's only temporary, it'll soon lift and you'll notice considerable improvement.' He then added: 'I cannot promise to give you the sight of normal eyes, young man, but I can promise that I will improve your vision considerably.' His calmness was soothing. 'I shall continue to visit you during your sleep state, because I can then more easily detach your spirit body from your physical body and give you the necessary treatment. I assure you I shall do everything possible to improve your vision.'

'I only hope you are right,' I said in desperation.

'Don't worry; don't worry, young man,' he repeated. 'I would like to see you again in about three months. Do you think you will be able to come?'

'Oh, yes, I'll come,' I acknowledged. 'But now I can't even see where the door is.'

'Don't worry, young man,' he said once again, and I heard a buzzer go somewhere outside, and then the door opening.

'Yes?' a female voice said.

'Ah, Margaret, would you see to Joseph please.'

'Thanks, Mr Lang, and I hope you are right and I'll be able to see.'

'Oh, you will, you will, it won't be very long.'

His voice was so reassuring.

I was led outside, and I asked to be shown to the front door. It was with the greatest difficulty that I groped my way to where we had left the car. I had a splitting headache and felt dizzy, and all my body was shaking.

What a fool I had been to give in to Pearl's insistence on my coming here, I thought. I may not have been able to see very much, but at least I was able to see *something* before all this hocus-pocus rendered me blind.

I sat in the car. Pearl and the children had gone off somewhere for a walk to stretch their legs and have something to eat. I fumbled for my cigarettes and lighter, burned my hand trying to light up, and sat cursing and depressed.

And then it began to happen.

I was gazing blindly in front of me when very slowly the shape of a tree started to materialise. At first I thought it was imagination. But no, it was not imagination. Like one of those trick cinematic effects, the outline of the tree sharpened and came into focus, and then I was able to distinguish the large branches, then the smaller ones, and finally the winter-naked twigs.

I closed my eyes in disbelief. When I opened them again I noticed that the windscreen was dirty and needed wiping. *The windscreen was dirty and I could see it!* I nearly cried the words aloud. I looked out through the rear window, and away in the distance I could see some people approaching. And then, with a surge of emotion I recognised the people. It was my wife, Pearl, and my own children, and even at this distance I could make out their faces.

I wept then, fully and freely, as I sat there alone in the car and waited for them.

HEALING HANDS

1

The Miracle

SITTING IN the front seat next to Pearl as she drove us back to Worthing, I found to my great joy that I was able to see much farther than ever before. And as early darkness crowded out the daylight, and street lamps and headlights were switched on, I discovered that they no longer dazzled me or hurt my eyes as they had done a little time ago.

My mind and heart were very full. I talked in long uninterrupted bursts, then became silent. Pearl understood and left me to my thoughts. It had been a day of happenings and mad emotional turmoil, and Pearl knew when to keep quiet.

On the following morning, a Tuesday, we were sitting quietly at breakfast, the familiar tones of Jack De Manio on his Home Service *Today* programme filling in the background. I was reading the morning paper. Presently I felt a hand being placed gently on my arm, and looked up to see Pearl standing there, smiling serenely down at me.

After a little while she said: 'Do you realise what you are doing. You are actually reading the paper. Isn't it wonderful? And you are holding it at least eight or nine inches from your eyes.'

She was right. I hadn't noticed, so rapidly does normality re-establish itself and come to be accepted without thought. Neither of us spoke after that. There was no need.

On the morning of the next day I woke up feeling

1

oddly different. It took only a moment to understand why. The cruel headache and dizziness which had been my waking companions for so many weeks had vanished. Gone too from my body was the aching tiredness I had long endured and I was filled with such a surging sense of well-being that I decided there and then to go up to London for the day and show my colleagues and friends the remarkable new man Joe Hutton had become.

Now that all the aches and pains associated with my liver condition had fled, a certain conclusion repeatedly suggested itself to me. But consciously, time and time again, I drove it out of my thoughts. I was wary. I wanted proof. I didn't want to go overboard on an imagined metamorphosis.

My friends in London, when I told them the remarkable things that had befallen me, were at first disinclined to show any great enthusiasm, though they were obviously glad for my sake that I was in such good form. They too, I felt, wanted some proof. Until then they had known me as a pathetically short-sighted man, so I decided to let them judge for themselves.

I saw down at a typewriter and began to type, and they saw at once that no longer did I have to crouch over with my nose to the keyboard. Nor did I have to jack-knife forward in order to read what I had typed. I was able to sit as upright as the next man. They crowded round me excitedly, their congratulations bubbling into my ears. Then I knew.

That night, when I undressed for bed, I noticed a long mark, a thick line about five inches long, on my body. I moved closer to the mirror to see what it was. Pink in colour, it had a series of dots above and below the line. It looked exactly like the scar of a surgical incision. I ran my fingers over it, but it felt quite flat. And yet it was plain to see, just as if I had had an operation on my liver!

On 22 January I went back again to Aylesbury, this time with someone who was in need of help and who wanted to be seen by the spirit doctor. I myself was seen as well, and after an examination on the couch, I was told: 'The operation was a success, young man.'

But I didn't have to be told. I knew it.

It was a miracle, and it happened in Aylesbury on a cold January day in 1964.

2

The Spirit Doctor and His Medium

CAN ANYONE deny that what happened to me was a miracle? I don't know how this assertion can be refuted, and, without meaning to be impertinent, I don't care. I am satisfied that it was a miracle.

I had first gone to Aylesbury as a sceptic, prepared to scoff – full of derision and suspicion.

I went there as a man who was seriously ill. Seriously ill and teetering on the brink of blindness.

I came away with restored sight and renewed health.

These are the facts.

For me, the proof of a miracle is more than conclusive. I am satisfied also that the late William Lang, F.R.C.S., was instrumental in bringing about my cure. I had never heard of him before. The name George Chapman meant nothing to me. But I am convinced that when George Chapman goes into trance as a medium, his spirit control is William Lang.

I do not expect you to believe what I believe, nor is it my purpose to convert you to my way of thinking. I want this to be understood from the outset.

All I am doing is putting down in this book the things that I found out throughout a year of travel and research. I have met all those people whose evidence I intend to present, and the words they speak are theirs, not mine.

I am not offering you a rounded story. It is entirely without any formal plot, and while it has a beginning and a middle, it has no end because it is still going on. It is just that I feel these things deserve to be told, and now is the time to do so.

One other point I would like to mention is that I have decided, for the sake of convenience and *not* as an attempt to influence any reader, to refer to the in-trance George Chapman as Mr Lang.

In March 1964 I went back to Mr Lang for a check-up, and afterwards talked to him for a very long time. Our conversation embraced many subjects, and I found him to be a charming and knowledgeable speaker. Eventually I steered the talk around to the possibility of my writing about him and his medium, George Chapman.

When I put it to him he seemed slightly bashful. He smiled a small shy smile and dropped his head down on to his chest in thought. Then he said:

'Well, I suppose one day such a book is bound to be written, Joseph, and if it has to be done I'd like you to do it. Go on, young man, write it, but there is one thing I want you always to keep in your mind – that George and I are only God's instruments. It is through His aid and His aid alone that I am able to use my skill as a spirit doctor to relieve suffering.'

I knew, though, that the project could be carried out only if Mr Lang agreed to talking to me fully and freely about his life on earth and in the spirit world, and of his association with his medium, George Chapman. I mentioned that such an arrangement could not but take up a great deal of his time.

'Oh, don't worry about that, young man,' he replied. 'Come any time. I love seeing you and your dear wife. It is good to meet people with whom one can speak so easily.'

I thanked him and said that there were many questions I wanted to ask George Chapman. 'I've never met him in his waking state,' I pointed out.

'That will be no problem. George is a nice man and you will like him, I feel sure. I suggest you write to him to enable him to make an arrangement with you.'

'Would there be any objection to my using a tape-recorder?' I asked. 'It is easier than having to make a lot of notes.'

'Of course not,' he said, 'I'm sure everything will work out satisfactorily.'

That was the end of our talk, and when I got back to Worthing I wrote immediately to George Chapman. It was much later (and then quite by accident) that I learned that many requests from well-known authors, journalists, television and film writers, had been received in the past. All had been turned down.

When my wife and I eventually met George Chapman at his house at Aylesbury, we found ourselves facing an extremely personable young man who looked to be in his late thirties. He was in fact then forty-three years of age.

During my three visits to the spirit doctor, I had had ample opportunity to study him closely. He had a distinctive way of holding his head slightly cocked in the listening manner of a much older man. Yet another indication of the seeming burden of years was an inclination to stoop. These were the characteristics of Chapman the medium but now they were no longer present. This was a person who walked easily and erect. His face was smooth and he was obviously a very shy individual.

The contrast in speech was equally striking. Chapman's voice, unmistakably Merseyside in accent, was that of a youngish man, and he spoke quietly because of an inherent diffidence, and Lang's on the other hand was cultured and assured, strongly Southern, peppered of course with medical terms, and high-pitched in the manner of the aged.

There were, however, certain attributes which were shared: exceptional friendliness and goodness, absolute unselfishness, and a powerful devotion towards helping those who, in medical terms, were considered incurable. Early on in my first meeting with Chapman I got the feeling that I had known him for a very long time.

3

Long Before the Beatles

THE MISTS were swirling around Merseyside on 4 February 1921. They were carried in from the sea by a gusty wind which whipped around corners and bit to the bone anyone abroad on the streets. Down river there was the mournful cacophony of ships' hooters. Along the docks, donkey engines whined on wet slippery decks, cargoes swung precariously on the ends of protesting hawsers, and men with inflamed hands cursed the winter.

High on the dirty grey-black mass of the building that dominates the Pier Head and the whole river front, the Liver Bird, gilded and scrawny, looked down on the drenched and depressed city of Liverpool. Further along the river, in the county borough of Bootle, a woman strained in the pains of childbirth, and when her sweating and agony had ceased, there was beside her the pinched-up face of a baby who would be christened George William Chapman.

These were uneasy times. In Ireland there was unrest and poverty and the black shadow of civil war. In England there were many young men who were old because of what a world war had done to them, and there were many middle-aged men who looked like walking cadavers. The limbless and the disillusioned peopled the streets, and the poor, as always, were hit hard and often.

But George Chapman was too young to know. So he was suckled and grew strong and learned to crawl and walk and talk. And then, suddenly the baby was a baby no longer, but a six-year-old boy who saw and felt many things.

In the mean streets he saw toughness and poverty, stablemates at any time and place. He heard the accents of the Irish, lived through Catholic-Protestant brawls, and was eternally shocked at the things people would do to animals either in fun or in anger.

Whenever he saw a boy creeping up on a cat or dog nosing at a dustbin for food, George would scream a warning to the unsuspecting animal in an effort to save it the pain of a well-aimed brick. There were times when he was set upon as a spoil-sport. It would be false to say he didn't mind. He did, and was as scared as any back alley youngster would ever be, but he didn't seem to learn the intended lesson.

As he became bigger and stronger, the instinct for survival became even more dominant and, full of confidence, he learned to use fast hands and feet in a manner which came to be respected. But he fought only when necessary, and more often than not he had to only if a cat's life was at stake. Or a dog's. That was the way it was.

However, there were more injured and stray cats and dogs in and around Bootle than George Chapman could ever have hoped to save. And the Chapman living quarters were far too cramped to allow even a small number of those animals that George wanted to shelter inside.

He needed some sort of place to house the strays. Not only did he not have any accommodation, but there was no spare money either to buy food for the animals he loved. Then one day he hit upon an idea. Why not go around the doors and ask if they wanted any messages done?

The first five or six doors were slammed in his face. Didn't they have enough mouths to feed without trying to find coppers to give to a snotty-nosed ragamuffin for running messages? But George Chapman wasn't that easily put off, and when he turned to the homes of older women with grown-up families out at work all day, he found himself a handful of willing customers.

8

Not a halfpenny did he spend on himself. It all went on food for the animals. Then one magic day, a lady offered him the use of her cellar as a sanctuary for his pets. In return, she wanted him to do all her shopping and a fair proportion of domestic cleaning. To George Chapman it was a fine bargain.

Young George's animal sanctuary was soon well known in the district. People began to talk about the boy who undertook any errand or job to earn a few coppers to buy food for his stray cats and dogs, and who put splints on their limbs and nursed them when he found them injured. He did what he could, too, to help the neighbours' sick pets when they brought them to the 'child vet'. To this day, some of the people in Bootle talk about the unselfish boy who nursed animals with such tenderness.

George left school when he was fourteen. It was into the cold harsh world of unemployment that he went, and for longer than was good for his mind and body he stood at street corners and listened to the gutter talk of his companions. The future, such as it was, appeared grey and hopeless. He knew nothing, and didn't want to know. Why should he? What had the world done for him? He was a drifter beginning to drift, so what the hell.

But one day he heard of a job going, and almost before he had a chance to tidy his hair, he was running to the garage where they required a pump assistant and general labourer. He got there before any of his mates, and they gave him the job. It wasn't riches, but it was better than hanging about street corners. What was more, he liked the job. It made him feel that he had a place in the world. Until the day he was lying under a lorry trying to loosen a stubborn screw on the oil sump. The edges of the spanner were worn, the corners of the screw rounded, and the spanner could get no purchase. Then it caught, held fast, and George pulled two-handed with all his might. The next moment the heavy spanner slipped and was pulled down on to his face with the full force of his strength.

The taste of blood running down his throat sickened the youngster, and he was hauled out with a badly lacerated nose. But there was scant sympathy from the garage proprietor, and the boy was sacked without wages. 'Bloody silly accident,' was all the owner said, and George Chapman was once again on the streets.

A few weeks later he was lucky enough to get a job as a butcher's boy, and though he often had to work from 6 a.m. to eleven o'clock at night, he liked the work. Soon, though, there was talk of another war and, when this became a reality, he told his boss that he intended to enlist. George had set his mind on joining the Irish Guards, and as soon as he picked up his wages, he took a bus to the Recruiting Office at Renshaw Hall. He looked at the guardsmen, tall and stiff and straight with their peaked caps low down on their foreheads, and tried to imagine himself in the same uniform.

But disappointment awaited him. As Chapman stood in front of a table, the recruiting officer glanced through his application form and then looked at the boy.

'You're too young, lad. You need another year to be able to join the army.'

George was just about to plead for a chance when he was told, 'Anyway, you're only five foot seven, and the minimum height for the Irish Guards is five foot eight. Sorry.'

But George's reputation as a boxer saved the day for him in an unexpected way. Across the hall, one of the N.C.O.s, doing paper work, recognised him and called out to the officer. 'That's George Chapman, sir, isn't it? He's a useful boxer and would be a good lad to 'ave with us.'

The officer looked at Chapman. 'So you're a bit of a boxer, are you young man?'

'Yes, sir, I do a bit,' George said.

'Mm-mmm.' The officer glanced through the form again. 'Let's see. Stand against the wall will you.'

George hurried now to the wall behind the officer's table, and the officer measured him for height.

'Looks to me like someone made a slight miscalculation in your height,' he said. 'According to the way I read it, you're just five foot eight. And what did you say about your birth date being wrong? You were born in 1920 you say, and not 1921?'

'Yes, sir, that's right, sir.' George said, taking his cue smartly. So they gave George Chapman a shilling, sent him to the Q.M.'s Stores, and he was in the Irish Guards. In due course he was ordered to Caterham, given a regulation haircut, a meal of liver and bacon, and assigned to a training squad.

'But the first time I went on parade,' he recalled, 'and stood in the centre of a group of six-footers, I knew how small I was. I felt like a pygmy in the company of giants.

'A few days after going there I was among a crowd of fellows in the barrack-room when someone came in. Everybody jumped to their feet, but I was doing some chore or other and I remained seated. The next thing I knew was that a young officer was standing in front of me, looking down. "Are you tired, or sick or something?" he said. And I said "No." Well, he nearly hit the roof. He asked me if I knew I was talking to an officer, and carried on something alarming, then turned and stormed out. The sergeant had a go at me then, and used language I could never hope to repeat for the sheer flow of its obscenity.

'Anyway, a couple of days later I was told I was being transferred to the Royal Irish Fusiliers, and I went along to headquarters to get my papers. The officer who saw me was not the same one who had bawled me out, but he looked me over and said, "Let me see now, you're – your name is George William Chapman?" I replied, "Yes, sir." He went on: "Your date of birth, Chapman?" And without thinking I said, "4 February 1921, sir." He started laughing then. "Hah!" he said, "I thought as much. Well, I'm sorry Chapman, but you're under age. We could do with chaps with your spirit, but

11

regulations have to be observed, you understand that. I'm sorry." And I was out.'

Back at Merseyside again Chapman managed to get a job on the docks, but his heart was still set on joining up, and after thinking things over for a few weeks, he decided to try to get into the R.A.F. By the time formalities were completed, his birthday had come around, and George William Chapman, civilian, became A/C Chapman.

Life in the R.A.F. was a crowded time for the young man from Bootle. His first posting was to Blackpool where he became a drill instructor. Then followed transfers to Tangmere and Merston. He met up with heavyweight wrestler Tony Mancelli, the Birkenhead boxer Jackie Parnell and several others who were useful performers in the ring, and as a squad they put on boxing exhibitions for the camps based around the South coast.

Then came a posting to Portsmouth for the purpose of gunnery training on H.M.S. *Excellent*. He buckled down to the tough practical tests and swotted hard at the theory, and eventually passed out as Instructor in Gunnery.

One day when a working party from Worthing arrived to lay a landing strip for Spitfires, one of the engineers, apparently in search of something to talk about, casually asked Corporal Chapman if he had ever considered the possibility of life after death.

Before he was able to reply, his mind was crowded with memories, many of which belonged to his childhood. He remembered, for instance, how one of his uncles, a solemn man, could talk of little else but life after death and Spiritualism. But his nephew declined to concern himself with questions that were beyond him.

'I'm not really interested in these things,' he told the engineer and left it at that.

The other man said: 'Yer oughta be, y'know.'

Chapman whirled on him: 'Don't give me any of that stuff, mate! There's enough happening here and elsewhere without my having to bother about what happens to me when I buy my lot. Get me? So drop it, eh?'

The engineer walked away.

In 1943 George William Chapman was transferred to R.A.F. Halton in Buckinghamshire, where he was promoted to Sergeant. And it was while stationed there that he met the girl who was to become his wife. A year after their wedding, Margaret presented her husband with a baby girl who was christened Vivian Margaret Chapman. The event brought the customary welling of pride in the hearts of the newlyweds, but their joy was all too soon tempered with tragedy, for the doctor called George Chapman aside and warned him that it was most unlikely the baby would live much longer than a month.

'I remember the tears I cried in the woods around the hospital at Ashbridge the day the doctor broke the news to me,' Chapman recalled. 'I wasn't a religious fellow or much of a believer in what religion teaches, but I'm sure nobody ever prayed harder to God than I did then. But when it was not possible to hope, I got to thinking that there just couldn't be a God who would let an innocent little baby die like that. Know what I mean? I was distracted.

'But she died. You know they say that tragedy never leaves us where we were originally. I found that to be true. We both did, Margaret and I. Somehow or other our baby dying drew us closer together, and when we had become reconciled to our loss, it kind of strengthened us spiritually.'

As the war drew to its grisly end, Sergeant Chapman became aware again of the problem of unemployment that would face him when he came out of the Royal Air Force. He had no special qualifications which would fit him for a civvy job, and he didn't particularly want to stay in the service. He was anxious to set up a permanent home for Margaret and himself and the children they hoped to have.

The coal mines were beckoning, but he had no yearning to spend the rest of his life below the ground hewing at the black seams and breathing in the black dust. The only two occupations that attracted him, even vaguely, were the police and the fire brigade. Nowhere else was there any hope of a job. Again his lack of height was against him, for the invitation to join the Aylesbury Police stipulated a minimum of five foot ten inches for would-be recruits. There was only one avenue left.

On 2 May 1946, Sergeant George William Chapman of the R.A.F. was demobbed. Within a few days he changed into a new uniform and became Fireman Chapman of the Aylesbury Fire Brigade.

4

The Die is Cast

W HEN FINALLY the time came for my appointment
to see Mr Lang, I told Chapman, and he said I had
better keep the tape-recorder plugged in as it would take
him but a short time to go into trance. I did this, and kept
my eyes on George Chapman.

He made himself comfortable in the armchair he had
been sitting in during my interview with him, closed his
eyes, and rested his head on the back of the chair as
though in sleep. My wife and I watched closely. We saw
the expression of the face changing into the look of an
old man. The mouth gradually twisted into a new shape,
and new wrinkles appeared about the eyes. One of the
hands came up slowly into a position I had noticed in Mr
Lang. The deeper the medium sank into trance, the more
he changed until he looked exactly the same as the person who had greeted me that first afternoon in January.
Then he stood up and came towards Pearl.

'Hello, young lady, it is nice to see you again,' he
began. He shook hands with her, then turned to me.
'And you, young man, it is good to see you too.'

'I am grateful that you have allowed us to come and
talk to you,' I said, and I shook his outstretched hand.

'Yes, yes . . .' he said in that delightful vague way of
his. 'Now let me see, it is Worthing you come from, isn't
it? Yes. You know I used to rent a week-end house there
once, in the early 'twenties I believe it was. Delightful,
delightful. But I mustn't waste your time young man.
You've come a long way to talk to me. I'll try to answer
all your questions.'

15

On 28 December 1852, Isaac Lang – a prosperous and well-liked Exeter merchant – sat waiting in his splendidly furnished drawing-room while his wife lay in labour in an upper room. He was not worried. He said later that somehow he *knew* there would be no complications and that he knew, too, the baby would be a boy. When the family doctor appeared, at last, to announce, 'Your wife has blessed you with a bonny . . .' Isaac Lang cooly interposed and said, 'Yes, I know, with a bonny baby boy.'

'How do *you* know?' the doctor exclaimed. '*I* was quite certain it would be a girl, and told you and your wife so on several occasions. I am not often proved wrong in these cases.'

'I said all along that we would have a boy but you wouldn't listen,' the proud father reminded him.

'Yes, but *how*?' the doctor pressed.

'I can't explain it – I just knew.'

The doctor left the house a puzzled man.

The baby was christened William, and on the day of the christening Isaac Lang made another prediction for his child, his fourth-born: William would break away from family tradition and become a very successful doctor – a noted specialist. Isaac Lang's relations and friends refused to believe him. For generations the Langs had been successful merchants and it was unthinkable that a Lang would go into anything else. They laughed at Isaac and said he was indulging in day-dreams. But Isaac Lang spoke with such conviction of the child's future that he made many of them think again.

'My life was one of pleasure,' William Lang told me as we chatted about his happy childhood. The tape-recorder was switched on, and I sat facing him in his Aylesbury surgery. 'Of course we didn't travel a great deal, because travel was rather slow in those days. If we went to Plymouth, for example, or anywhere in Devon, it took a long time to get there.

'We spent most of our young lives in our large house in Exeter. We never attended any school. No, we had a

16

very capable tutor who used to come to the house. He was very strict but, although we liked and respected him, we used to play him up a lot because we were as mischievous as are most children. When we went too far, father would be called, because our tutor wasn't allowed to spank us. Father usually punished us much harder than the tutor might have done.'

At the age of twelve, William was sent to the then famous Moravian School in Lausanne to receive higher education. Although his tutor had prepared him well enough to justify his acceptance by the Swiss boarding-school, the youngster from Exeter nevertheless found it difficult at first to cope with Latin and several other subjects new to him. But, right from the start, the Senior Master, Pirie, took a liking to the small country boy from England and helped him to overcome his initial difficulties. The boy proved himself a keen student and soon went to the top of his class. He distinguished himself in chemistry, which was one of his favourite subjects.

'You may know that Swiss boarding-schools are very strict,' Mr Lang recalled, 'but we had quite a lot of fun there. The standard of education was high and we had to work hard, but we were allowed to visit the town and the surrounding villages, and we also went to Germany on several occasions. My fellow students came from many different nations, and so we learned a good deal about the habits and life of our respective countries.'

While studying at Lausanne, William made up his mind to become a doctor. Knowing the family tradition as merchants, he feared opposition from his father. When, eventually, he felt bold enough to acquaint his father with his desire to study medicine, the old man's answer amazed him.

'It is your life, William, and I want you to have a profession which you'll really like. Become a doctor by all means.'

In 1870, at the age of eighteen, William Lang entered

the London Hospital in Whitechapel as a medical student, and from the very start of his career studied with tremendous energy and enthusiasm.

'When I went to live in the East End of London,' he recalled, 'I met some very likeable people. In and around Stepney lived many people of diverse religion and race. Many were extremely poor – and somehow I became more friendly with them than with anyone else.'

The year 1874 was a notable one for the then twenty-two-year-old medical student. He qualified as M.R.C.S. – Member of the Royal College of Surgeons – and married his second cousin Susan. It had been an idyllic love affair for both of them, and the wedding was the commencement of a very happy union which only came to an end when Susan died in 1892.

The young surgeon was so devoted to medicine that he would spend many hours with his patients, talking to their relatives and doing all he could to discover more about the actual cause of disease; and, when he decided it was necessary to operate, he would arrange to have patients brought into the hospital an appreciable time beforehand, would visit them daily, gain their confidence and learn something about them as individuals.

'I always tried to touch a person's soul so that he or she had the *will* to get well,' Mr Lang explained to me. 'My fellow-surgeons used to think I was wasting my time. Some of them even voiced the opinion that "William Lang spends too much time talking with his patients". Well, maybe I did, but thank God, my patients seemed to do remarkably well. I was . . . eh . . . quite successful – and I hope I don't sound boastful. I don't mean to be.

'I remember my wife Susan saying to me one day: "You know, William, you must have quite the longest list of lady patients of any surgeon in London!" I said it must be because of my good manners!'

In every surgeon's life there are cases which, despite all his tireless efforts, he finds himself defeated. I asked Mr Lang what he had felt about this aspect of his work.

'Yes, you are quite right,' he answered. 'Sometimes

18

when I examined a patient I knew immediately that he would die, that it didn't matter who operated, the patient would not survive. But as a surgeon, you never give up hope until the last heartbeat has long stopped.

'Now whenever I lost a case I became deeply, deeply depressed. It is an experience common to every doctor. You feel you have failed. Failed a human being. You feel responsible. Your rational mind will tell you that you were *not* responsible, that you did everything in your power, but you are still left with the feeling of having failed. And you look around at the heartbreak of those relatives who have to face life without the one who has died, and somehow their suffering becomes your responsibility too. Oh, I remember that so clearly. It was very hard. Very hard.'

He spent a great deal of his time on the sociological side of his work. One thing that always had an effect on him was when he heard that old people were about to be sent to the workhouse. Such a possibility would have him leaving the hospital or surgery at the first opportunity to beg and plead with the relatives of the old person *not* to send the old lady or old gentleman away. And when he succeeded (as he did on many occasions) he would go away happy that the old person would be able to live out the last few years in surroundings which were familiar and comforting, rather than in a poor-law barracks where human dignity was stripped away.

William Lang served as House Physician and House Surgeon at the London Hospital in Whitechapel for nine years. Late in his stay there he was Demonstrator in Physiology and Anatomy in the medical college, and it was then that he met and came under the influence of James Edward Adams, a famous ophthalmic surgeon. Such was the dedication and power of Adams' personality that Lang became engrossed in ophthalmology and began to study it. Adams encouraged him at every opportunity, and when Lang got his fellowship of the Royal College of Surgeons in 1879 and was offered a position at the Central London Ophthalmic Hospital, he accepted it.

19

His years at Whitechapel had been very happy ones, and when the time came for him to leave he was heavy in heart and rather afraid that he had made a wrong decision.

5

A Brilliant Career

WILLIAM LANG, F.R.C.S. was appointed Ophthalmic Surgeon to the Middlesex Hospital, London, in 1880. Four years later, when an irony of fate forced his friend James Edward Adams to resign from the Central London Ophthalmic Hospital (later Moorfields Eye Hospital) in London's City Road because of increasing blindness, he succeeded Adams to his position at the hospital, and also took over his private practice.

Being a devoted ophthalmic surgeon, Mr Lang realised that there was a vital need for a society of eye specialists and, together with colleagues and professional friends, founded the Ophthalmological Society in 1881. Despite his strenuous work at his private practice and at the Middlesex Hospital, he always found time to take a leading part in the activities of the Society. In 1903 he became its Senior Vice-President; later he held an additional post – President of the Ophthalmological Section of the Royal Society of Medicine.

'I haven't been a prolific writer – in fact I found writing and speaking in public quite difficult,' Mr Lang told me. 'You know, I used to go through agonies of mind if I had to write a medical thesis, make a speech, or take part in a public function.'

Nevertheless, his output was considerable and his more important publications of great significance. The many cases he brought forward at the meetings of the Ophthalmological Society usually made the subjects of lengthy and fruitful discussions.

In 1882 – when he was thirty – Mr Lang published, with

Mr W. A. Fitz-Gerald, a study on the movements of the eyelids in association with the movements of the eye. It was his first contribution of importance in which he was able to pinpoint the function of the inferior rectus muscle in the downward movement of the lower lid.

The publication created considerable controversy. He was accused of 'availing himself of unconventional methods', since Sir William Gowers had previously stated that the lower lid was depressed by the pressure of the limbus upon the margin of the lower lid. Sir William was eventually proved wrong, and Mr Lang's theory accepted by ophthalmologists throughout the world ever since.

He was for many years the editor of *The Royal London Ophthalmic Hospital Reports*, and contributed, in collaboration with Sir James Barrett, some very important studies.

Among other notable contributions to ophthalmology was that entitled *The Retractive Condition of the Eyes and Mamalia*, published in 1886. This study was the conclusion of extensive examinations on a great variety of animals – 185 pairs of eyes in all – which established that the majority were hypermetropic. At this time Mr Lang was a member of the committee which reported on 211 cases of sympathetic ophthalmitis, and he published an elaborate study on *The Action of the Myotics on the Accommodation*.

Greatly impressed by Mr Adams Frost's suggestion of a then revolutionary operation – the insertion of an artificial globe into Tennon's capsule after excising the eye – Mr Lang investigated the possibility very thoroughly and wrote his own account of it in 1887. In the same year he also published, in collaboration with Sir James Barrett, *The Action of Myotics and Mydriatics on the Accommodation* – a work that had considerable practical importance and led, ultimately, to the use of cycloplegics in refraction work.

This study was a record of a patient supported by careful investigation, and was introduced as an enquiry into the action of a mixture of homotropine and cocaine – often known as 'Lang's Drops' – and of the extremely ingenious oily solution of these alkaloids. It was shown in this work how easily and safely the action of these drugs could be controlled by the subsequent use of eserine.

These listed are only a few of Lang's published works.

Mr Lang was at all times concerned with the practical side of ophthalmology and here he was a master. He improved many of the instruments in common use.

The McHardy Perimeter, for instance, was ameliorated by Mr Lang in many ways, and his modification was extensively used everywhere until it was surpassed by better models. His speculum with solid blades is still in use, and his twin-knives for dividing anterior synechiae marked an epoch in the improvement in cataract extraction because, by using them, he drew attention to the importance of avoiding the inclusion of lens capsule in the wound.

As a clinical observer and all-round ophthalmologist, Mr Lang was at his best. His operating technique and resource in difficult cases was admired and remembered by those who were his House Surgeons. The delicacy, certainty and speed with which he worked, made him a surgeon to be remembered. His students (he called each of them 'dear boy') were always loath to leave him for he had so much to impart, and did so with brilliant fluency. This I found out for myself in doing the preparatory work for this book. Mr Lang, they said, was extremely patient, the essence of courtesy, and rarely showed himself to be of short temper. Indeed, when driven to the limits of his patience, the most violent expletive he was known to use was 'Dash my wig!'

Lang married again, and with his second wife Isabel and his son Basil, once again found the contentment that he thought had deserted him forever when his first wife died. It was a matter of deep satisfaction to him when Basil, as a young scholar, revealed interest in medicine. It was an interest which was to develop into a vocation, for Basil Lang, too, became a distinguished surgeon.

During one of our tape-recorded interview sessions at Aylesbury, Mr Lang suddenly interrupted his train of thought and said: 'You do smoke, young man, don't you?'

I said: 'Yes, I do, but I was asked not to smoke while I was with you.'

He passed no comment on this but went on:

'Today they say that smoking causes cancer of the lungs. In my days they used to say that central scotoma – the blind area in the field of vision – was caused through smoking. Although I never smoked myself, I couldn't believe that smoking would cause central scotoma and, being the kind of person who liked to get to the bottom of any problem, I decided to put my distinguished colleagues' theory to the test.

'I chose a young doctor, who was one of my patients, as my first "guinea pig". He was ideal for my research work because he had been troubled with central scotoma for a number of years and also smoked quite heavily. I outlined to him my colleagues' theory about the relationship between smoking and scotoma and said: "Let's try something, shall we? Now I want you to stop smoking." He agreed to collaborate and stopped smoking completely. He received the same treatment as before but his eyes did not improve – in fact they became worse.

'This was sufficient for me, but I realised I would have to offer much thorough proof if I wanted to substantiate my findings and convince my stubborn opponents. I made many other tests on different patients who were troubled with central scotoma and finally got together enough evidence to show conclusively that smoking could not cause central scotoma. I wrote quite a lot about the extensive research I had done, and my papers on the subject started a controversy.

'My learned opponents attempted to brush aside my findings and said: "Lang can't be right, it can't be as he says." This was because they had accepted their own theory for so long that they did not like to be proved wrong by anyone, and especially not by "a know-all", as they put it. However, some of them decided to carry out their own experiments on a number of patients, and as you know, they eventually admitted that central scotoma was *not* caused through smoking.

'I was of course grateful at having been proved right because I always tried to make a point of it that there can be *many* causes for *any* disease. If a person has a central scotoma it can be caused by so many factors. If you have an irritation of the eye, then smoking can make it worse of course but it *can't put* the disease there – as it *can't* put cancer in your lung – the disease must *be* there, and then smoking can make it worse. . . .'

Lang's father, Isaac, had been at the centre of many a strange happening at their home in Exeter. The word 'psychic' would have meant nothing to the children. It was never used. What did impress them were the unaccountable sights and sounds in a room they knew to be empty of people. And it was always their father who sought to reassure them by explaining the phenomena.

'They are spirits,' he would say, 'and there is nothing to be afraid of. Spirits won't hurt you. They just come to visit us, to be around and help us.'

So it was that early in his life William was made aware of an unseen world. Life after death was a topic he had heard much discussed. As he grew to manhood certain beliefs grew strong in him, but of course as an eminent man of medicine he realised that it would be unwise to advertise too much what was, after all, a very personal thing to him. In any event, his beliefs were unpopular then, as they are now, and he didn't want unnecessarily to lay himself open to derision.

Three men who came into his life provided him with the outlet he needed to discuss these matters. They were distinguished medical men, knights all of them – Sir John Bland-Sutton, Sir Arnold Lawson and Sir William Lister.

'They were splendid people,' Mr Lang said to me at Aylesbury. 'We would talk with each other about everything – everything you can think of – but our favourite subject was life after death. I remember, I used to say to them: "The knowledge of life after death is very consoling, because we know that even if we do our best for a patient when we operate on him but nevertheless fail, he will live on." They agreed, but whenever any of us had to reckon with a case in the operating theatre when the pendulum could swing either way, we forgot that line of thought and did everything humanly possible to save, or at least prolong, the patient's life. . . .'

One of the great joys of Mr Lang's life was the pleasure he derived in the career of his son Basil who had followed in his footsteps and become a surgeon. Father and son often operated together, and nothing gave the senior Lang greater pleasure or satisfaction than watching Basil engaged in very difficult and complicated surgery and bringing many an "impossible" operation to a successful conclusion.

Then Mr Lang's happiness was dealt a cruel blow. Basil fell ill with pneumonia and, although the best medical skill did everything that could be done for him, it was not possible to save him.

'All my hope went then, all my hope,' Mr Lang said, reliving the tragedy. 'My world collapsed, and with it all my dreams of Basil's brilliant future. He was my son. He was also a wonderful, a very wonderful surgeon, and I could not bear the thought that he would never again be seen in the operating theatre. I lost interest in everything, and went to Crowborough in Sussex because I wanted to get away for a little time from my house in Cavendish Square – it held too many painful memories for me. . . .'

Many of his famous colleagues and friends came to see him and offered help, but there was really not much they could do. Mr Lang was then already in his eighties.

One of the doctors who came to see him was a Dr Alexander Cannon – a very capable medical practitioner who was not, however, looked upon with favour by the profession because of his views about life after death. Dr Cannon believed in the projection of the astral body and spoke to Mr Lang at great length about it as well as about many other psychic aspects.

'We became rather well acquainted,' Mr Lang told me. 'I did not accept *everything* Dr Cannon said and, at times, I thought he had quite mad ideas. But I rather liked the way he stuck to his guns if he believed a thing and his never giving up what he was doing, even though it sometimes landed him in trouble.

'When Dr Cannon came to see me one day he said: "I could cure you by drawing away your spirit body a little and giving you treatment." He was very kind and went out of his way to help me but, I suppose, I had grieved too much and no longer had the will to pull through, so he couldn't really do much.'

On Tuesday, 13 July 1937, William Lang's heart stopped beating. He was holding the book *The Life of Jesus** in his hands.

* By Ernest Renan, Member of the French Academy (Mathieson & Company).

6

The Moment of Death

COUNTLESS TIMES during our interview sessions I sat and peered intently at the figure seated in the chair opposite me. My thoughts occasionally wandered into wondering just what I was doing. But it was not a fantasy I was experiencing. The constant muted hum of the tape machine kept me reminded of where I was. This was reality and I was doing a straight job of hard interviewing for what I hoped would ultimately turn out to be a bit of good factual reportage.

There was one question I wanted to ask, but wasn't quite sure if I had the courage. Suddenly, I felt I had to know.

'Can you remember exactly what it was like when you died?'

'Oh yes, yes. It is perfectly clear to me. You see on that day – 13 July 1937 – I knew my time on earth was up. I said to my dear friends who were sitting around my bed that I was going to die. One of them said: "Well, William, we shall all meet one day in the spirit world, and when that happens we shall have the privilege of watching you operate once again." I nodded my head. I was unable to talk because suddenly I felt very very tired and began to drift into a deep sleep.

'I knew a good deal about life after death, that somehow or other I would continue to exist. But I didn't know what to expect when I drifted off into sleep and passed into spirit. I was not aware of the fact that my heart had stopped beating. I felt somehow content, free from troubles and worries and I thought I'd suddenly got better.

'Then I saw my two dear wives, Susan and Isabel, dear Basil, my son, and quite a few of my best friends standing around me. It didn't dawn upon me at that moment that spirit people know when a person ends his time upon earth and so gather around him, to be near him, to help him. I thought it was just a dream. And, as I asked myself, "Where am I? What am I dreaming about?" I saw myself lying lifeless on my bed with my surgeon and doctor friends sitting around it. I could distinguish strange sounds, but not voices. Obviously they could neither hear nor see me. It was all quite worrying and I did not know what to make of it. Then I fell into another deep, dreamless sleep and was spared from worrying.

'I do not know how long this period lasted – whether it was seconds, hours, or even days? I never attempted to find out because it was not really important to me, but I did find out that during this period of unconsciousness spirit doctors and helpers attended to me, that they relieved me of this ailment and also of the worries that had been on my mind.

'Quite suddenly everything changed, and I could clearly see my two dear wives, Susan and Isabel, standing there with outstretched arms; dear Basil was of course with them, as well as the rest of my family and some of my closest friends. We could speak with each other, and I was no longer kept in doubt as to whether I had left earth or if everything was only a strange dream, because one of my medical friends said: "William, you are with *us* now in the spirit world." I then saw many of my patients whom I knew on earth and who, I'm afraid, passed on before me. They came to thank me and I felt happy, very very happy.

'My wives and friends told me they would show me round this new world, give me a holiday, so to speak. It was all very beautiful with magnificent flowers and lovely scenery, and I felt a deep peace at being able to talk with my dear family and friends again.

'As a child I used to wonder, "What is God? Who is God?" I was brought up in the Church of England faith but, throughout my life got on well with most people –

29

Church of England, Catholics, Jews, and those of other faiths. I wasn't what you would call a very religious man because I didn't spend much time in church praying, but I used to give an awful lot of thought to God. When I used to see my patients before an operation, I always prayed for them.

'When I was ill and knew my time on earth was running short, I expected that the moment I passed into the spirit world I would be brought before God to account for my life. Nothing of the sort happened. When we pass over here, we see God every day of course, but no one is brought before Him. He is not an imaginary legendary figure. God is what I see in you; God is what I see in everything that is good; and when I am healing I am doing the work of God. God is simply a Great Love, a great feeling of doing good. You see, God is a very good, a wonderful God – that is if we understand this God, and *I* feel I do understand Him. We are here to do God's work – you, George, I, anyone else; and by doing this, we get near God and are given God's favours.

'When you pass over here, you retain the same personality as you had on earth. Some people who come to see me, say: "You are such a wonderful spirit person, Dr Lang," and I tell them: "Now, look here, young lady, or young man, when I lived on earth, I liked to live my life to the full. I tried to do good and not to wilfully harm anyone, but I was *never* the *perfect* being. And now that I have passed into the spirit world, I am still the *same* William Lang as I was upon earth. I know a little more about my work, but as for changes in myself – there are none, I am still the *same* person." You see, people believe that when you pass over here you become very wonderful, but you do not. You remain the same.

'Well, having passed into spirit, I soon had a yearning to once again do something positive. I told my friends who were with me. I said: "Medicine was my whole life. I knew little else, and I would like to use my knowledge and my experience once more to help people. Can you help me?" It was then they showed me into the hospitals here, which are quite similar to other hospitals I have known. I was able to see how patients who had passed over in an imperfect state received treatment from spirit doctors and nurses. I immediately noticed that treating patients in the spirit world is very different from the way which we employed on earth and I was eager to learn this specialised technique as early as possible.

'"You won't find it difficult to learn to operate on the spirit body, William," my dear friend Bland-Sutton, who had come over here a year prior to my arrival, enlightened me. "We all had to go back to student days to acquire this new method which is vastly different from working on a physical body, but it is the only way for a spirit doctor to help his patients over here."

'I was very interested and keen to return to some work and at once started studying the art of spirit surgery. Although the spirit body is more or less identical with the physical body, it is none the less rather difficult to explain to anyone living on earth exactly *how* a spirit doctor operates upon a spirit body or engages in any other form of treatment, because it would not be understood *fully* anyway.

'Together with a number of medical friends I operated on many people who had passed over in an imperfect state, and helped to free them from all their troubles. It was very rewarding work, but I thought eventually: "I am not *really* needed here as a doctor. There are plenty of highly skilled surgeons and physicians here who are quite able to look after the spirit people. Perhaps I could help people suffering from serious ailments on earth." I spoke about this to my friends and, having considered my idea carefully, they said:

'"The only way in which your ambition can be realised is to find a medium for you through whom you could reappear on the earthplane. It is very hard to find the *right* medium, but it is possible."

'"Well, let's try to find one," I suggested.

'"You must be perfectly certain that returning to the earthplane and giving medical help to the people living there is really what you want to do, *before* the *right* medium is found and trained for you," they went on. "The reason for this is that when you find your medium, it means that you will have to stay with this medium, complete your work, and then, when the medium's lifespan on earth is finished, your work as a spirit doctor will be finished as well."

'"Well, I have made up my mind that I want to return to earth as a spirit doctor and I am perfectly willing to carry on the work as long as possible," I assured them. "Will you now assist me to find the *right* medium?"

'"You can rest assured, William, that everything will be done to help you," my friends promised. "You must be patient of course because, as we told you before, it is difficult to find the *right* medium. Don't forget that there are many doctors over here who have the same ambition as you, and who desire to return to the earthplane to work as spirit doctors through mediums; for very few of them has a medium been found. You may, however, be luckier than the others. There is a young man living on the earthplane who could be trained to become your medium. But it is an involved business and full of imponderables. For the time being you must continue your work at the hospitals here. Perfect your skill as a spirit doctor. *We'll* do our best to have experiments carried out with this young man so that he can be trained for you."'

7

A Transformation

NOT LONG after George Chapman joined the Aylesbury Fire Brigade, one of the officers was complaining about pains in his back.

'What you need is some Yoga,' Chapman said, believing it might help.

His colleague looked up in surprise and said: 'I didn't know you were interested in Spiritualism.'

Chapman replied: 'What has Spiritualism got to do with it?'

The other man then began an explanation that was almost a minor lecture, the nub of it being that it was possible to receive spirit messages if people sat round a table, put their fingers lightly on an inverted tumbler and waited for it to spell out words. Chapman was interested enough in what his fellow-officer told him to decide to try it one day just to find out what would happen.

Shortly afterwards he made friends with another man in the station who claimed he knew all about the reception of messages from spirits via the inverted glass method. It turned out that this person had taken part in Spiritualist seances while serving in the forces during the war, and consequently he knew how to conduct a glass seance. Chapman proposed to a few of his fellow-officers that they should try a seance. At first there was a laughing reluctance, but a few days later they gathered together in a group and held a successful meeting. The inverted tumbler moved from letter to letter on a sheet of paper on which the alphabet was written in a circle, and spelled out general messages for all those sitting around the table.

From then onwards the urge to give Spiritualism a try became stronger in Chapman's mind and prompted him to attend Spiritualist meetings and sit in circles. Time and again he was given messages from spirit. The most recurring one was that he would become a healer.

'I found I did not get anywhere in the circle and only wasted my time as far as my own Spiritualist development was concerned,' he told me. 'Consequently I came to the conclusion that the only way to really find out anything was to try sitting on my own. I thought, "well, nothing can happen to me because I know I am master of my own mind, I know what I want, and if any spirit comes, he certainly won't frighten me. Might perhaps even help me to find out more about it."

'So I started sitting on my own in my bedroom – every day, Saturdays and Sundays included – and I meditated for hours on end. I found my psychic development coming on in leaps and bounds, and one day I decided to try something new. I now know it to be astral travel. I just lay down and it happened straight away – I seemed to know what steps I should take and no one needed to tell me, "you ought to do this or that or study books about the other".

'At first I used to watch myself moving about in different parts of the house while my body remained lying on my bed – I used to let myself look in different rooms downstairs. Then I tried to send myself farther afield.

'Another stage in my development was that I used to go to sleep, and when I woke up, I knew consciously where I had been. As I matured still further, I would find myself falling into a very heavy sleep, but when I awoke I didn't know anything of what had happened. This was the start of my being able to go into deep trance.'

Most people without mediumistic faculties are interested to know what a medium feels when going into trance, so I interrupted Chapman to ask him.

'Well,' he said. 'I sit down, and after a short while I feel a heaviness on the head. A strong pulling sensation appears to take place at the base of my skull. Soon I feel very tired and fall asleep – or so it seems. In this state I experience all kinds of dreams – some quite ridiculous and fantastic, and others instructive and interesting. I have, however, no recollection whatever of what my spirit control is doing when he takes full charge of my physical body.'

I took this opportunity to enquire if it was *always* easy for him to slip into the state of trance whenever required and wherever he was or if there were instances when he encountered difficulties of some sort or other.

'To get into trance doesn't ever create *any* difficulty for me,' he said. 'It doesn't make the slightest difference to me where I am or under what circumstances I have to do it. I just sit down, make myself comfortable, and the rest you already know.

'There was only one occasion when I experienced some difficulty and could not slip into trance with my usual ease. This happened ten years ago in the Midlands – in the autumn of 1954.

'A woman there had been given distant healing for some time for internal trouble, and one day she wrote to me and asked me to visit her to give her contact healing. In those days I was able to visit patients in urgent need of contact healing, so I made an appointment and drove to where she lived.

'When I arrived she asked me if I could wait until her husband arrived, as he was also in need of help but refused to have anything to do with Spiritualism or spirit healing. She hoped that by watching William Lang giving her treatment, her husband might be convinced and, perhaps, agree to receive healing. I'd had requests of a similar nature previously, and as she assured me that her husband would arrive home very shortly, I agreed to wait for him.

'When he came in and his wife told him what she had in store for him, he was quite adamant and determined not to have anything to do with spirit healing. He was a highly intelligent man, but of stubborn determination. I remember wondering what his job was, but I was not told and was not inclined to enquire. Anyway, he eventually yielded to his wife's persuasion – probably out of courtesy to her and because of his curiosity about what would happen – and he led me into the lounge. He said he'd "have to go first". He had a spine injury, and I noticed that he walked with considerable difficulty.

'When we retired to the lounge, I endeavoured to go into trance, but for the first time in my association with William Lang, I experienced difficulty. As soon as I felt near to it, unknown faces materialised and a strange odour – which reminded me of death – pervaded the room.

'I mentioned this difficulty to my patient, who had not had the chance to have his customary bath and change of clothes since arriving back from work. He smiled and stood up. He walked to the door, and, as he went out, said, "I'll be back shortly."

'When eventually he returned to the lounge, I again composed myself to go into trance. This time I succeeded without difficulty and very shortly William Lang was able to take full control of me. He attended to the patient, performed an operation on the spirit body and succeeded in curing the man almost instantaneously. Afterwards the wife was operated on and her internal trouble disposed of.

'A little later, when we were having a cup of tea, the husband mentioned my difficulty in going into trance. "As I told you," I said, "I kept getting a most peculiar smell, and all these faces kept materialising. And it was a smell of – I hope you'll excuse me – a smell of death."

'The husband inclined his head slightly and smiled. "I think I can explain why," he said. "You see, I'm a surgeon. Today I was doing post mortems." The conditions which I'd picked up in the first instant were undoubtedly those of the dead bodies the surgeon had examined that day.'

But this carries us ahead of George Chapman's development as a medium.

The process was slow, and at first very far from spectacular. There was little of the sensational associated with it which might have convinced the easily-swayed into instant acceptance of the extraordinary.

But one day in 1946 Chapman was hurrying along a street on his way to the fire-station. As he rounded a corner he came across an old man whose ragged clothes betrayed the fact that he had seen better days. Apparently, the old fellow had been standing at the kerb for some time trying to cross the stream of traffic. High Street was crowded, and he was standing there isolated and helpless.

George Chapman stopped when he saw him and said: 'Trying to get across, are you dad?'

The man turned rheumy old eyes at him, and nodded, mouthing frustrated curses at the traffic and his own lack of mobility.

'Here, I'll get you across,' Chapman said taking hold of the man's arm.

They moved slowly forward, Chapman once or twice holding up a hand to restrain the speeding vehicles.

As he held the stranger's arm, Chapman realised that the old man could hardly have any use of the limb, so locked did it feel on its bent position. He made no comment, however, but laid his free hand on the fixed joint. When they reached the other side of the road, the old man suddenly shouted:

'It's free! It's free!'

Chapman did not say anything. He left the stranger, and walked quickly away. When he had gone some little way, he looked back and saw the old man still standing on the edge of the pavement, moving his arm up and down and crying excitedly:

'He's made it move! It's free! It's free!'

There were other people in the Aylesbury district who, as time went by, were helped by the fireman with the soft voice and the Merseyside accent. And since Chapman was fully conscious on these occasions he, too, was often amazed at the things that happened.

It was raining outside in the Aylesbury streets and a

cold wind was whipping the freezing drops against the windows. It was one of those treacherous days when driving demanded great care and concentration. All the way from Worthing, Pearl, my wife, had listened while I talked but had said nothing. She was keeping her eyes on the road. It was only when we got to Aylesbury at last, and had to slow down, that she relaxed. We were both hoping that the weather would clear by the time the interview with Mr Lang was concluded.

He was sitting in his usual chair, back to the window over which the venetian blind had been drawn shut. The red wall lights made a soft warm glow in the room. The reels on the recorder were revolving at their slow 15/16 speed. Lang was talking, and his words were being preserved on the thin brown tape.

'. . . and so Joseph, my friends in the spirit world came to me and said they had been successful in finding the right medium for me. They had prepared and tested him and were quite confident that we should be able to work perfectly together.'

'This testing and preparing, how long did it go on?' I asked.

'Oh, I think five years or thereabouts. But you can check that. Yes, my friends told me that my medium was a young man named George Chapman who was living in Aylesbury. He was a member of the local Fire Brigade. Well, of course I found George to be an extraordinarily nice chap.'

'Can you tell me what it was like the first time you worked through George Chapman?' I said.

'Yes, yes of course. You should know, by the way, that in his period of preparation George had been the instrument of a number of cures.* These were carried out by

* I checked this and found out that George Chapman had become well known around Aylesbury at this time. It was known that he frequently travelled at his own expense to patients who could not come to him, or who could not afford the fares. So, while still a serving fireman, he was winning a reputation as a healing medium.

some of my colleagues from the spirit world, notably by two Scotsmen. One of them was Dr McPherson who, I understand, attended to George's mother in Bootle in the 1920's. The other was my Scottish-born surgeon friend McEwen. I think I told you on a previous occasion that he was a noted bone specialist.

'But now to the first time – I remember it well. As soon as I was told: "You have completed your training and your medium is ready", I went to take control of George. He just went into trance (it has always been easy with him, he can sit and go into trance anywhere as if he is going to sleep) and I was able to control him straight away. My colleagues, the other spirit doctors, had done an excellent job and enabled both George and myself to embark on a working association which has always been ideal.'

'Is George Chapman your only medium, or do you work through others as well?' I asked.

'Only through George,' Lang said decisively. 'I couldn't work through any other medium. Why do you ask this question?'

'Because certain healers and mediums have said that you are also working through them when you are not using George.'

'That's nonsense!' the spirit doctor exclaimed emphatically. 'I have *never* worked through any other medium but George, and indeed I wouldn't be able to. I told you a little while ago that George and I were trained for each other and that before George's training as my medium started I had to make up my mind once and for all whether or not I wanted to stay with him throughout his life span on earth. I made my decision to do so, so you see, even if I wanted to leave him and work through someone else I couldn't. But of course I don't ever want to leave him. I am very fond of him as I've told you already, and our association is ideal.'

'I can't understand how people dare state for a fact that you're working through them if it isn't true.'

'Well, you know how it is,' Lang said. 'George and I are by now well known, so other individuals try to enlarge their numbers by pretending that I am working with them – that they are in good hands, so to speak. But that doesn't worry us. It is sufficiently well known that my *only* medium is George and that's all that matters.'

I also asked George Chapman what it was like the first time the spirit doctor took full control of him.

'Well, he conveyed to me that he had been a man named William Lang,' George Chapman told me. 'Said he'd been a surgeon working in London in the last part of the past century and right up to some years before the Second World War.'

I said: 'What was your reaction to this?'

'Don't get my meaning wrong,' he said, 'it wasn't that I didn't believe it, you know, but I wanted to, well, put it to the test. So the next time I went into trance, I got one of my mates from the Fire Brigade to come along and get all the details down. I can't remember anything that goes on and is said when I'm in trance, and I wanted to have some details to check on.'

8

'There's No Doubt About It'

From the day in 1951 Mr William Lang, f.r.c.s., returned as a spirit doctor, he endeavoured to establish that he was *the* William Lang who had been born at Exeter on 28 December 1852, and passed away on 13 July 1937. In order to satisfy his medium of his true identity, he revealed many episodes from his life on earth – things that could only have been known to a circle of intimate friends – and requested that his information should be corroborated.

When George Chapman studied these revelations which his colleagues had recorded for him while he (Chapman) had been in deep trance, he was pleased that his spirit doctor control had given him something to go on. As an ordinary layman he had not heard of a surgeon named William Lang. This was not surprising, because during his life Mr Lang had not been what one could call either 'famous' or 'fashionable' and his name was consequently not bandied about in the popular press. Although he had distinguished himself in many ways as an outstanding ophthalmic surgeon, he had been far from a spectacular figure, and his skill more familiar among the profession itself.

Chapman was satisfied that his control was highly skilled because he had already had ample evidence. A number of patients who had come to Chapman's house to be treated by Mr Lang had already been classed 'incurable' by their own doctors and specialists. Lang, working through Chapman, cured these 'incurables'. But Chapman was eager to know as much as possible about the past life of the man who controlled his body while he himself was in deep trance. To corroborate what had been told to him by his control Chapman asked his friends to look up details about Mr William Lang, F.R.C.S., in the public libraries. This was done to the best of their ability but the searchers drew a blank.

Unaware of the fact that details about Mr Lang could not be found in this way, they jumped to the conclusion that corroboration did not exist. Was this evidence of fakery somewhere? One of Chapman's helpers said to him: 'It would appear that your spirit doctor has given us fictitious information about himself because we can't find a single book or pamphlet that contains any reference to a surgeon named Lang around the time he claims he was alive.'

Mr Lang was disappointed with the 'poor' attempts that had been made to authenticate his statements. He said to George Chapman: 'Of course you won't find anything about me in the books published for the general reader; look up literature which was published for members of the medical profession and you'll find out that everything I've told you is correct.'

The British Medical Association was then approached with an enquiry as to whether anything was known about a Mr William Lang, F.R.C.S., born on 28 December 1852, died on 13 July 1937. No further details were given. In due course, a reply from the B.M.A. was received, and it confirmed all the details the spirit doctor had revealed about his medical career. Chapman and his friends then accepted as a fact that the spirit doctor was the same Mr William Lang, F.R.C.S., who had started his medical career at the London Hospital, and who had later distinguished himself as an ophthalmic surgeon at the Middlesex and Moorfields.

Some time later even more striking proof was furnished that the spirit doctor controlling George Chapman during his trance state was indeed *the* brilliant William Lang, F.R.C.S. This unsolicited evidence was supplied by a number of people who had met Mr Lang either at the Middlesex or Moorfields Hospitals, or at his private practice. There were people who vividly remembered the dapper, kindly ophthalmic surgeon.

When going to George Chapman's sanctuary to seek the spirit doctor's help, Mr Lang's ex-patients and friends just expected to be seen by *a* Dr Lang.* As soon as they met and talked with him, they were astonished by old familiarities in speech and manner. Here was someone they hadn't seen in years, someone who had died before the Second World War! And, yet, he was able to recall instances from long ago meetings, matters known only to themselves. They were more certain than ever that no possibility of mistaken identity existed.

One of the personalities to identify the spirit doctor as Mr William Lang, F.R.C.S., in 1961 was Dr Kildare Lawrence Singer, M.R.C.S. (Eng.); L.R.C.P. London, 1917, Middlesex; Capt. I.M.S., who remembered Lang well. He had first meet him while a student at the Middlesex Hospital, where he received instruction in ophthalmology from him. Later, after he had qualified as a doctor, a friendship with his distinguished senior developed, and their devotion to each other continued until Lang's death.

Dr Singer's recognition of his old friend was entirely unexpected. Singer suffered from cancer and when he found out that a spirit doctor named Lang had cured some patients also afflicted with the malady he decided to consult him. It never occurred to Dr Singer that there could be any connection between this *Dr* Lang and the *Mr* Lang, his old mentor and friend, but when he entered George Chapman's sanctuary and the spirit doctor greeted him with the familiar: 'Hello my dear boy, I *am* happy to see you again,' Singer knew immediately he was facing William Lang, F.R.C.S.

Mr Lang talked with his 'young' friend for some considerable time and sometimes about long-forgotten episodes from their past.

* The spirit doctor is generally known as 'Dr' Lang although as a surgeon his correct description is Mr.

'I have been given ample evidence that he is, without a doubt, the Mr Lang I met at the Middlesex Hospital for the first time in 1914,' Dr Singer said immediately after the confrontation. His next visit strengthened this conviction.

Mrs Katherine Pickering of Aylesbury identified, in 1952, 'Dr' Lang as Mr William Lang, F.R.C.S., with as much certainty as Dr Singer had done nine years later. She had first met Mr Lang almost sixty-one years ago, had been under his care for fifteen years and consequently was able to claim she knew him fairly well.

'I was four years and nine months old when I had a serious attack of measles and German measles which affected my eyesight and were suspected of having contributed to my alarming myopia,' Mrs Pickering told me when I visited her at her Aylesbury home on 26 August 1964. 'I was taken to the Ophthalmic Department of the Middlesex Hospital and became Mr Lang's patient.

'I was a rather shy child and was usually frightened of strangers, particularly doctors, but as soon as Mr Lang sat me on a chair and started talking to me, before even looking at my eyes, all my shyness and fears were gone, and I felt as though I was speaking to an uncle or a relative.

'He was not tall, like some of the other doctors there, and he spoke so kindly that I took to him right from the start.'

'It's extraordinary that you can remember all these details,' I cut in. 'It's over sixty years ago.'

'Well, not quite,' Mrs Pickering explained. 'I *was* Mr Lang's patient for *almost fifteen years* – till I was nearly twenty. You would be surprised how clearly one remembers things in one's life if they made a sufficient impression at the time. Mr Lang made a very great impression on me. I was shy and frightened, as I told you; and this is doubtless the reason why a childhood memory of a man who was so kind and gentle is so deeply engraved in my mind.'

44

'What made you so sure that the spirit doctor is the same Mr Lang under whose care you were at the Middlesex Hospital?'

'Well, as soon as I walked into Mr Chapman's sanctuary in 1952, Dr Lang greeted me with the words: "It's nice to see you again after all these years, Topsy. I remember you when you were so high," and he held his hand out. Now, he'd always called me "Topsy", as a child, and the way he said it now and put his hand on my shoulder – well, I mean who could possibly have known a thing like that about me from over sixty years ago? I'd not met Mr Chapman before. I'm convinced that it was, is, Mr Lang.

'He examined my eyes and the way he said: "Oh dear, they are still not too good," made me remember that he frequently used this very same phrase when I went to see him as a teenager. I really felt myself back at the Middlesex Hospital. To have found Mr Lang after all these years was quite astonishing.'

Mrs Pickering told me that Mr Lang had performed a spirit operation on her eyes and that, as a result of it, her vision improved to such a degree that she can now read without spectacles – something she could not do before her visit to George Chapman's sanctuary. She added that she had not told Chapman nor Mr Lang about her suffering from internal trouble for which she had gone to see him to receive help; Mr Lang had nevertheless diagnosed her complaint precisely without asking her anything about symptoms. He had performed some additional spirit operations, given her spirit injections, and had relieved her from her complaint and suffering.

'I was brought up of old Quaker stock – my people have lived in Buckinghamshire for three hundred years – and my father always instilled in me the obligation to speak the solemn truth,' Mrs Pickering went on. 'I'm mentioning this to make it absolutely clear that I never say anything in public without being perfectly certain of my facts. When I say that I believe the spirit doctor and Mr William Lang are one and the same person, I am absolutely sure of it.'

Mrs Pickering is indeed very much concerned about checking everything before making any statement. Since childhood she has kept diaries, concise but descriptive accounts of the people she has met and the things and events that have impressed her. Before answering any of my questions, Mrs Pickering consulted her records. She didn't, she said, want to rely on recollection which can be fallible.

At the time of Mrs Pickering's treatment, George Chapman had no idea of what William Lang looked like. He had been unable to find any photographs, and all he had to go on were the descriptions given him by Mrs Pickering. Then one day he came across a reference to a Mr McDonald who called himself a Psychic Artist. It was a description which intrigued George Chapman.

Mr McDonald, it appeared, claimed that he could paint portraits of people who had died, with no more help than the signature of the person who required the portrait. Wondering just what he would get back, George Chapman wrote a simple letter which said: 'I should like a portrait of my spirit control.' Apart from the address and his own signature, there was nothing else on the plain sheet of note-paper.

In due course a thin oblong parcel was delivered at Chapman's house. When he opened it, he was to see a picture in colour of an elderly man wearing wing collar and cravat. A note accompanying the painting explained that the spirit control's name was William Lang, and that he had been a medical man.

Chapman had never met this Mr McDonald. He had never spoken or written to him, other than to send the request for the portrait. Yet here was McDonald's note already identifying the spirit control as William Lang. George Chapman, for the umpteenth time in his life, was astounded. Nevertheless, the exchange remained incomplete. Chapman wondered how good a likeness had the Psychic Artist managed to make.

A few days after the portrait arrived, Chapman met Mrs Pickering. As soon as he could decently interrupt her conversation, he said: 'Oh by the way, someone sent me a picture the other day. It's of an elderly man. Very nice picture too. It's an original. Would you like to come and have a look at it?'

Mrs Pickering looked mystified at this strange request, but returned with Chapman to his home to see the work of art. As soon as she saw it, she put her hand to her mouth in an involuntary gesture of surprise and said: 'Oh but this is Mr Lang! Didn't you know?'

'Mr Lang, you say?' Chapman said by way of reply.

'Yes, yes, of course it is.'

'Look Mrs Pickering, how sure are you that this really is Mr Lang?' Chapman pressed.

'My dear Mr Chapman, how could I ever mistake him? I *knew* the man, attended him for fifteen years, right through my childhood and teens until I was twenty! Don't you understand? One doesn't forget a face you've known all that time, you know.' She turned away from Chapman to look back at the portrait. 'Why I even remember that cravat he's wearing. Extraordinary. Quite an extraordinary likeness.' She stood there looking at it for some minutes. When she left, it was with a strange quizzical stare at George Chapman.

Some months later, after persuading friends to search all sorts of unlikely as well as likely sources. Chapman managed to get hold of an old medical publication which carried a photograph of William Lang at the height of his career.

He brought the book with him, found the page with the picture of Lang, and then compared it with the portrait.

The similarity between the painting and the photograph was remarkable.

The success achieved by George Chapman as the medium of a spirit doctor quickly became known and marvelled at not only in Aylesbury and throughout Hertfordshire but all over the country.

His achievements were startling. Many persons suffering from incurable diseases visited him and were able to leave his house and pass on the news of miraculous cures affected by the 'dead' doctor – the spirit doctor named William Lang. Soon the number of patients who sought out George Chapman to be treated by Mr Lang became enormous.

9

The Voice of Authority

PERCY WILSON, M.A. (Oxon) – Technical Editor of
the journal *The Gramophone*; former Vice-President
of The College for Psychic Science; one of the world's
leading authorities on psychic research and phenomena;
and Chairman of Psychic Press Ltd – is one of the few who
not only met George Chapman in the early days of his
mediumship, but who also continued to meet him and the
spirit doctor at frequent intervals. But, unlike the others,
Mr Wilson did not, in the first instance, seek out the
medium for the purpose of healing. As a critical but fair-
minded investigator, his object was to establish whether
George Chapman's claim to being controlled by a spirit
doctor was genuine or whether the young man was a victim of self-deception.

'I first met George Chapman some twelve years ago in
London and we sort of gravitated together,' Mr Wilson
told me when I interviewed him on 11 December 1964. 'He
was one of the people I wanted to meet because I was
anxious to establish by means of serious research whether
or not this young man was indeed controlled by a spirit
doctor and, if that being so, he was sufficiently developed
to enable his spirit control to work efficiently through him.

'Of course I did not really suspect the young man of any
consciously fraudulent intention, but there are so many
people who so much want to be trance mediums that frequently they are apt to fall victims to involuntary
self-deception; they trick themselves into the belief that
their imagination is fact. Although there may be no calculated imposture, they are nevertheless as dangerous as

deliberate frauds because they mislead, and often greatly disappoint, those who come to them in good faith. In this way they throw a stigma on spirit healing and Spiritualism as a whole. One can therefore never be too careful when investigating trance mediumship.

'Now, in the case of George Chapman, I had to be particularly thorough because he not only claimed to be a trance medium who was controlled by a spirit doctor, but even stated that his control was a certain William Lang, F.R.C.S., who had died in 1937 and who, during his lifetime had been a surgeon and consultant specialist at a number of well-known London hospitals. Well, if the result of my investigation satisfied me that this was a fact, it would be a wonderful and significant contribution to spirit healing and Spiritualism in general, and I would do everything I could to help the young man and his spirit control in every way. However, if my research convinced me that the claim was unfounded I would of course have to make it known that in my view this was not a bone fide case of spirit healing. A step like this would, indeed, have been my duty, because, in spirit healing in particular, every possible precaution must be taken that only those people are accepted as spiritual healers whose bona fides have been proved beyond all possible doubt.'

'Having been an active Spiritualist for over half a century and having engaged extensively in psychic research, are you satisfied that you could not be tricked in any way by a very clever and cunning imposter?' I enquired.

'Well, I believe I am qualified to carry out these investigations quite competently. During the past fifty years or so I have studied the phases of mediumistic trance through many notable exponents,' Mr Wilson replied. 'I should think it is true to say that I have more direct experience of trance mediumship, and more knowledge of its different aspects, than any other person alive today. That may sound rather strange because there are plenty of trance mediums who have more direct experience of *being in trance*. But a person who goes into trance doesn't necessarily know the intricacies of trance mediumship and the variety of it, or its peculiarities or even techniques. If I investigate a form of trance – or supposed trance – I can tell quite quickly whether it is genuine or whether it is just self-deception, or perhaps even deliberate fraud. Quite a lot of so-called trance is self-deception.'

'Did you investigate George Chapman's claim when you first met him?'

'Well, no. I met him in London as I said, and at that time he was in his normal state of consciousness. To be able to investigate his claims, I needed to see him in trance. So, all I could do at our first meeting was to arrange to meet him when he was under spirit control.

'I talked with him of course about his mediumship and work, and I was in no doubt that he was a sincere young man who was imbued with the desire to be of service to suffering humanity. Unfortunately this was no guarantee that he was indeed a genuine trance medium – his desire to help suffering people could well have been the root of involuntary and quite innocent self-deception. But of course I didn't make up my mind either way, because if I was to engage in serious research I couldn't afford to arrive at any conclusions before I had unearthed all the relevant facts by careful investigation.'

Mr Wilson kept his appointment with George Chapman, and when he entered Mr Lang's consulting room he found the medium already in trance.

'When I first went to Aylesbury and saw Dr Lang, I got a most favourable impression,' Mr Wilson said. 'I could tell at once – and anybody who is experienced in trance mediumship can do this – that it was not only a genuine trance, but one of a very high order.

'I got a definite impact that I was meeting an entirely different personality – entirely different from George Chapman an old man, a wise old man at that, whose medical background stood out a mile so to speak. I should have taken him for a Harley Street specialist straight away, you see, both from his general attitude and from the fluent and almost casual way he spoke about medical things.

'After I'd carried out a very thorough investigation which furnished me with conclusive proof that this was definitely a case of a very high-grade mediumistic trance, I once more met George Chapman as soon as he had regained his normal state of consciousness. Though I had already collected all my evidence that here was a really outstanding medium who was controlled by an identifiable surgeon, I cross-examined him very searchingly once again in his normal state of consciousness. There were lots of things I wanted to know from him.

'In these early days of his mediumistic association with Dr Lang it was clear that George Chapman's own medical knowledge was very much less than mine, and that, apart from this, he was a very simple, genuine and honest character. Yet Dr Lang was unquestionably an expert. The difference was marked.

'Moreover, in those days George Chapman was not what you could call an intellectual type of man – he was quite simple in some respects, and indeed was perhaps inclined to be a little *gauche*; but as his healing mediumship developed and he came more and more under Dr Lang's influence, he's become more and more cultured and more intellectual. He's learned a lot through Dr Lang, but even now, after thirteen long years of close association with his spirit control, he's still as entirely different in personality from Dr Lang as he was when I first met him in his normal state of consciousness.

'When I left Aylesbury that particular evening in 1952, my considered verdict was: It was one of the most interesting and thorough forms of trance mediumship that I've ever seen. And the more I met George Chapman and Dr Lang in these later years, the more I have confirmed the verdict I'd arrived at thirteen years ago.'

Mr Wilson also met Mr Lang as a patient when he went to consult him ten years ago to receive help from the spirit doctor, help which he could not get through orthodox medical treatment. The complete cure of his ailment was so speedy and striking that whenever he felt in need of medical advice he went to consult Mr Lang as well as his own doctor or specialist. And he was so impressed with Mr Lang's abilities and achievements that he took a considerable number of relatives and friends to Aylesbury for spirit operations and healing.

'One of the people I took to Dr Lang was my niece, who'd been a medical problem ever since she was born,' Mr Wilson said. 'When she was sixteen weeks old she started suffering from tummy trouble and couldn't keep any food down. The hospital doctors operated on her three times to try and find what the trouble was. They didn't reach any definite conclusion, but fortunately the operations seemed to have the desired effect and for some years she was free from trouble.

'Then, five years ago, she suddenly had a recurrence of it. Her parents took her back to the hospital. The same specialist who'd performed the operations before was still there, and after he'd examined her again, he said it was the old trouble and that they'd have to operate again to try to detect the cause.

'At that stage, however, I took my niece to Dr Lang. As soon as he examined her he said: "Oh, this is a very peculiar inflammation of the stomach, a very peculiar one. It's an inflammation of the interior walls. I'll operate myself and we'll put that right." He performed an operation on her spirit body and she has not had any recurrence since.

'That was five years ago. The specialist at the hospital, who'd had her under observation for years, was – and still is – puzzled by the miraculous recovery, which occurred before he'd had the chance to operate. Well, there she is. She's a highly intelligent child who is doing very well at school. I asked her only about a month ago whether she'd had any further trouble, and she replied: "No, nothing, not the slightest little bit." Well, I've taken quite a few people like that to Dr Lang. Not a single one has failed to have considerable relief from Dr Lang's spirit operations and healing.'

Mr Wilson also recalled the following case of a lady whom he had taken to Mr Lang but who was already beyond help even through spirit healing:

'When he'd examined her, Dr Lang told me candidly that he did not think he would be able to save her earthly life because he'd been consulted too late. This is one of Dr Lang's unique qualities. If he knows he cannot help, he never misleads anyone by lulling them into false hope, though of course he says it diplomatically so as not to upset or frighten the patient. This candidness is very important because one knows that if, on the other hand, he says he can help a patient, it's not just a frivolously made statement.

'Well, according to the family doctor's prognosis, the lady was expected to live another two or three weeks. When I spoke with her the day after Dr Lang had seen her, she told me: "I'll have breakfast with Dr Lang next Monday or Tuesday" I said: "Why do you think so?" She looked at me with one of those knowing looks and said: "Dr Lang is very cute."

'On Monday evening she passed away calmly and peacefully.'

During his many visits to Aylesbury over the past twelve years Mr Wilson has had ample opportunity to study Mr Lang's behaviour and healing techniques, and he summed up his findings as follows:

'I am always impressed by the fact that Dr Lang goes out of his way to explain things to a patient – and especially a new patient – and by the way in which he almost immediately gains everybody's confidence. I am equally impressed by his explanation of how he detaches a person's spirit body so as to be able to perform his operations on it or give it other forms of healing treatment, and particularly by the clear-cut words with which he makes it understandable to everyone that there is a difference between the spirit body and the spirit itself.

'Still another thing about Dr Lang that impresses me is his sure touch on *everything*, his sure touch in every way. Mind you, I have good reason to know that when he's doing his diagnosis and explains things to a patient, he's quite diplomatic about it. It's one of his great subtleties

54

that he never blurts out things on impulse which would give the patient a shock or even a wrong impression of any kind. And he only promises to be able to cure a complaint if he is completely sure of himself. Even then he usually only says "I think we might be able to help you" and that's, generally speaking, as far as he goes.

'Apart from his healing, I think even more striking is his uncanny power of diagnosis – his X-ray eyes, as I put it. His description of a patient's symptoms and even the medical history is always accurate and so is his prognosis of the effect his operations and treatment of the spirit body are to have on the physical body.

'One is never in doubt when listening to Dr Lang that here is an old and learned and experienced medical man. And this is not merely my own opinion, but also that of many members of the medical profession, some of whom indeed were his friends and pupils when he was at the Middlesex Hospital in his earth life.'

Mr Wilson's testimony as to the genuineness of George Chapman's mediumship carries with it an immense amount of authority. Those involved with psychic research are only too keenly aware of the stringent tests they are required to set up to prove the veracity of the claims made by those who think themselves gifted with psychic qualities. In the area of psychic science and research, the name of Percy Wilson is a very considerable one indeed.

10

A Policeman's Lot

REGINALD ABBISS of Aylesbury – a retired Super-intendent of Police who spent thirty years in the force – was one of the people who went to George Chapman's sanctuary during the early stages of his association with Mr Lang.

I wanted to know how it came about that a senior police officer with a sceptical mind went to seek a spirit doctor's help instead of consulting his own medical practitioner?

'Well, I'll tell you,' Mr Abbiss said when I saw him at his Aylesbury home on 16 September 1964. 'A friend of mine who'd served with me in the police force since 1929, and who knew that my wife was in poor health, told me about how wonderfully Dr Lang had helped a friend of his who had been hopelessly ill. He thought the spirit doctor might be able to do more for my wife than orthodox medical treatment which had not, frankly, shown too good results. Actually I found out later that this friend of mine had been thinking about it for some time before approaching me. He was afraid I'd blow up at the mention of unearthly things. At the same time he didn't want my wife to be deprived of something that might bring about a cure. So, first he told me all about the remarkable things that Dr Lang was doing.

'I'd never come in contact with anyone or anything connected with Spiritualism or spirit healing before, but I was interested to learn from my friend that Dr Lang worked through his medium, Mr George Chapman, and how the spirit doctor actually worked and helped his patients. I was so intrigued with what my friend told me that I decided to visit Dr Lang to find out for myself what it was like to meet the spirit of a "dead" man.

'My friend arranged an appointment for my wife to be seen by Dr Lang at Mr Chapman's sanctuary and I went along with her. From what I had learned by then I had some idea of how things were but I did not really know exactly what to expect.

'When my wife and I entered Dr Lang's consulting room, a courteous old gentleman, or so it seemed to me, with his eyes shut, welcomed us and extended his hand in greeting. He conversed with us for a while and we spoke of all sorts of things. When he learned that I was a retired Superintendent of Police, he said I was his first patient of this sort and spoke with me about how very much easier police work was in his day.

'It was an unusual, in a way overwhelming, experience. It was the first time in my life that I had ever seen anybody in trance. In fact, when I spoke with the spirit of a "dead" man through the medium as freely as with any person, I thought, "I wonder what I've missed by not having attempted to find out about these things before."'

Mr Lang requested Mrs Abbiss to lie on the healing couch and, as he touched her fully-clothed body lightly with his hands, he diagnosed her complaint in every detail. He then explained to both Mr and Mrs Abbiss that every person had a physical and a spirit body, that he treated the spirit body only, in an attempt to achieve a corresponding effect on the physical body.

Then Mr Lang performed some spirit surgery on Mrs Abbiss, her husband the whole time looking on and noting what was happening.

'I was surprised when he wanted to examine *me* because I had not arranged to see him myself – I'd just come to accompany my wife,' Mr Abbiss continued. 'As a matter of fact, I had been troubled for some time with a little internal discomfort but hadn't bothered about it, and I had certainly not mentioned anything about it to anyone. I wondered how Dr Lang could know about it.

'I did of course as I was told, and, as soon as I lay on the healing couch and Dr Lang – his eyes still shut – touched my fully-clothed body lightly with his hands, he told me exactly what was wrong: that I had been suffering from something to do with my pyloric opening which needed attention because of the constipation and discomfort it caused. He then explained that he would perform a spirit operation which would relieve me of the trouble.

'I must say that I felt a most pleasing sensation as he did his work.

'Dr Lang was perfectly right in everything he said. The day after he'd operated on me, I felt a slight improvement. Don't think that this was brought about by wishful thinking or willpower. Anyway, within about a fortnight I was in the clear, proof enough that Dr Lang had indeed cured me.'

'Are you telling me then that you accepted the whole thing right from the beginning?' I asked.

'Well, when I first entered Dr Lang's room you know, not knowing exactly what to expect, I must confess that I was on the alert to see if everything was above board,' the ex-Superintendent replied. 'You see, it is only natural that during my thirty years of service in the police force I had become accustomed to looking at things critically in an endeavour to differentiate between the genuine and the fraudulent. I watched every movement Dr Lang made closely.

'Any possible suspicions of any sort which I may have harboured were quickly dispelled and, in a way, I became ashamed of having been suspicious at all. The whole atmosphere in that room was one of sincerity and desire to help anyone in need.

'Yes, I was convinced that I was facing a genuine spirit doctor who spoke and worked through his medium. What is more, I was – and am – greatly impressed with Dr Lang. I felt I was talking to an old doctor whose mannerisms and demeanour proclaimed his profession and I had no hesitation in saying that I accepted him absolutely. My speedy recovery confirmed my faith in him.'

Ex-Superintendent Abbiss accompanied his wife to

George Chapman's sanctuary for continued treatment from Mr Lang. On one occasion he met George Chapman when the medium was not in trance.

'What a marked contrast there was between Mr Chapman and Dr Lang!' Mr Abbiss said to me. 'Physically Mr Chapman was a much younger man, and his speech too was entirely different. The older doctor always spoke as an elderly consultant, but Mr Chapman spoke with a distinct Northern accent. Their mannerisms were very different and I was left in no doubt whatever but that I was indeed meeting two completely separate individuals. Incidentally Mr Chapman was then still an officer in the Aylesbury Fire Brigade.'

Mr Abbiss regularly accompanied his wife when she went for treatment. On one occasion, a long time after the first visit, Lang unexpectedly asked him to lie on the healing couch.

Abbiss was surprised at the request, as he told me.

'"There's nothing wrong with me, Dr Lang," I said. "You've cured me completely of my trouble." Dr Lang answered: "I'd like to have a look at your eyes, young man." Well, I did as I was asked and Dr Lang performed a spirit operation on my eyes. He told me he had rectified the weakness and, to be sure, I soon noticed a considerable improvement in my vision. I used to wear glasses when driving, but since Dr Lang's operation, I no longer need to wear them.

'I am by no means an exceptional case – I know many others who have benefited from Dr Lang's operations and treatment just as strikingly as I did.

'It would not be right to assume that all Dr Lang's patients are convinced Spiritualists prepared to accept everything without questions. Quite the contrary. The patients in Mr Chapman's waiting-room come from all walks of life. A substantial number of them are not Spiritualists at all. I remember hearing a patient being asked by another whether she was a Spritualist and her prompt reply was: "No, I am not. But, what on earth has that got to do with healing? I am receiving wonderful help and I don't need to know or believe any more than that."'

11

The Knife is Cheated

DURING GEORGE CHAPMAN's earlier association with William Lang he agreed to visit patients in need of help whenever he could find the time. Sometimes it meant making long trips which he paid for himself. One such visit took place in 1954, when he set out to see Mrs Winifred Holmes at her home in Chester.

Mrs Holmes had been suffering from gall stones for a considerable time. Having failed to receive noticeable relief from orthodox medical treatment, and being reluctant to consent to an operation (like so many people, she had an inordinate fear of the surgeon's knife) she decided to try spirit healing. She had heard of some of Mr Lang's successes and wrote to George Chapman to arrange distant healing from the spirit doctor. This was arranged but failed to produce any noticeable alleviation and Mrs Holmes then asked if she could undergo contact healing and if it was possible for Chapman to come to Chester. He agreed and arranged to visit her on 3 September 1954.

When he arrived at Mrs Holmes's house, she asked him if he would wait until her husband returned home from work.

'He too is in need of treatment,' she explained. 'He is not a believer in spirit healing – in fact he has no time for Spritualism or anything of the sort – but I am hoping that if he witnessed my treatment he can be convinced of its worth and agree to being treated himself.' She added that her husband was receiving medical attention at the hospital but didn't appear to be improving.

While they waited, Mrs Holmes told George Chapman about her husband's trouble.

'He had an accident some time ago, and ever since he's been in a very bad state – often in agony,' Mrs Holmes said. 'The X-rays disclosed it was a slipped disc, a condition from which he has suffered on three previous occasions without being able to secure any permanent relief. He's a steel worker and you can imagine how difficult it is for him to wear a terrible steel corset. The doctors have now decided that a plaster jacket might be better for him. I pray that Dr Lang may be able to relieve him of his suffering and put him right. . . .'

'I am sure he will do everything he can,' Chapman replied.

When John Holmes arrived, he was introduced to George Chapman, and immediately showed strong antipathy towards anything connected with spirit healing. He said he wanted nothing to do with it, but Mrs Holmes was a persuasive wife and broke down his resistance. Reluctantly, he agreed to undergo treatment by the spirit doctor, although he remained very sceptical if somewhat curious. But he made it plain that he had yielded simply to please his wife.

The two men then retired to another room where the medium went into trance with his usual ease. Shortly afterwards Mr Lang was able to take full control of him.

'I am pleased to meet you, young man,' Mr Lang greeted Holmes. As he touched the patient's fully clothed body with his hands, he added: 'I am very happy that your dear wife wanted you to see me because I think I'll be able to put your slipped disc permanently into its right place. There won't be any need for you to wear a steel corset or a plaster jacket afterwards – you'll be perfectly all right, young man, and will be able to work with the same ease as you did before your accident. And when you go to the hospital for your next examination, the doctor will confirm it.'

Holmes was surprised that the spirit doctor had not found it necessary to question him but knew at once the nature of his illness. He began to feel much less sure that nothing would come out of the strange experience.

Mr Lang performed a spirit operation and, as he flicked his fingers and gave orders to his son Basil and other invisible assistants, John Holmes felt a sudden sharp pain.

'It was remarkable,' Mr Holmes stated afterwards. 'Dr Lang did not actually touch my body – his hands were all the time hovering just above it. When I felt the stab of pain during the "operation", I realised his hands were still an inch or two away from me.'

At first the so-called spirit operation appeared to be a failure. Far from feeling better, Mr Holmes was convinced that his condition had worsened. He thought himself all sorts of a fool for having allowed himself to be persuaded into something he had disbelieved from the start. Why hadn't he stuck to his own convictions? Women – they were always meddling! Now look at the condition he was in!

Holmes was about to give vent to his feelings when he was told: 'Very well, young man, you can try to walk and move about now if you wish.'

Holmes restrained his anger and raised himself up on the couch. Amazingly, it was easier than he expected. He slid his legs down over the side and pushed himself into a standing position on the floor. No twinge. He took a tentative step. It was painless. Then he walked across the floor to the other side of the room, and back again, and could feel himself starting to laugh with sheer relief.

But there was still one thing he wanted to try. Memory of past pain inhibited him. But he knew that if he didn't try it, he'd never know whether what he thought had just happened had *in fact* taken place. He summoned up courage, then slowly, expecting every moment to lock stiff with agony, he began to bend down as far as he could reach. He made it without the semblance of a twinge and then, as successfully, made the return journey. He had done it! There was no pain! He was cured!

John Holmes stood staring at the hunched figure watching him. 'Well, there you are young man. Feel better now?'

Holmes couldn't talk. He nodded his head.

'Now I want to see your good lady. Would you ask her to step in here please?'

Holmes went out and called his wife. When she saw his face there was much that she wanted to ask him – particularly about the inane grin he was wearing. But there wasn't time for that now. Mr Lang was waiting.

John Holmes stood and watched while the spirit operations were performed on his wife. And when they were done, he saw his wife sitting up, a smile on her face, pain lines already appearing to smooth away. She walked across to him after thanking the spirit doctor, and held out her hands. 'John,' she said, 'I feel much better. No pain any more, and I won't have to have an operation. Isn't it wonderful?' She turned back from her husband. 'Oh Dr Lang, thank you so much. Thank you, thank you,' she said.

John Holmes never wore a steel corset again.

When he visited the hospital a few days after his cure by Mr Lang, he was told that his slipped disc had gone back into place. The examining doctor expressed amazement, and also confirmed what Mr Lang had said – that there would be no further need for the steel corset or a plaster jacket. Mr Holmes kept quiet about the spirit doctor.

In January 1965 I located the Holmeses. Neither had been in touch with George Chapman or William Lang since that single occasion some ten years previously.

'There was no need to contact them,' Mr Holmes told me. 'I have worked at my old job as a steelworker ever since without a day's illness. It's many a year since I felt so well.'

Mrs Winifred Holmes too has been in good health since that September day in 1954.

12

Miracle Girl

O F ALL the cases I investigated, that of the Amersham housewife, Mrs Dorothy James, was the most astonishing and moving. Apart from wartime, I have never come across anyone so appallingly injured; fractured skull, shattered limbs, loss of sight, loss of memory – her condition appeared so hopeless that a priest had been called to administer the last rites.

But on a June day in 1964 I met Mrs James and heard from her and her husband of what had happened on 12 November 1954. Mrs James was a lively and delightful person.

'I remember getting off the bus on the way to work,' she recalled. 'And as usual, I waited until it pulled away from the stop, and I could see in both directions. I was always over-careful when crossing – in fact it was a joke with my two sisters. They always said that I never would be killed by getting knocked down by a car, because I was "too much of an old woman!" Anyway, as I say, I waited till the bus pulled away, and I must have been pretty certain nothing was coming before I took a step forward. That is all I am able to remember.'

Mrs James's husband took up the story:

'Dorothy was hit by an Aston Martin whose driver was trying it out for the first time. It was a present to him on his twenty-first birthday and he admitted to the police that he had been doing eighty miles an hour. He said he had looked away for a moment at the lovely autumn fields he was passing and when he saw the road again Dorothy was right in front of him. He slammed on his brakes but hit her. She was tossed on to the bonnet and her head went through the windscreen before she was finally flung over the top of the car and on to the road behind. She lay there broken and covered in blood.

'When the ambulance arrived, a cottager who had covered her body over with a blanket, told the crew: "You've come too late, she's ready for the mortuary, not the hospital." But the ambulance driver pulled the blanket away and, after a quick look, answered: "No, there's still life in her, let's get her to the hospital at the double." This much was told to me later.

'When Dorothy arrived at the hospital, the doctors found she had a fractured skull and that both legs were broken. She was terribly lacerated and her condition so critical that she was not expected to survive longer than a few hours. They bandaged her head, put her legs in plaster and called the priest.

'I was practically demented at this stage,' Mr James told me. 'I mean, I could hardly think straight. All I knew was that my wife was smashed up and dying. And then I was listening to some woman talking about a spirit healer who could save my wife. I cannot remember ever having given Spiritualism a thought. But I told myself, "anything, anything at all that might help." And I said to the woman: "No, I have no objection. But if he can do anything, for God's sake get him to hurry."'

George Chapman was contacted, informed of the plight of Mrs James, and asked if Mr Lang could commence distant healing as soon as possible. Meanwhile, at the Bucks Hospital, Mrs James was dying.

'The nurses,' she said, 'told me afterwards that there was an orderly from a men's ward nearby who used to come in at least once a day, sometimes twice, and again during the night, and would look at the chart at the end of the bed and ask the nurse questions.' Mrs James continued, 'When they asked him to explain his interest in me he replied, "It's all right, it's for Mrs James's good. I have to tell a friend of mine exactly how she is." Afterwards, a long time afterwards, Mr Chapman told me that a friend of his who had been working in another ward provided him with a daily account of my condition. This enabled Dr Lang to give me the most effective distant healing. But of course I knew nothing at all about it at the time. In fact it was ages before I knew anything.

'The hospital doctors were of course not aware of my being given distant healing and they couldn't understand how it was that I was alive. First they said I would never live. When I didn't die they said I would never see, or talk or walk again, and if I did indeed survive, I would have to face a future in a Mental Home. You see, the specialists had diagnosed that my brain was damaged, my whole nervous system affected, and that this damage would result in mental deficiency and permanent blindness; apart from this, my right leg and ankle were crushed.'

'Dorothy was semi-conscious for nearly six weeks,' Mr James put in. 'At times she came round, but she had no idea where she was or what had happened.

'The doctors and nurses used to refer to her as The Miracle Girl. She was taken on several occasions to the operating theatre where her wounds were stitched and where the amputation of her crushed right leg was considered. And, had the surgeon not refused to operate because he feared that she would die on the operating table (he thought the injuries to her brain too serious to subject her to such an ordeal) she would have lost her leg.'

Mr James was repeatedly told by the hospital's medical staff that he must be prepared for the worst to happen at any time. It was the opinion of the doctors that if Mrs James survived she would be blind, possibly severely mentally affected and would have to be found a place in a mental hospital.

Distant healing was given continuously by Mr Lang, and although Mrs James still remained only semi-conscious and on the danger list, she slowly grew stronger. Five weeks after the accident she recovered full consciousness for the first time. Let's take up Mrs James's story again in her own words:

'When I first woke up, I asked a lady in the next bed to

tell me where I was, but instead of replying she called the ward sister who explained that I'd had a very bad accident and had been there for almost six weeks. She called me Mrs James but I told her that my name was Dorothy Danielson* and that I wasn't married. She then went to the locker beside my bed, showed me a photograph of a little boy and said he was my son Martin. She put the photograph in my hand and helped me to hold it, because my right side was completely paralysed. I looked at the photograph and thought: "What a lucky person a woman would be to have two such lovely boys." I remember saying what lovely twins they were. Sister told me that there was only one little boy in the photograph and I told her I could see two.

0 'Sister then called the staff nurse and another young nurse to stay with me while she went to the telephone. I asked the staff nurse to give me a looking-glass so that I could see if I was Dorothy Danielson, but she said, no, the doctor had said it wasn't time to see my face yet (because it was ugly with all the stitches and raw skin). She also told me not to touch my face as otherwise my wrists would have to be fastened to the sides of the bed. My husband told me later that, during the first weeks, my bed had been like a baby's cot – sides had been fixed to the bed to stop me trying to get out, and my wrists had been tied because I had kept trying to pull the stitches from my face.

'Sister came back with some doctors, and one of them said he was so pleased that I had awakened and could see. He asked me to look at the clock on the wall and tell him the time. I did as I was asked and I also remember saying that it was rather silly having two clocks so close together, and he said: "Thank God, sister, she's told us the correct time." Then they walked away, talking about half a battle being won.

'I was trying so hard to think things out after they left my bedside, but I just couldn't remember anything. I remember my father kissing me on the forehead and saying: "God bless you, my dear, there are others who need you

* Mrs James's maiden name.

67

more than I," so when he'd gone I asked the patient in the next bed what he'd meant. She told me *no one had been at my bedside* since the doctor had left. As I was to realise, much later, my father had died some years ago.

'My fellow-patient also told me that Jeff had almost lived at the hospital for nearly four weeks – he'd stayed day and night and had fed me – and that the photograph of the little boy was really my own son Martin. She told me that my sisters and my mother frequently came to see me, and many other relatives as well. I asked her when was visiting time and she said: "You needn't worry, your family and relatives can visit you when they choose." I didn't understand what she meant. I wanted to know why *I* was so special that I could have people coming in at any time. She told me then that I had been on the danger list.

'Then sister came back. She had a person with her whom she said was a priest. I don't know his name. Sister said: "Here's a friend you'll be very pleased to see, Mrs James," But I didn't know him. For some unknown reason I was afraid of him and, as soon as he began to speak, I didn't want him to come near me. I expect I sub-consciously knew that he was the priest who had given me the last rites, I don't know. Anyway, every time he came again and I heard his voice, I used to pretend I was asleep.

'But on the day I was going home, he and sister between them caught me. Sister had ordered a special dinner – chicken, etc. and Christmas pudding – and I had a wish-bone on my plate – I still have it at home as a souvenir. For the first time I was allowed to be propped up in my bed to feed myself. We were all ready to start and then two nurses pushed a little trolley on wheels to the bottom of my bed. The trolley was made like an altar with candles and a cross in the centre. They lit the candles and in came the Dean with sister and he said: "Oh, I've found you awake at last!" We all laughed about it, the whole ward. Then he conducted a little service and it was really lovely.

'There are just a few things I can remember while I was in hospital.

'One was that a very kind man used to be nearly always

there with me – he used to feed me – and he had loving eyes. I found out afterwards that it was Jeff, my husband.

'Another time, I can remember, the surgeon telling a lot of other doctors that it was *his* case and he did *not* intend taking off my leg – he was going to patch it up, and if one was a little shorter than the other, I could always have a special shoe built up. The ward doctor told me that I hadn't been quite unconscious in the operating theatre.

'Then, on another occasion, I can remember being on a stretcher and it seemed as though my right leg was put into an oven in the wall. The ward doctor was standing beside me and I could hear his voice saying to someone: "She's coming round, shall I give her the needle now?" The next thing was that I was in the ward and all the screens were drawn around my bed. Sister and the ward doctor were on each side of me. I was in most awful pain and the doctor said something to sister about having the plaster sawn off and a new one put on. I don't remember anything after that. Later the nurses told me that the house-doctor was at my bedside all through that night.

'I also remember once seeing my sister-in-law, but they told me later that she came every day. You see, I was not quite aware of everything that was going on around me.

'One incident I remember clearly. A very old lady in a bed opposite mine cried because the nurses said she was to get up and sit in a chair. It was for her own good they said, otherwise she would never get better. I called out to sister to let me get up in her place and not to worry the old lady, but sister called across the ward to me not to be a silly girl, as it would be months before I would be allowed up. I then tried to push the clothes back, but found I couldn't move my right arm. I pushed some of the clothes away with my left, but could not move my legs.

'Sister then came to my bed and showed me the plaster around my legs. She sat on my bed and told me that there was a great possibility that I'd never walk again. But I just laughed at her and said: "Oh yes, I will, even if the doctors have to cut both my legs off. I'll have artificial ones." Sister then said: "Yes, my dear, if it ever comes to that, and please God it won't, I am quite sure you will be able to master it." She told me that in her whole nursing career she had never come across anyone with so strong a will to live and such a determination to do just the opposite of what was expected.

After I'd been in hospital six weeks I was just beginning to realise who I was, and to know that Jeff was my husband. I longed to go home and find out if I could remember my son. It was almost Christmas and I asked the surgeon if I could possibly go home for the holidays. The doctors talked it over and the next afternoon Jeff arrived and I was taken home by ambulance by the same men who had rushed me to hospital. They just could not get over the fact that I was still alive.'

Mrs Dorothy James was released from Buckinghamshire Hospital just for Christmas 1954. It was made clear that after New Year's Day she would have to return.

On arriving home she discovered to her dismay that she could not recognise anything. She was not convinced Martin was her son and not even sure whether or not she was Mrs James.

George Chapman called to see Mrs James immediately after Boxing Day during his off-duty time at the Aylesbury Fire Brigade. He talked with her for a little time about her accident and about the hospital but, while he was still talking, she fell into a deep sleep. Only when she woke up after a long and refreshing slumber did she find out from her mother, who had been in the bedroom, that George Chapman had gone into trance, and that Mr Lang had performed a number of spirit operations and had then ordered that the patient was not to be wakened, but allowed to sleep on.

'When I awoke I asked my mother: "Where's the gentleman gone?"' Mrs James continued. 'Instead of telling me, my mother said: "Don't try to pull yourself up in bed, you'll hurt yourself!" I told her: "No, don't touch me, I can do it myself." I remember putting my right arm down – the arm that I couldn't use or feel before – and I cried out, "I can lean on my arm!" And oh! there can be only one explanation – the gentleman must have done it. Why isn't he still here? Where is he? He must think me very rude going off to sleep in the middle of a conversation. You see, I didn't know who he was or what he could do, or anything. They hadn't told me about it – my mother had just introduced him to me as the gentleman who wanted to enquire about my health. It was now that my mother told me about the spirit doctor, Dr Lang, who had performed spirit operations on me while I had been asleep.

'The next morning Mr Chapman came again – straight from the fire service and still in his uniform. He hadn't been home to have his breakfast. He wanted to see what progress, if any, I had made since the previous day. I said to him: "I'm very sorry that I fell asleep yesterday – I'm not really as rude as that." He only laughed and said: "You didn't fall off to sleep, Dr Lang put you to sleep." He then explained that he was Dr Lang's medium and assured me that he and Dr Lang would do all they could to help me.

'On this occasion I saw Mr Chapman go into trance. He took off his wrist-watch and put it on the side-table, and then went over to the corner and muttered a prayer. I watched him and noticed that his body went down a little bit. I thought that my eyes must be playing tricks on me again, and I felt upset because since his first visit the previous day I had had no eye trouble at all.

'When he spoke to me a few moments later, Mr Chapman's voice had changed completely. It was not Mr Chapman's quiet voice, it was a deep husky voice and it seemed to me as though the words were sort of blurred. He came over to me, moving his hands and flicking his fingers and I had the impression he was talking to doctors and nurses, asking for instruments and things. He never touched me, but was obviously working on my head and I felt a strange sensation. Then he started working on my shoulders. My arms had been pulled out from my shoulders during the accident, and the right one hadn't been set back properly. Again he didn't really touch me, but I could feel the bone moving inside the socket. It didn't hurt, it went sort of numb.

'He was talking the whole time, and moving his hands, and he moved right down my body. When he got as far as my knee – you must remember my legs were still in plaster – he suddenly said: "I'll say goodbye for today, young lady, but I shall see you again in two day's time." I don't remember any more – suddenly I fell into a deep sleep. When I woke up, my mother was sitting by my bed, knitting, and she told me that Mr Chapman had left two and a half hours ago.

'During that afternoon and the following day I improved rapidly. I felt so much better – my speech was better, I could move my arm much more easily and my vision was so much clearer. For the first time since my accident I really started feeling on top of the world.

'When Mr Chapman came again – that was on the day before I was due to go back to hospital – I saw him go into trance for the second time, exactly in the way he had done so on the previous occasion. And when Dr Lang operated, I noticed something very interesting. When he was Mr Chapman, he used his right hand; but when he was Dr Lang he used his left. In fact, when I first noticed it I said to him: "Have you hurt your right hand, Mr Chapman?" and he replied: "Dr Lang you are speaking to – I have the honour of Mr Chapman allowing me to come through him to you to help you."

'We talked for a little while and out of the blue he said: "You do believe that I am going to make you better?" I assured him that I did, but I told him that I had to go back to the hospital next day. "I've no intention of staying there," I said. "No, you won't have to, young lady," he said. "I shall see you again next week – here in this house." He then went on performing further operations and suddenly said: "I'm afraid you won't be able to say goodbye to me today either because I am going to put you to sleep."

'After this I don't remember any more. I can't tell you what operations he performed this time. I'd slept longer than ever that day and when I woke up it was already afternoon. And again I felt very much better.'

Mrs James was taken back to hospital the following day but she was convinced that she would not be requested to stay. When the doctors examined her it was to find an improvement in her condition that was beyond their capacity to explain. They agreed to her request that she should be allowed to return home, because, they said, they believed the home atmosphere might be beneficial.

From then onwards Mrs James was taken to and from Buckinghamshire Hospital twice, sometimes three times a week. The hospital doctors invariably greeted her with 'Ah, the Miracle Girl!' or 'How's the Miracle Girl today?' Mr Lang continued to visit her regularly at her home.

'When they took the plaster off at the hospital, my right leg was three-quarters of an inch shorter than the left, and they said that I would have to have a special surgical shoe built,' Mrs James told me. 'Well, I didn't want to have this, and I fervently hoped that Dr Lang could do something. So I told him about it when he came again through Mr Chapman, and of my dread. I could see he understood my feelings. While he was operating on me that day, I suddenly had this funny feeling, as if someone was lifting my leg and putting weights on the end of it.

'Next thing was someone slapping my face lightly. It was Mr Chapman himself. He said: "Come along, come along, Dr Lang didn't want you to sleep all day, wake up. I've put the kettle on for a cup of tea. Are you feeling all right? What happened?" Evidently he doesn't know what happens, so I told him as much as I could remember, and he said when I finished: "Come on then, let's try your legs." He measured them. The right one was still a little shorter than the left, but it was longer than when they'd measured it at the hospital. Anyway, when I returned three days later to the hospital, the doctors were flabbergasted when they measured my legs and found that they were both the same length!

'There was another remarkable thing. When they set the ankle and put pins in my bones they set the ankle-bone too far forward. When they took the plaster off and discovered it, they made arrangements for me to be operated on in April 1955 so that they could try and correct it. I told Mr Chapman about it when he came the next time and I said: "You know, Mr Chapman, I feel I just can't stand any more operations." He said: "Well, I don't know anything about such operations – I expect they did their best for you under the difficult circumstances."

'While we were talking, he changed in his chair and Dr Lang came through. Almost immediately he started operating on my ankle, moving his hands and fingers and talking, and truly I could feel things being done. As soon as he had finished, I could see that the ankle-bone had been moved into its proper place. Before he left, he told Jeff to 'phone the hospital in four days' time and tell them that the proposed operation was no longer necessary. Well, Jeff did as Dr Lang had asked, but the hospital didn't take much notice of what he said. They insisted that I come in for the operation, but when they examined my ankle, they were speechless. They said they just couldn't understand how my ankle-bone could have gone back into its right position without an operation or treatment. And they said that they wouldn't need to have me in to do anything on my ankle at all.'

When the Aston Martin tore into Mrs James and did its grisly job on her body, it did not neglect her face. Her features were ripped and crosshatched by scars. When she was strong enough she was sent to the famous Stoke Mandeville Hospital for plastic surgery. This is what she told me about that episode in her life:

'Having had all those operations at the Buckinghamshire Hospital, I was frightened of what lay in store for me again, and the next time Mr Chapman came I told him about it. To cut a very long story short, Dr Lang performed a plastic surgery operation on my face. When he'd finished he wanted to know exactly when I had to go to hospital, and I told him that it was to be in a fortnight's time. He then said: "Oh, by then it'll be cleared up. Don't forget to bring that to the doctor's notice, and ask whether you can have your name taken off the list." Well, I did, because my face became as it is now – with powder on you can't see a thing – and when the lady doctor from the Stoke Mandeville Hospital examined me she was stunned. She couldn't understand it. She said there was no need for plastic surgery now. Once again Dr Lang had performed a miracle.'

It was a long time before Mrs James fully recovered from the injuries she had sustained in the accident. Although Mr Lang and his specialist colleagues in the spirit world had restored her brain and nervous system, there were no *immediate* results – she regained her full mental self only step by step. However, barely six months after her terrible accident, she was able to go out. She had to learn to use crutches, but slowly her strength and co-ordination improved. She picked up once more the threads of social life. The doctors at the hospital kept a continuous watch on her and then, on the anniversary of her accident, they classified her 'almost normal'. The Miracle Girl had lived up to her descriptive nickname.

'When Dorothy was fit enough, I used to take her to Mr Chapman's house in Aylesbury to save him coming to us,' Mr James told me. 'I was present when Dr Lang per-formed his operations, and several times I actually watched how Dr Lang took control of Mr Chapman. Mr Chapman himself used to more-or-less shrink slightly; the features, the whole body seemed to change, and the voice changed. Mr Chapman's quiet soft voice became, well, gruffish and old, if you know what I mean. Mr Chapman is very shy when he is himself, but Dr Lang knows exactly what he wants. He has an authority that you'd expect from a man used to handling a staff of assistants, nurses and doctors.

'What Dr Lang has achieved for my wife is really won-derful. He improved her eyesight with every operation. She had three changes of spectacles. Now she doesn't need them at all. His operations brought back the smell in her right nostril, he took away her awful headaches and

75

relieved her of the dizzy spells – she used to have complete blackouts and did not even know they were coming on . . . I could go on and on telling you all the many, many things Dr Lang did for her.

'When she came home from hospital, she was really in a terrible state. I remember one occasion when she had made a trifle after she'd learned to cook again, and when the door-bell rang, she just dropped the bowl with the trifle on the floor, just like that, so that she could open the door! Another time, when she wanted to put coal on the fire, she went to the pantry, got a handful of eggs and threw *them* on it. This shows you how mentally disturbed she was – in those days there was no telling what was going to happen.

'Look at her now – she is as well as she was before the accident. If it had not been for Dr Lang, and she still survived, it would only have been to spend the rest of her life in a mental hospital.'

13

Birth of the Birmingham Healing Centre

THE NEWS of incredible healing successes spread slowly but steadily through patients who had first contacted the fireman-cum-medium in despair, and had experienced the 'dead' doctor's painless spirit operations and treatment. The number of patients grew from day to day. Consultations with Mr Lang were free of charge to *any* patient.

Despite the fact that there was hardly any time left which Chapman could call his own, he never refused to travel any distance if a sufferer from ill health genuinely required the spirit doctor's help. It came about that he embarked on such a journey to Birmingham in the early part of 1956, and this was in fact the first step towards the setting up of the Birmingham Healing Centre.

For a considerable time, Mrs Joan Smith – crippled with arthritis and bed-ridden – had no other alternative but to accept the doctors' and specialists' verdicts that nothing could be done to get her on her feet again. Then she learned about how the spirit doctor William Lang had cured a patient suffering from an almost identical ailment, and Mrs Smith hoped that she, too, might benefit from spirit healing. She wrote to George Chapman, explained her circumstances, and asked if he could come and see her at her Birmingham home. To her surprise and delight she got a reply saying that he would visit her.

A frequent visitor to Mrs Smith's home at the time was Mrs Hilda Carter, a kindly woman living at King's Heath, Birmingham. When I met Mrs Carter in June 1964, she told me about the concern she used to feel for Mrs Smith.

On her regular Tuesday visits she would try to be out-wardly cheerful for the patient's sake, but inwardly felt sorrow at the plight of her bed-ridden friend. And the fearful thing about it was that nothing could be done.

'Then one day she told me about what she had learned of Mr Chapman and his spirit control,' Mrs Carter said. 'And she told me she'd asked Mr Chapman if he could come to Birmingham to try and help her. I was most interested in all this because I hadn't heard a thing about Mr Chapman or his spirit doctor Lang at this time. I knew of course that Mrs Smith had tried a lot of healers in the past but didn't get any real benefit because here in Birmingham we are very short of good healing mediums. Well, I hoped that Mr Chapman might be able to extend proper spirit healing in Birmingham, and I asked Mrs Smith whether she thought he might be willing to take a small group here, because I knew of quite a few people in urgent need of help. Mrs Smith approved of my idea and suggested: "Well, if you like I'll give him your address and then he can write to you and see what arrangements he can make."

'In due course Mr Chapman wrote and told me that Dr Lang agreed he would like to help patients living in Birmingham. We arranged that when he came to visit Mrs Smith he would also attend to some patients whom I would have waiting for him at her house.'

From the moment George Chapman set foot in Birmingham and went into trance at Mrs Smith's house, Mr Lang stood up to the great expectations the sick woman had had. He diagnosed immediately that Mrs Smith suffered from rheumatoid arthritis and performed a number of painless operations on her spirit body. But, although he made it clear from the start that he could not bring about quick and striking results, and that improvement would be rather slow with regular long-term treatment essential, Mrs Smith none the less felt the first signs of relief straight away.

After Mr Lang had concluded his treatment to Mrs

Smith, he attended to the group of twenty patients Mrs Carter had waiting for him. The visit was an astonishing success and Mrs Carter asked Mr Lang whether he would agree to give a public healing demonstration. The spirit doctor readily consented.

The public exhibition of his unique skill and ability to help the gravely ill made Mr Lang and his medium the talk of Birmingham – and not just among grateful patients and believing Spritualists, but among those people who had witnessed his public display and passed the word on. In the Press, although some correspondents expressed their doubts about Spritualism and allied subjects, it was recorded that 'the "spirit healing" which a number of patients received from the fireman-cum-psychic-healer, who claims to be controlled by the spirit of a dead doctor while in trance, was striking and convincing.'

After his first visit to Mrs Smith's house in Birmingham in the early part of 1956, George Chapman revisited the city frequently. Mrs Carter received so many SOS calls for spirit healing from people suffering with serious complaints that Mr Lang found it necessary to attend to his new patients at Birmingham itself.

The more the contented patients talked about the wonderful help they had received from the spirit doctor, and the better Mr Lang and his medium became known in the Midlands, the more often reports about their activities – and especially about the spirit doctor's public healing demonstrations – appeared in the Press. On 17 September 1956, for instance, the following report appeared:

'Last weekend was a very busy one for Mr George Chapman, the spirit healing Aylesbury fireman, who came to Birmingham to demonstrate in public how his spirit Dr Lang attempts to help sufferers of various illnesses by means of "spirit operations" and treatment.

'These healing demonstrations were conducted at the Birmingham districts of Moseley and King's Heath.

'The first healing demonstration was held last Saturday afternoon at the newly erected Queen's Bridge School,

Moseley, and had a large attendance. Among the audience were some people who had travelled from as far as Leamington Spar, Stafford, Walsall, and other distant places.

'Dr Lang selected cases and, after describing the condition of the patient, commenced spirit treatment. In every case the patient confirmed that the diagnosis which the "spirit doctor" had given by merely touching his fully clothed body with his medium's hands, was correct and corresponded with the diagnosis his own or hospital doctor had expressed. Quite a few patients attested that they felt considerable improvement after having received treatment.

'Dr Lang maintained interest by his remarks both to patients and the audience throughout the demonstration, and kept every one in a happy frame of mind. Many remained after the meeting to speak to the healer who speedily regained his natural state.

'Sunday morning and afternoon were fully occupied with healing given to those who required it privately, but a further public demonstration was given at the evening service of the Silver Street Christian Spiritualist Church, King's Heath. The Spiritualist Church was packed and some people who did not want to miss the performance stood in the porch outside throughout the meeting.

'Both on Saturday and Sunday, I interviewed a considerable number of people – some of whom had received spirit healing from Dr Lang on Mr Chapman's previous visits to Birmingham. They testified to the benefit they had received from spirit healing.

'Mr Chapman gave a promise that he would come again in the very near future.'

The promise was kept.

One of the people healed by Mr Lang in that autumn of 1956 was Mrs G. Fletcher of Birmingham, who had suffered since 1949 from stones in the kidneys. She was rarely free from pain, which was accompanied by vomiting, bouts of colic and the acute discomfort of passing stones. Regular morphia injections kept her from becoming crazed with pain.

Mrs Fletcher was under permanent medical care. It was eventually decided at the hospital that there was possibly a growth on the parathyroid gland which upset the calcium output and distribution in the body. This caused the calcium to crystallise in the kidneys and form stones. The surgeon and doctors responsible for the diagnosis believed that surgery was the only way in which the condition might be corrected, but nevertheless a positive result was by no means certain unless the surgeon succeeded in dealing with the parathyroid gland, from which excess calcium could affect the whole body, lungs, chest, skeletal structure, etc., and lead to a fatal result.

Having been informed by the surgeon that, 'if the proposed operation fails to produce the result based on the tentative diagnosis, further complications are to be expected', Mrs Fletcher decided against the operation. Instead she went to a friend who was a healer and underwent treatment. Improvement was minimal. Suffering remained her bedmate. And yet, at the back of her mind, somewhere, was a conviction that spiritual healing would one day cure her.

Then, after seven years of suffering, Mrs Fletcher heard of George Chapman and his spirit control, William Lang, and decided to find out whether he could do anything for her. She was first seen by Mr Lang in October 1956, and was greatly impressed by his accurate diagnosis of her complaint. Mr Lang made it clear to her that it would take a long time to relieve her of her complaint and this would only be possible if she received regular treatment. When she told him she was determined to co-operate, he performed the first of several operations.

Immediately after this very first confrontation, Mrs Fletcher felt better. Eight years later I read her case history at Aylesbury. Her name had come up at random and I wanted confirmation of the claims made in pen and ink. I jotted down the address alongside many others I had entered in my note-books. On 16 November 1964, I finally got around to contacting Mrs Fletcher. Here is what she had to say:

'I have not consulted the medical profession since receiving healing from Dr Lang, although I did pass several stones after my consultation with him. The last was in 1961. It was painful, yes, but I didn't suffer nearly as badly as during my previous attacks when X-rays showed my kidneys were full of stones. I have visited Dr Lang in recent months and he informed me that I have no stones now or any disease whatsoever. I know this must be so because since 1961 I haven't been troubled with this painful and depressing complaint.'

In March 1957 Mrs Hilda Carter suggested to George Chapman that he should come to Birmingham every Saturday at five to six weekly intervals; Chapman agreed to a trial period of twelve months. On one occasion, when Mr Lang spoke with Mrs Carter before starting his healing session at Silver Street Christian Spiritualist Church, he predicted that 'a house very near the Church will become vacant and will be our permanent Healing Centre'.

Mr Lang's prediction came true.

At a time when the number of patients had reached such large numbers that it was difficult to deal with them at the Spiritualist Church, the house next to the church became vacant. It was turned into George Chapman's Birmingham Healing Centre in 1958.

14

Killing a Cancer

NORAH OSBURNE of Folkestone, M.O.A.T., S.R.N. and Matron, fell ill in 1943 while working at Guy's Hospital during her training as a nurse. Three specialists confirmed the hospital doctors' verdict that her condition was due to gland trouble in the throat. They advised her against having an operation.

'Cancer was never mentioned,' Miss Osburne told me when I saw her at Folkestone in September 1964. 'At the same time I became most frightfully worried and depressed. One of the specialists told me: "I don't know what you're worrying about, it will clear up." It was obvious that the doctors thought I was making a fuss about nothing. But I was the one who was in great pain.'

For ten years Miss Osburne bore her suffering. Then, in 1953, her father – a doctor and superintendent of a mental home in Cork, in the south of Ireland – fell ill and asked his daughter to come home and help. She went back to Cork.

'Then my illness really flared up because, after my father passed away, I was working too hard,' Miss Osburne continued. 'The doctor I saw in Cork aspirated the gland in my neck, but it got steadily worse.

'For the next two years it was "grin and bear it" for me. The pain became harder to endure and I knew I had to get some sort of treatment. It so happened that I got hold of a copy of the *Psychic News* while over in England for three days' holiday, and I looked at the column containing "Spirit Healers". For some reason I picked out the name of George Chapman and wrote to him, asking if he could arrange distant healing for my pain and nervous apprehension. He answered my letter immediately, told me that he was controlled by a spirit doctor named William Lang, and assured me that distant healing had commenced on receipt of my letter and Dr Lang would do all he could to help me. I found it rather interesting and gratifying.

'When distant healing commenced, there was a very slight relief, but I couldn't honestly say that I felt really better. I was pleased when Mr Chapman wrote to me that Dr Lang considered contact healing necessary. It meant that I would have to travel from Cork to Aylesbury – a long and costly journey – but I decided I'd go anyway. That was in April 1957.

'I arrived at Mr Chapman's house half an hour early, and met him and his wife while he was still his own self and not yet in trance. He seemed a very pleasant, sincere person and very quiet. You sometimes see mediums who are rather talkative, but Mr Chapman seemed a very ordinary type of man – he hadn't a lot to say really. And from what conversation we had, he didn't appear to have a clue about medicine.

'I saw him going into trance after he'd taken me into the sanctuary. He was sitting down, and suddenly I saw him look up and smile. I had a queer sensation, a shiver – probably due to excitement, I suppose.

'Then he stood up and greeted me. "How are you, young lady?" His voice was very different from Mr Chapman's. He struck me as rather old-fashioned – a type that one doesn't meet nowadays, a type I still remember from my grandfather.

'After we'd chatted with each other about all sorts of things, he said: "What a dreadful mark on your neck." I told him the doctor in Cork had aspirated it, and he commented that the doctor had made a mess of it. He asked me to lie down on the healing couch, and after he'd examined me, he gave me his diagnosis. Listening to it, I decided he possessed vast medical knowledge.

'He performed a spirit operation and it seemed that he was cutting the invisible spirit body with unseen instruments. I could almost see myself in the operating theatre with him. I mean, I could visualise the operation he was doing – he was draining the thing out. You see, I'd put a lot of duty in the operating theatre during my time at the hospital. . . .

'After he had finished the painless spirit surgery, he told me that he would attend to my eyes because there was a weakness there. This was quite true. Things used to get blurred a bit if I was looking at bus numbers or anything else in the distance.

'Dr Lang performed an operation on my eyes, and when this was done I asked him if I would have to wear glasses. I had worn them for years. He replied: "No, it won't be necessary, but avoid bright lights and just use your glasses for reading, and perhaps when you go to the cinema or theatre." He really succeeded in achieving something extraordinary. Since the operation on my eyes, identifying buses at a distance or anything else, is no longer a difficulty. I no longer wear spectacles and am able to drive a car.

'But to go back – when I left Dr Lang on that first occasion I felt terribly ill. I returned to Ireland with pains worse than ever. I hoped that my next appointment in May would show greater benefit. I did not blame Dr Lang for my being worse than before I saw him – quite the contrary – for some inexplicable reason I felt convinced that he would eventually be able to help and cure me.

'I was so sure of his ability to do this that I spoke at length about him to my mother. You see, she had serious trouble with her eyes – she had been complaining of see-ing floating objects before them, and a specialist diagnosed an early cataract and gave her six months before her sight failed altogether. To cut a long story short, my mother welcomed my suggestion to see Dr Lang when I went to Aylesbury for my next appointment in May.

'When Dr Lang examined my mother, he said: "This is not a case of cataract, it is scotoma – black spots inter-fering with the vision. I'll soon put this right." And, as he performed his spirit operation on my mother's eyes (having asked me to stand behind the healing couch), he told me exactly what he was doing. I felt once again as if present in the operating theatre, watching intricate surgery being performed. It was all so real, all so true to life.

'Dr Lang kept his promise and cured my mother – on the spot. When we left Mr Chapman's sanctuary, mother suddenly exclaimed: "My eyes are all right, no more floating objects!" And when she went back to Cork and went with me to the eye specialist, I was enthralled by the look on his face. Utter amazement when he examined her eyes. He kept testing and testing them, and in the end looked across at me and said: "They seem to have cleared up – extraordinary! Your mother is all right now!" I'll never forget the look on his face!

'My mother thought Dr Lang was wonderful – he was of the same generation as her father who'd been a surgeon. I come from a medical family – five generations – father, grandfather, great-grandfather, and so on, were doctors and surgeons and the mental home in Cork was handed down through the family.

'But to return to my own case, when Dr Lang had finished his operation on my mother, he asked me to occupy the healing couch and, having examined me, said: "Oh dear, this is very bad, I am sorry about this. I'll have to drain the poison off again from the gland." Then he operated on me and I distinctly felt some very slight pain – as if incisions were being made. Afterwards he asked me to go upstairs, and rest in the sitting-room for about ten minutes without talking. When I came down again, he performed still another spirit operation.

'When he was finished he said: "Don't do anything, don't go to any doctor now, don't have an operation yet; wait for me to tell you when it is safe to operate." He explained that the gland at the back of my neck was full of poison, that he wanted to dispose of it and was doing his best to drain it into a carbuncle-like thing down the front so that it could be easily dealt with. He didn't tell me anything about cancer, but when my mother re-visited him for a check-up on her eyes two days after her operation, he told *her* I had cancer. He made it clear, however, that if given time he could cure me completely.

'I went back to Ireland immediately, leaving my mother behind, and still knowing nothing of cancer, to return to my duties at the mental home. The train journey from Dublin to Cork nearly finished me off. The pain – I'd never experienced such agony in my life!

'Within a week, the gland on my neck started to work down – it came from the back to the front and was hanging down like a carbuncle. In the end I had to send an express letter to Mr Chapman to ask his advice because Dr Lang had impressed upon me not to do anything. Dr Lang replied through Mr Chapman that I had reacted so well to the spirit operations that I could go and see my doctor and have the gland opened. But he added I must not have it *removed* at this stage. I must wait for him to tell me when it would be safe to do so. I was still unaware of the fact that this was due to the cancer not yet being cured – my mother kept this secret from me.

'I saw my doctor, who was quite amazed by the transformation. He said: "I've never seen anything like it happen before." He made a slight incision into the carbuncle-like gland, and the pus just poured out. The pain lessened and lessened.

'During the following three months progress was very slow and pain sometimes drove me to near madness. I received distant healing from Dr Lang and knew that he came to visit me. I couldn't see him of course, but I sensed his presence time and again. Sometimes I used to say to my sister: "Dr Lang is here." She'd ask: "How do you know?" and I'd reply: "I just know he is here." He told my mother that I had psychic faculties and knew when he was there. And, sometimes when I meditated, I felt a strange tingling in my body. All this proved to me that regular contact was being maintained between Dr Lang and myself.

'One of the things Dr Lang insisted I must do to help him cure me was to rest as much as possible, and to go to my bedroom not later than eight o'clock in the evening for ten minutes' quietness. I did as I was asked, but one night, instead of going up to my bedroom at eight o'clock, I remained sitting in the drawing-room longer than usual. Suddenly I heard a loud clicking of fingers – the same sound I knew so well from my visits to Aylesbury when Dr Lang clicked his fingers while operating and asked for the invisible instruments. I knew immediately that Dr Lang was there and thought: "My goodness, I'm late." I flew up the stairs. My mother and sister, with whom I had been talking, also heard the clicking sound, but they didn't think anything about it at the time because none of us could see Dr Lang. I realised, however, that it was a sort of reminder from Dr Lang for me to go upstairs. . . .

'In August 1957 I saw Dr Lang again. There was another spirit operation and, when he had finished, he said: "It's cured now, you can have your operation for the removal of the gland at the hospital. Don't be annoyed with me because of the time it has taken and all the suffering you had to endure, but it was malignant." I had gathered that, and I assured him that I was most grateful to him for what he had done for me. It was only then that I found out that I had suffered from cancer, but that now I was completely cured.

'In September I entered hospital and had the operation for the removal of the gland. When they operated, it became septic – I had an awful time with it. Afterwards I was completely paralysed in my left arm, and the physiotherapist confirmed the doctors' and surgeon's opinions that the paralysis would remain because there was nothing that could be done to remedy it.

'When I saw Dr Lang again in October, he told me I was a very lucky person. Anybody else in my condition would have been in the next world by now. He told me: "You may wonder why *I* didn't remove the gland? I'll tell you. After my spirit operations and treatment, it was only like a dead growth, which had to be removed, and it could be done easier and speedier at a hospital." He went on to say that he was not competing with the earthly medical profession – that he liked nothing better than to co-operate with his "living" colleagues as much as possible.

'He then said that the paralysis of my left arm was due to the nerve and muscles having been damaged during the operation. He performed a spirit operation and afterwards I asked him whether I should go to a physio-therapist and have heat treatment. "No," he said. "Not heat treatment, but gentle massage and exercises. And take a hot bath daily." I went to the physio-therapist and did the exercises.

'A month later, I visited Dr Lang again. I felt very much better, and he was quite pleased with me. "Oh, the muscles will come back," he assured me, and he was right. You can see for yourself that my arm and hand are completely normal. They are perfect, and they were so after Christmas 1957. I've had no trouble of any sort ever since and I have worked very hard. I can truly say that I have seen a miracle take place before my eyes.'

Miss Osburne looked in splendid health. She is a fine matron, respected and admired. Her case impressed me profoundly. There is no dubiety about the details.

15

*Mirabile Dictu**

THE CASE of Mrs Barry Miron of Saltdean, Sussex, is in my opinion the most important contribution to this book. Hers was undoubtedly one of the most difficult and trying cases which Mr William Lang ever encountered – not only during his distinguished career on earth, but also throughout his practice as a spirit doctor.

When I met Mrs Miron in October 1964 to obtain details of her illness and treatment, I had the good fortune also to meet her husband, Mr S. G. Miron, L.D.S., R.C.S. (Eng.), who agreed to explain to me all the complex aspects of this unusual case in medical terms. Indeed, Mr Miron was possibly the best person qualified to give me a full medical account, because he was not only a dentist of considerable experience but had also engaged extensively in oral surgery at hospitals during his long professional career.

Trouble for Mrs Miron started in the late summer of 1957 when her upper left first molar was removed. The extraction had been difficult and, due to the fact that a small piece of bone adhered to the root of the tooth, a perforation into the antrum occurred which led to an infection of this hollow – a complaint considered by the medical profession to be one of the most difficult things to clear up. But let the surgeon give us his interpretation of how such an unfortunate mishap could have occurred.

'The roots of this particular tooth are in very close proximity to the floor of the antrum. The roots of the tooth don't project directly into the sinus, but the bone covering

* Latin 'Marvellous to relate'.

the roots often comes up in waves into the floor of the sinus, as you can see on X-rays. Well, in removing the tooth it can happen that a small piece of the bone adheres to the root and causes a perforation into the sinus. If this perforation is very tiny it can heal up under its own volition.

'In my wife's case, however, it was unfortunately not a very tiny perforation, but was what is known as an antro-oral fistula – a great hole from the mouth into the antrum. This was in consequence of a so-called dry socket after the extraction of the tooth – a very painful affair which brings with it a certain amount of bone infection. As this was attended to, a mistake in treatment had been made in so far as a type of dressing had been used which set rather hard and forced the tissue to open to such an extent that I could have put my finger in the hole. This gives you an idea of how extensive and serious the opening was.

'Now, when you have an acutely infected antrum, any doctor will tell you that it is one of the most difficult things to clear up. An antral operation is a gamble, a toss of the coin. You never know the result. In about fifty per cent of cases people with antrum trouble suffer some types of recurring discomfort for the rest of their lives. It is one of the most unsatisfactory operations you can possibly think of.

'I was on the hospital staff myself at that time, and from my experience of oral surgery – surgery in the mouth – I knew that this was a job for plastic surgery. So I took my wife to the Churchill Hospital in Oxford where she was seen by the maxillo-facial people who suggested flapping the soft tissues together and sewing them up. Owing to my experience in this field which I had acquired from years of hospital work, it was my considered opinion that trying to stitch it up was just a waste of time because too much of the bone was missing and there was nothing to support the soft tissue. I was, however, not in charge of the case and could not very well argue with the surgeon, who was of a different opinion. To cut a long story short, they had a go at it, but it was unsuccessful. It was just impossible to tackle the problem this way – the hole was too big for closing it by flapping the soft tissues together and sewing them up. It was a clear case for plastic surgery.

'Two days after the futile sewing-up my wife was released from hospital. She was in great pain. In the end she was seen by a leading plastic surgeon, who stated at once that a graft was the only way to close the opening to the antrum and suggested the operation should be carried out as soon as they had a bed available at Stoke Mandeville Hospital.

'This type of graft operation is the same type as a skin graft. They take a flap of tissue from inside the cheek, turn it back over the opening and then stitch it up inside the palate. The flap of tissue has got to have a blood supply from the live tissue to stay alive until it has grafted itself on, and is consequently only severed from the live tissue when the grafting has proved successful. It is a lengthy and unpleasant process, but it is the only means of closing up an opening in the antrum of such size.'

Having been advised that this operation could not be carried out for another three weeks or so, because a bed was not available, Mr and Mrs Miron decided they would meanwhile consult Mr William Lang. They knew a good deal about him and his successes as a spirit doctor and hoped that spirit surgery and treatment might put the trouble right, or at least lessen Mrs Miron's suffering until the hospital bed was available.

'I had a rotten time,' Mrs Miron told me. 'It was extremely painful and throughout I had to have the hole stopped with large cotton-wool plugs. If you have a thing like this you have to have it plugged, you can't have it open, because if it is unplugged it feels as though you are underground in a huge cave – everything echoes and reverberates in your own head. If you swallow anything, it immediately goes into the hole and down through your nose. I know only too well.

'Anyway, I went to see William Lang, and after he'd examined me he stated: "I *think* there is a very good chance that I may be successful." He did not *promise* success, but pointed out he would know whether or not he was able to help me after he performed the necessary spirit surgery. This seemed fair enough and I asked him to go ahead with what needed to be done.

'He performed the operation on the spirit body. After he'd finished, he said that he had been successful and added: "The hole will heal. Ask your husband to watch it." He then made it clear that I must come back to him frequently for observation and further spirit operation.

'A most interesting thing happened while I was on my way home from Dr Lang. I told you I had the hole plugged with a large wad of cotton wool. Well, as I was about half-way home – it took about three-quarters of an hour to get to William Lang's door from where we lived then – I began to feel pressure on the cotton-wool plug. In other words, there was a tightening up process going on from either side, a distinct feeling of a growth of some sort going on, and it continued, slowly but steadily. As this continued, the plug had to be made smaller and smaller, till the opening to the antrum closed down to the size of a pin point. But I am ahead of events – all this took quite some time.'

Mr Miron had this to say. 'I watched it and treated it day by day – by treating I mean I saw to it that it was kept clean and covered with the smooth plastic plate we had made for this purpose,' he said. 'I examined it daily, X-rayed it myself at least once a week and, well, the soft tissue gradually flapped over it – I mean it just closed up.

'There was not a shred of doubt in my mind that this was due to the spirit surgery William Lang had carried out, because during the time of waiting for the hospital bed and the graft operation to be carried out, my wife did not receive medical attention from *any one*. William Lang's prognostication that it would close up was correct. If in ordinary surgical practice a specialist had said anything of the sort to me I'd probably have thought, "the chap is a bit round the bend, he's probably overworked", because no one could say things like that and, in fact, no one *would*. William Lang, however, had said that the hole would close up and that I should watch it, and *it did close up!*

'I accompanied my wife several times when she went to see William Lang, and I saw him perform his spirit operations. He worked an inch or so *above* her face, at the floor of the sinus and around the site of the wound. He was asking for instruments which were handed to him by his son Basil and a large number of assistants and I knew the instruments he was using because I used them myself.

'Quite apart from the fact that he was telling me exactly what he was doing – he was building up the tissue, not in the physical sense but on the spirit body – I knew precisely the type of surgery he was performing from the movement of his hands and from the various instruments he asked for. I mean, had he been carrying out a physical operation, as a physical man in an operating theatre, everything would have been the same in every detail – the only difference would have been that I'd have seen it. Everything he was doing was a hundred per cent correct – it was the correct technique for flapping tissues over a great hole, for building a plastic graft over it.'

Before Mrs Miron went to see the plastic surgeon at the end of the waiting period, she saw Mr Lang. He was very pleased with her progress and declared that a graft operation would not now be necessary as the hole was closing up. 'I'll do my best to impress upon the surgeon to leave it alone,' he said. 'He is a sensitive man and we might succeed in influencing him.'

'We do not know of course whether William Lang succeeded with the plastic surgeon or not, but it is an irrefutable fact that when the gentleman examined me prior to my entering Stoke Mandeville Hospital, he decided to give it a further chance,' Mrs Miron recalled. 'He told me that under the unexpected circumstances he would postpone the operation for another three weeks so as to find out whether the progress had continued. If it had, a plastic graft operation might not, after all, be necessary. He made it clear, however, that if there was even the slightest setback I must see him immediately.'

Mrs Miron continued her frequent visits to Mr Lang. Additional spirit operations were performed. The opening to the antrum continued to get smaller and smaller.

After the expiration of the second waiting period, Mrs Miron again saw the plastic surgeon and he was amazed to discover that the opening to the antrum had become even smaller. He decided: 'We'd better let it go and see what happens to it.' He did not know that the patient had been receiving spirit treatment – Mrs Miron did not consider there was any purpose in telling him.

'I wanted to know what he would say, so I asked him how he explained that such a large opening suddenly grew smaller and smaller, because one must remember that he had asserted all along that *only plastic surgery could close up the hole*,' Mrs Miron continued. 'He replied: "Well, of course very occasionally nature does take over and it is possible that these two separate bits of skin could grow together, but cases like this are *very, very rare*." He added candidly that during his long career as a plastic surgeon he himself had not met with a similar development in a case where there was such a large opening.'

'With all due respect to the plastic surgeon, who is a specialist with vast experience and skill, I whole-heartedly disagree with his explanation and affirm that it could not have happened by nature having taken over,' Mr Miron told me. 'Let me be a little more specific about this. There is no point in my humbly saying he knew more than I did because he didn't. He is of course a plastic surgeon of the highest repute and experience, performing countless plastic operations on various parts of the body, but I specialised in *oral* surgery at the hospital and, therefore, I know more than he does about what can or cannot happen in the *mouth*. I say this with all modesty but it is true. If one realises that the skin that covers the body is much harder and tougher than the soft tissue in the mouth, it will be understood that there is considerable difference between graft surgery on any part of the body and graft surgery in the mouth, though the operating technique is very similar.

'Taking everything into account, I say most emphatically that the tissue just could *not* have grown together by the normal laws of nature as we know them. Look, I watched the opening close up. I plugged it, X-rayed it regularly and we made a little plastic dental plate to cover it, and I recorded every stage of the progress until the opening was covered with a thin floor of skin. If one remembers that the hole at one time was so big that you could put your finger up it, as I've already told you, you'll appreciate how considerable the opening was. *Nobody* who has the least knowledge of medicine or surgery can tell you that where there is such a great loss of bone, soft tissue can span nearly half an inch and grow firmly together. It is just not possible. However, it *happened*, and that *is* a fact.'

After a short pause, Mr Miron added:

'I am by no means trying to belittle the plastic surgeon's experience or skill. He had no knowledge of my wife having received spirit healing and was faced with the fact that something like a miracle had happened. Having been asked to explain rationally how the closing of the opening in the antrum was possible, it is understandable that he attributed it to nature having taken over. Quite frankly, had I not known that it was the result of William Lang's spirit operations and treatment, I don't know what I would have thought had I come across a similar case. I would probably have said that something inexplicable had happened.'

As Mr Lang continued treatment, and the opening grew together to a minute hole which became almost invisible to the naked eye, he warned Mrs Miron:

'You must exercise great care. Owing to the floor to the antrum being very thin and having no bone structure to support the tissue, there is at this early stage the danger of breaking it open again. Until sufficient time has elapsed for the tissue to grow stronger, you must be terribly careful how you blow your nose when you have a cold, because the force of the pressure could break the tissue down again.'

This is what, unfortunately, did happen.

Quite apart from the antrum trouble, Mrs Miron was at that time very low in health and became the victim of endless colds and attacks of influenza. She fought a losing battle and developed a further infection in the antrum. Because of this, the healing broke down and, although the hole did not get nearly as large as it had been formerly, the trouble started all over again.

'If you can get over here every day, I can prevent this getting worse,' Mr Lang then told his patient. When she replied that the best she could do was to come to Aylesbury once a week, he comforted her: 'Don't worry, I'll do all I can to keep this accumulating poison at bay.'

For a long time his efforts were successful, but suddenly Mrs Miron became much worse.

'During the next six months I became progressively more ill, because, due to the hole having opened again, I was swallowing poison,' Mrs Miron described. 'It was physically a most revolting and filthy ordeal because I was aware all the time of an endless trickle of poison which I tried to spit out. The taste was awful and made me feel ill. It was draining into my stomach and poisoning my entire system. I became extremely distended, my skin turned a peculiar yellow, and I became exhausted. However, I carried on to the best of my ability and even went with my husband on a summer holiday we had planned. I felt the only thing I wanted to do was to rest in bed.

'By agreement with William Lang we went to see an ear, nose and throat specialist at Oxford, but on no account was he to be allowed to operate. Dr Lang explained his reasons as follows: "The poison has got into the marrow of your bones and your system, and if the specialist is permitted to operate, the poison will still remain in your system, and regardless of how successful the actual operation might turn out to be, it will still gravely affect your health. I am doing my utmost to remedy this by giving you contact healing here every week and working on your spirit body every night during your sleep-state. I am trying to localise the poison. This will take time, but when I have succeeded, you can ask the specialist to operate because it will then be safe to carry out surgery." I realised how very difficult, if not impossible, it would be for me to tell the specialist what he should or should not do, but I was determined to comply with my instructions as closely as I could.

'To give the specialist his due, he was not awfully keen on operating. The X-rays showed that pus had spread out everywhere under the orbit of the eye, and he said quite candidly that an operation did not appear advisable. He gave me several wash-outs, which William Lang did not like at all (he said they did a lot of damage to his treatment) but *I* couldn't stop him doing it.

'Eventually Dr Lang succeeded in collecting the poison into a localised area and it felt as if a terrific weight was under my eye. He told me then that I was to see the specialist without delay and tell him to operate.

'I called on the specialist and said: "I am sorry to have to say this, but I feel terribly urgently that I ought to have this operation now." I felt awkward telling an eminent surgeon what to do. He didn't say anything as he examined me, and for some time he just walked about the room. Then he turned round and said: "Do you know, I don't know why I am saying I will operate because I don't think it will be a success. The normal thing I should say should be: 'No, I won't operate,' but I will." He did. After the operation he told me that it was the worst case he had ever encountered.'

'My wife had a Caldwell-Luc operation, which is a bad thing because the result is generally fairly indifferent in fifty per cent of cases,' Mr Miron explained. 'It is a crude operation and one which is only performed because it is the only thing that can be done, but no real surgeon likes having to do it. Very often the result is a chronic sinus which doesn't completely clear up and is always giving trouble. In my wife's case, however, it was completely successful. I saw the ear, nose and throat surgeon after the operation and he told me that he was highly delighted and a little surprised at the completely satisfactory result.'

'The usual thing after this kind of operation is that the pain is so terrible that the patient is given morphia for twenty-four hours,' Mrs Miron told me. 'Well, I was sitting up in bed and eating a meal within six hours and smoking quite happily, which they thought was extraordinary. They all came to look at me in astonishment and said: "How is it you are so cheerful and free of pain?" In the end I said to the sister: "It is because I am having spiritual healing." Her remark was: "Oh, no wonder."

'After my comparatively speedy release from the nursing home where the operation was performed, I was to come straight away back to William Lang, and of course I did. For another week I received regular treatment from him, and then rapidly started to recover my full health. He succeeded in effecting a complete cure – I had no return of any sort since William Lang's spirit treatment terminated in April 1959.'

'If you take into consideration the various stages of this case, you'll arrive at the conclusion that William Lang actually cured my wife in record time,' Mr Miron summed up. 'During the first part of his treatment he successfully closed up the oral fistula. During the second stage came the complication of the infected antrum which was due to my wife's lowered health. The third period saw the breaking down of the tissue that he had built up, and this occurred because of the infection. Finally, he succeeded in gathering the poison from all over the body into one central point and was then able to rebuild the tissue a second time.

'In my considered opinion he succeeded in making the impossible possible.'

16

Full-time Healing

GEORGE CHAPMAN found it increasingly difficult to continue his dual occupations and the time came when a decision had to be made. He could continue in the secure and pensionable career of a public servant, which had already earned him his Long Service Medal as an acknowledgment of ten years' service, or become a full-time spirit healer, acting as medium for Mr Lang. He had his wife and family to think about. Would they be able to live without a steady, guaranteed income? He pondered long over the problem and on 31 October 1957, resigned from the Aylesbury Fire Service.

With plenty of time now for spirit healing, Chapman was not only able to cut down the waiting list of Mr Lang's patients, but to accept many more sufferers as patients. The regular journeys to the Birmingham Healing Centre no longer created difficulties. In the past he had frequently been obliged to ask colleagues to change duties with him so that he could travel to the Midlands. Now that particular form of worry was at an end. And, above all, he could now fulfil his desire to make Tuesday the day for a Free Clinic where anyone in need of spirit healing could receive attention from William Lang without being involved in any payment.

From the day George Chapman became a 'professional' medium, his sanctuary never lacked patients. Quite the contrary. So many sufferers from every type of disease requested consultations with Mr Lang that he was often required to stay in trance from 10 a.m. to 5 p.m. Indeed there were many occasions when the crush of patients in need of lengthy spirit operations and healing was so great that Chapman remained under Mr Lang's control until well into the evening. Yet, even the longest working hours were never too much for the dedicated medium – the thought that he was compelled by his spirit control to spend an excessive amount of time in a trance never entered his mind. He had devoted his life to healing and accepted wholly whatever conditions were necessary.

On 1 November 1957, he spent his first day as the full-time medium of William Lang, F.R.C.S.

One of the early patients to come to Chapman on his first day was Mr Cyril G. Woodley of Brill. I got in touch with him to learn how his illness had fared under the treatment of William Lang. This is what Mr Woodley told me:

'Around about seven years ago (in 1950) I began having pains in my legs. After trying every known embrocation and ointment to no avail, I was finally forced to go to the doctor, who said it was fibrositis, and suggested a period of rest. As time went by the complaint got steadily worse, however, and I was sent to hospital for X-rays. They then said I had inflammation of the spine. I had eight weeks' heat and massage treatment with no apparent benefit. I was X-rayed again and finally told that I had a serious complaint called spondylitis.

'In 1953 I had a spell in Mount Vernon Hospital where I was given deep ray treatment. When I was discharged, to be frank, I felt even worse!

'After two years on National Insurance, I had another eight weeks' heat and massage treatment, but again, it seemed useless. I started work again in my shop, but I found it hard to stand for any length of time. I was attending a hospital clinic the whole time, and all they could do for me was to give me some tablets which I was supposed to take every time the pain got bad.

'Then my wife Jessie, who'd heard from Mr Maurice Barbanell about Mr Chapman and Dr Lang, persuaded me to try spiritual healing. I agreed in the end and made an appointment to see Dr Lang in November 1957.

'When Dr Lang saw me and examined me, he diagnosed exactly what was wrong with me. He was quite

101

frank with me and said he'd be able to help me get right enough, but that it would take some time, and that I'd have to be patient and come to see him often. I told him that I was willing to do as he said. After all, I had been suffering for seven years and didn't expect a cure to happen overnight. In fact, I thought, if he succeeds in curing me, he'll be doing something doctors have failed to do.

'Dr Lang then carried out what he called an "operation on my spirit body" and, although I didn't feel a thing at the time, I was a heck of sight better by the time I got home.

'I kept every appointment Dr Lang made for me, and each time I went, he did something for me that made me feel much better afterwards. By February 1959 I felt nearly one hundred per cent again, and since I was due for a check-up at the hospital, I was very curious to learn what their verdict would be. I can tell you the doctor was flabbergasted, and that's no exaggeration. He muttered something about "inexplicable things sometimes happening". I told him then about the treatment I had had from the spirit of Dr Lang. He listened and didn't say anything. He asked me to call again in two years' time. I did of course – in February 1961 – and, after examining me again, most carefully and thoroughly, he said I needn't come any more as I was completely cured. Oh and he said something to the effect that it was an extraordinary occurrence and hard to believe that anything of the sort could happen.'

On 6 December 1964, Mr Woodley kindly gave me the following information about the ongoing state of his health:

'I'm happy to say that though it is now more than seven years since I first consulted Dr Lang, I am practically one hundred per cent fit again. Since we moved to our present house, I have managed the upkeep of our garden which is two hundred feet at the back and thirty foot at the front. With the help of my son I have managed the heavy digging – it's clay, and that speaks for itself!'

When Mr Woodley first visited Mr Lang on 1 November

1957, his wife Jessie accompanied him. She was equally impressed with Mr Lang and his effective spirit healing, for she had been suffering from high blood pressure and accompanying ailments for many years, and the doctors had not been able to do more for her than prescribe tablets. Her regular visits with her husband to Mr Lang enabled the spirit doctor to cure her completely of her complaint, and she, too, confirmed in December 1964 that she had enjoyed good health ever since Mr Lang had given her treatment.

'You may be interested to know that I spent more time in bed in winter before I went to see Dr Lang, than I was able to be up and about, owing to bronchial asthma,' she stated. 'It's wonderful now to be active in wet weather and fog with only an occasional wheeze! My usual bronchitis would start any time after September, but all that belongs to the past now. I guess you can imagine how glorious it is to breathe freely and deeply – thanks to Dr Lang's cure.'

When Mr and Mrs Woodley came to George Chapman's sanctuary in August 1958, a leaflet was handed to them as well as to other patients. It was a request for notification to be given if any phenomenon was noticed arising out of treatment by Mr Lang.* Mrs Woodley complied with the request and sent George Chapman the following letter:

'I am writing to let you know of some of the experiences my husband and I had when consulting Dr Lang.

'During our consultation with Dr Lang in January this year, he told me that he had injected deeply into my chest in two places and warned me not to become alarmed if marks apeared on my body. I didn't feel anything and I didn't think any sort of mark could appear. I was quite wrong. Two marks did appear on my body! Quite distinctly. And they remained there for four days.

* A considerable number of Mr Lang's patients also complied with the request expressed in the leaflet and notified George Chapman. Some of these discoveries of phenomena are included in patients' case histories.

'Twice during the winter I was unable to visit Dr Lang and he told my husband on both occasions that he would visit me. Each night I was awakened by a kind of electric shock. It was a tingling sensation from my head down to my feet, as one gets from stinging nettles, and lasted for perhaps a minute. On both mornings I felt fine and was able to get up.

'After Dr Lang had treated my husband and myself on our visit to him last June, he explained to us that he had drawn some fluid from my husband's spine. There sure enough was the wet patch on the cover of the healing couch! This was most remarkable because, as you know, Dr Lang *only* performs *spirit* healing and *never touches* the actual *physical* body. I always watched him very closely and saw his hands every time some short distance *above* the *physical* body.'

When George Chapman received Mrs Woodley's letter it provided the explanation to a puzzle that had irked him for the past two months. When he regained consciousness on a day in June 1958, after Mr Lang had attended to the last patient, George had noticed a wet patch on the cover of the healing couch. He could not find any explanation as to how this had come about and, without thinking a phenomenon could have occurred, he just changed the soiled cover for a clean one. But Mrs Woodley's letter provided the answer.

17

'I Shall Not Look Back in Anger'

As I sat opposite Miss Ilse Kohn and listened to her account of an accident that had befallen her seven years previously, in 1957, I could feel again the horror that wells up in me whenever I think of human beings being catapulted into physical trauma. About this accident there was the appalling familiarity that characterises so much of the slaughter and near-slaughter that takes place daily on our roads. A hospital matron on her bicycle, a car, a crash, twisted steel, and the maimed body of a woman lying, head bleeding, on the road. Then the mercy dash to Amersham Hospital, the examination, and the cataloguing of its findings – fractured skull, right eye gravely injured, fractured nose and fractured ribs.

'I was unconscious for ten days and nights. When I came round I didn't know where I was or what had happened. You see I'd had concussion, and after it one usually has no recollection of what has happened,' Miss Kohn told me. 'I couldn't lift my head off the pillow – I didn't want to. And I felt completely exhausted. I was really glad to be in bed.

'A few days after I'd regained consciousness, a number of doctors were standing around my bedside talking, discussing my case. I heard one of them saying quietly to another that he was concerned about my eyesight. One of his colleagues said something to the effect that he doubted whether I'd ever be able to see again. They didn't know I could hear what was being said. I had it on the tip of my tongue to say, "*I know* I'll be able to see again." They had replaced an eye which had been torn from its socket and had then closed the lid for protection. But they had left a part of it open in the centre, and through this I could see a fraction of the sky.

'I was determined to get better. When I heard a specialist express his doubts on whether I would fully regain my mental balance, and explain that it would take a long time before I could resume my duties as Matron I regarded it as a challenge to get well quickly. I think the doctors were amazed to see how soon I recovered. Within three weeks I had learnt to sit up straight, to stand and walk again, to look after myself and talk with other patients. Then I was discharged and allowed to return home.

'A very trying time followed. I was terribly weak and my right eye was still closed. I frequently suffered from intolerable pains in the head and it was very alarming to find out that I was unable to think clearly and logically. At times I wondered whether the hospital specialist had been right after all when he'd said it would take a long time (if ever) until I was fit enough to resume my duties as Matron. And when a psychiatrist friend said: "She'll have to start from the very beginning, as if she'd just been born, and go through every period of her life again," I was shocked. I thought: "My God! That's something to hear at the age of 33!" I found it terribly difficult to swallow this bitter pill, but eventually I accepted it.

'After a month at home I had to return to hospital to have my right eye opened. It was frightfully painful, almost like experiencing another accident. When I returned home, I had a relapse and felt weaker and worse than ever.

'Shortly afterwards I went to a convalescent home at Farnham and made good progress. I wanted to show that I was well enough to resume my duties as Matron, but apparently my mind was still not quite normal.

'As much as I tried, I couldn't meet my own challenge and everything I attempted seemed to fail. I couldn't understand it. Looking back I'd say it was because I was trying to rush things all along the line. And you can't *force* the pace of getting better beyond what nature will accept.

'There were times when I gave way to depression and the nights were bad, too. Unable to sleep, I could only weep and felt terribly alone, despite the sympathy and love of friends who cared for me as much as my parents would have done had they been alive. But I couldn't appreciate it. I felt as if I were in a prison, with no one to talk to. Deep within myself I think I knew that the misery was of my own making. It was like being in a cruel trap and feeling you'd never get out and would die.

'There was little change in my condition until after the New Year when it was suggested to me that I should consult the spirit doctor William Lang to see if he could help me in any way. Not being a Spiritualist, however, I wondered if anything could come of it, but I was curious and very willing to try anything.

'When I eventually met Dr Lang in February 1958, it was a very pleasant experience. There was so much friendliness about him that I felt at ease immediately.

'As he walked towards me, he reminded me of a German professor with whom I had enjoyed working in hospital. I at once thought: "I'm in good hands, here's someone who understands." I realised I had done right in coming to see him.

'Dr Lang talked with me for a while about all sorts of things. He wanted to know from where I came, what was my work and how the accident came about. He then asked me to lie down on the couch and examined me by touching my body very lightly with his hands. He said very little about my condition, but somehow gave me the feeling that I could rely upon him to help me.

'While I lay there, he explained that he would perform a number of painless operations on my spirit body. He talked to invisible assistants and asked for surgical instruments. His hands hovered an inch or so above my body as if delicately holding some instruments and performing an operation, but I didn't feel a thing. I knew instinctively that he would help me, though I wondered *how*.

'When I left I felt much easier, so much lighter and gayer. I felt that something had happened, though I didn't know exactly what. It was as if somebody had opened the door of my imaginary prison.

'At first I didn't know how to enjoy my new-found freedom. In my subconscious mind I feared that this wonderful feeling of being free, of being myself again, might not last, but I consoled myself with the thought that in a fortnight's time I would be seeing Dr Lang again, and he would then be able to help me still further. As the days went by, I was delighted to find that the free-dom of mind neither vanished, nor even diminished, but, in fact, grew more real and permanent every day. I felt I was no longer alone.

'When I went to Aylesbury on the second occasion, I met Mr George Chapman before he went in trance. He was a much younger man than Dr Lang, and I noticed that he spoke differently. Being a trained nurse, I naturally spoke about medical matters, and particularly about my case. He had no knowledge of medicine, and was anything but a doctor.

'Dr Lang again performed some operation and gave me spiritual healing, and again I felt better. This im-provement was, in fact, so remarkable that I became fully capable of resuming my duties as Matron.'

After her third and final visit to Mr Lang, Miss Kohn knew she had at last reached the stage of well-being when she could carry out her onerous duties with the same proficiency she had been able to show before her accident.

'I didn't feel on top of the world all the time, but Dr Lang somehow succeeded in implanting in my mind the sure confidence that I would get better,' Miss Kohn told me. 'Of course, there were difficulties still to be met, but in the end I managed to overcome them.

'For years now I have felt very well – I could not wish to be better. I enjoy life and I enjoy meeting people. I am reading and writing more than ever before.

'I shall never look back in sorrow and anger. When

sometimes I think of all that happened to me I wonder whether, in fact, I should have found the road to happiness had I not met Dr Lang. I pray that God will preserve the strength in me to help those who need me, as once I needed help.'

18

The Quest for Co-operation

ONE OF the first things I became aware of in my talks
with William Lang in the preparation of this book,
was his earnest desire to establish greater co-operation between himself and members of the medical profession. It
was a subject he touched on often. This longing was not
prompted by the idea that help from earthly doctors
would enable *him* to achieve even more striking results.
The catalogue of these spoke for themselves. But he
wanted to impart, in some way, something of his own
unique ability and knowledge to man whose horizons were
limited in the field of healing.

The ambition was fulfilled to some extent. A number of
his patients who attended their own doctors or hospitals
for periodic examinations spoke about the spirit doctor
and his painless operations which had cured, or improved,
their ailments. Many members of the profession of course
would have none of it, or would refuse any comment, but
there were some doctors and surgeons who agreed that
divine or spiritual healing should not be dismissed or
pooh-poohed. Some of them, in fact, went so far as to
advise their patients to continue to receive treatment from
Mr Lang, and also to attend at regular medical check-ups
so that their state of health could be observed clinically.

One such gentleman was Mr G. S. Miron, L.D.S., R.C.S.
(Eng.), whose co-operation with Mr Lang has already
been told in the chapter 'Mirabile Dictu'. He also co-operated with the spirit doctor whenever he believed it would
help the patient.

Other instances involving both doctors and distinguished consultant specialists could be cited.

Although this co-operation with certain members of the medical profession was a remarkable and most welcome achievement, it only partly satisfied Mr Lang's greater ambition, for he aimed at working closely with as many doctors as possible.

He made his first decisive move in this direction in 1958, for while controlling George Chapman one day, he dictated the following letter and asked it to be sent to the Registrar of the Royal Ophthalmic Hospital (Moorfields Eye Hospital):

'I know that this is a strange letter for your hospital to receive, but both I and my son Basil were active members of your staff for many years.

'If you will look into my past records you will find much about me, e.g. I wrote a book entitled "The Medical Examination of The Eye" and my son wrote a number of books on the examination and approach to a patient.

'It is my wish to invite members of your active medical staff, or indeed past members, to contact my medium, George Chapman, with the view to having appointments with me.

'I know that in eye surgery and technique I can be of great help and I am sure that many of the staff who are so interested and love their work will enjoy meeting me.'

No reply was received. When I asked Mr Lang during one of our interviews if he'd been upset by the Registrar ignoring his letter, he replied: 'Ooh no, I wasn't upset, no. I didn't really expect the Registrar to reply – it's perhaps too much to ask a gentleman in such a position to correspond with a "dead" man – but I just felt I had to write the letter to let them know I'm back and always willing to help in any way I am allowed to, but I don't consider it a wasted effort. I didn't receive a reply to my letter, but as a consequence of it some of the dear boys came to see me.

'A fortnight after George sent off the letter he received a communication from ——, I must not mention his name, it was a private consultation; but I can tell you that he is a very capable and skilled specialist. I didn't know the dear boy personally, he was one of Basil's colleagues, but I enjoyed talking to him.

'At first he marched into my room like a prize fighter,' Mr Lang continued. 'From the questions he hurled at me it was obvious that he intended to establish that I couldn't be the William Lang I'd claimed to be in my letter. He asked me very intricate ophthalmological questions and I answered each one in detail and also spoke about various treatment approaches. At the end the dear boy apologised for his hostile attitude and then enquired if I would permit him to consult me if ever he was faced with a problem he did not quite know how to tackle. Of course I said I would.

'Over the years we became quite good friends and he visits me quite often. In fact, he saw me only a few weeks ago about a case in which, I am pleased to say, I was able to assist him.' He looked at me in a mischievous way and added with a smile: 'I helped him of course in my own way. I was present in the theatre as he performed the operation and was able to guide him. Afterwards I visited the patient during his sleep state and attended to his spirit body. Of course the dear boy doesn't know any of this and I prefer him to believe it was his own care and skill that saved the patient's sight.'

During this interview it came to light that a number of specialists from various ophthalmic hospitals come to see Mr Lang now and then to discuss complex cases.

These visits to Mr Lang resulted in news of the spirit doctor spreading to other specialists and practitioners in other fields of medicine. George Chapman has a considerable file marked 'Confidential'. It contains letters from hospital and private doctors – some of them well-known specialists, others less notable practitioners. Many of them had asked for appointments with Mr Lang because they wanted to discuss with him some of the cases which worried them and which they hoped might be cured, or at least improved, by treatment from the spirit doctor; every letter showed that the patient had not reacted to orthodox medical treatment and was, as far as could be judged, incurable. There are letters openly requesting appointments for patients to be seen by Mr Lang so that spirit surgery and treatment can be tried. Since these communications are all marked 'Private and Confidential' the identity of the writers cannot be revealed. But I assure you I have seen them all and read them. And the names of these correspondents would probably startle you.

One prominent Harley Street specialist wrote: 'I am relinquishing my practice which will be taken over by —— who was trained at Guy's Hospital and was a —— prizewinner. —— spent a year at a Clinic in Canada, specialises in industrial injuries and polio cases, and has spent further periods at two hospitals (names stated) in London. I hope that —— will call and see you, and that you will afford him all the help you can.'

The specialist's successor in fact came to see Mr Lang to discuss with him a particular case which was causing him considerable concern. Mr Lang gave his advice and, unknown to his visitor, commenced distant healing for the patient. It was successful.

George Chapman continues to receive letters from members of the medical profession. One of the most recent written in December 1964 said: 'Next month I open my new department at —— Hospital. Please ask Dr Lang to give this medical department his blessing and to give me the strength, awareness, calmness and confidence to run it, I will look to Dr Lang for his help.'

Ultimately, Mr Lang's letter to the Registrar at Moorfields served its purpose, though not officially. But Mr Lang is never concerned with officialdom or public acclaim – his sole aim is to assist any sufferer in need of help. If he can obtain support from the medical profession and, through medical co-operation, bring about a patient's recovery, he is quite content.

Some years ago journalist Desmond Shaw wrote: 'The day will come when no great medical man, physiologist or pathologist, will dream of attempting to cure diseases without speaking to the spirit world, any more than he would dream of going into the operating-room without his scalpel.' Perhaps Mr Shaw's prophecy is on the brink of coming true.

19

Open the Doors of the Mind

DOCTORS ARE just as self-opinionated as anyone else. Because they have qualified in university and medical school, presumably they are reasonably intelligent people. But when it comes to the expressing of opinions, they are peculiarly hesitant. The most vociferous and the least vociferous share at least one quality – a massive inhibition centred on the public use of their names in connection with their views on certain subjects.

I spoke to many doctors in the cause of preparing this book. Some of them went in off the deep end at the mention of spirit healing. They laughed, they denigrated, they dismissed, they scorned. Others smiled condescendingly or shrugged their shoulders, or offered unfinished phrases such as: 'Yes, well, you know how it is . . . ' or 'Well, people are entitled to believe what they like, but I, well, how should I put it . . .'

One was left with the impression that as far as the main body of the medical profession is concerned, spirit healing was beyond the pale. Not only was it a thing they either didn't understand, or plainly disbelieved, but it didn't even warrant objective investigation.

Only a fraction of those doctors with whom I spoke would agree to allow me to quote their names together with their opinions. This is something I don't pretend to understand. Why the fear?

Even those doctors who had come in contact with George Chapman-William Lang showed some reluctance. And it wasn't as if I was simply in search of favourable opinion. I would have been pleased to quote the 'anti' spirit healing (or anti-Lang) opinions as well as the 'pros'. But the response I encountered was almost a wholly 'VER-BOTEN' attitude.

One of the doctors who met the spirit doctor on several occasions, and kindly permitted me to name him, was Dr Theodore Stephanides. After half a lifetime's experience as a doctor, he served during the Second World War as a Major in the R.A.M.C. and afterwards joined the staff of Lambeth Hospital, London, where he worked until his retirement from hospital service in 1961.

'I first met Dr Lang at the beginning of 1958,' Dr Stephanides told me at his Chelsea flat. 'A friend of mine, Mr Eric Raymond who comes from Haddenham, and who suffered from deafness (he had progressive sclerosis of the tympanum – hardening of the eardrum), asked me to go along with him to Aylesbury. He'd decided, he said, to go to a spirit doctor, and he wanted me to hear what the spirit doctor would have to say and see what he might do.'

'Had Mr Raymond had any medical treatment before he went to Aylesbury?' I asked.

'Oh yes, he'd tried orthodox medicine for a long time, without getting any results at all,' Dr Stephanides said. 'Unfortunately, Dr Lang was unable to improve Mr Raymond's deafness either. But this, I think, may have been an unfair test as far as Dr Lang is concerned, because you see sclerosis of the tympanum is known to be a progressive condition, practically impossible to cure by orthodox medicine. It goes on and on until a person becomes quite deaf. Practically nothing can stop it.

'Anyway, when we went to see Dr Lang at the beginning of 1958, he rightly diagnosed Mr Raymond's condition. He *didn't promise* that he'd heal him; he said he *hoped* that he might improve his hearing. He performed what he called an "operation" on Mr Raymond's "spirit body" which he said would result in virtual surgery on the ear-drum. This "operation" was of course performed without any visible instruments or assistants.

'Immediately after the treatment Mr Raymond's deafness did seem a little improved, but this didn't last. I saw

Mr Raymond about a fortnight ago in fact and there's no appreciable improvement there I'm sorry to say. But, as I have said before, this wasn't really a fair test and Dr Lang's failure was no indication that he lacked success with other cases. To take this view would be manifestly unfair – and of course illogical.'

'Speaking as a doctor, what impression did Mr Lang make on you?' I enquired.

'Oh, competent, kindly, slightly pedantic. Like a medical practitioner of the old school,' Dr Stephanides replied. 'During my talks with him – I accompanied Mr Raymond about eight or nine times to Aylesbury – he never made any medical mistakes. But as I was present as a guest and not as a scientific investigator, I never asked him any test questions of any kind.

'It appeared to me that there was vast medical knowledge there but of a time gone by, if you understand me. He didn't seem to mention any of the modern developments – things like penicillin, etc., but that may of course have been coincidence. But what he spoke about at various times clearly indicated that he had a great deal of medical experience and knowledge.

'I have personal knowledge of an incident during one of my meetings with the spirit doctor which made quite an impression on me.

'In February 1958 I had an operation at Lambeth Hospital for retinal detachment of the right eye. The following June I visited Dr Lang with Mr Raymond. On that occasion Dr Lang came up to me and stood in front of me (with both eyes firmly closed as usual), and told me that he was pleased that my operation for a "retinal disorder" (he didn't use the term "retinal detachment") had been so successful. There were no outward signs of any kind which would betray the fact that I had had the operation, and I hadn't at any time mentioned it. Nor had Mr Raymond; I confirmed this with him afterwards.

'Of course, there is no absolute guarantee that the information in question could not have come from some person connected with the Lambeth Hospital, but I don't think this probable because, as far as I know, Mr Chapman hasn't any connection there.

'Another possibility is, of course, telepathy; but here again I don't think telepathy comes into my case because I certainly wasn't thinking about the operation when I went to Aylesbury. There was no reason why I should be thinking about it. The operation had been performed four months before my June meeting with Dr Lang and I had no trouble afterwards.

'When Dr Lang told me about the operation, I was surprised, most surprised. I myself incline to the opinion that Dr Lang made or sensed the diagnosis by what I would term "super-normal" means.'

During my interview with Dr Stephanides it came to light that he had met George Chapman in his non-trance state during one of his visits to Aylesbury. I asked him about his impressions.

'Well, they seem to be two entirely different people,' Dr Stephanides said. 'Of course I never knew Dr Lang – or Mr Lang to give him his right title – in real life, but I think that people who had known him and spoke to Mr Chapman in trance, when he was under the influence of Dr Lang would recognise him and find a resemblance. His manner of speaking and the way he holds himself, among other characteristics, were quite different from Mr Chapman's.'

'Do you believe that George Chapman is in fact controlled by Mr Lang?' I asked.

'This is a very difficult question to answer. Let me put it this way: Either Mr Chapman is an extraordinarily good actor or he *is* controlled by Dr Lang.'

'If Mr Chapman was just an extraordinarily good actor, how could he achieve his wonderful healing results?'

'Well, there of course I can't speak from *personal* knowledge because the only case I saw for myself was the inconclusive one of Mr Raymond,' Dr Stephanides replied. 'But let me say this: I believe that spirit healing actually takes place. The only thing is that, so far, we don't know the laws of spirit healing or how it works.

117

'Although I haven't had any first-hand experience, I have read a good deal about spirit healing. So far we haven't discovered enough about its laws. Very often, people who don't believe in spirit healing are cured, and yet others who do believe in it find that the effects are sometimes negligible, even negative.

'The healer himself appears, too, to have his ups and downs. Over a period he may have a long chain of successes and then suddenly, and for some time, lose some or all his power. Even if he doesn't do this, another curious phenomenon may occur in which, sometimes, he may treat three patients in succession and achieve good results with two of them while the third, whose case seems exactly similar, will show no improvement. And that's the reason why it's difficult to assess exactly what the overall results of spirit healing are.

'There is also the great difficulty of knowing how far auto-suggestion comes into it. This is a very important force indeed, because it can make a person better or worse. I mean, a person can imagine himself to be far worse or better than he actually is.'

'Is it possible to cure cancer, for instance, by auto-suggestion?' I cut in.

'Personally I don't know of any case myself where it has been done or tried, but so little is known of the forces of the body itself as it were, that one really cannot say what auto-suggestion can or cannot cure.

'Auto-suggestion seems to be a very strong force. Cases have been known – let's say for instance in an epidemic of plague in India – when people die of fear because they convince themselves they have indeed got the plague. Incredible as it may seem, these victims of auto-suggestion die with many of the symptoms of the disease, although post-mortem examinations prove that the bacillus is absent.

'It is also well known that where a patient has an illness – practically any illness – and the doctor tells them, "Oh, you'll soon be better," the patient has a much better chance of recovery. But if the doctor were to shake his head and say: "I don't think much can be done, you'll be dead in a few days," the chances are that the patient will get worse almost immediately.

'There is a huge gap in our knowledge of what exactly influences the human body. There's where I think research ought to be done to try and find out what I'd call the *laws* of spirit healing. Then one would know more about it and could assess easier which patients would benefit from spirit healing and those who would not.'

'Generally speaking, do you accept that spirit healing might help a patient who doesn't respond to orthodox medical treatment?' I asked.

'Yes, I think so,' Dr Stephanides said. 'I think there is ample evidence of the great effectiveness of spirit healing. Take Lourdes, for instance. No one can deny that countless cases have been treated there with most remarkable success. And not only at Lourdes, but also at the Island of Tinos in Greece, where the Virgin of Tinos has achieved, and daily achieves, most wonderful healing results. My father lived many years in India and he said that similar healing results were obtained by people who bathed in the Ganges. It is not just a case of a particular religion being able to bring about miraculous healing results. Lourdes is the healing grotto of the Roman Catholic Church; Tinos is the healing island of the Greek Orthodox Church; and the Ganges is the healing river of Hinduism. Here alone we have three different religions practising spirit healing and I believe there are others who bring about exactly the same sort of fantastic healing results.'

'If you had a patient who didn't respond satisfactorily to orthodox medical treatment, would you advise him to seek William Lang's help?' I asked.

'I'd advise him first to try orthodox medicine and then, if that didn't succeed, to try spirit healing.'

'I am sure you realise that your views are quite exceptional,' I said. 'Because my own experience with members of your profession is that they refuse to entertain the idea of the existence of a spirit body. They see nothing beyond their own sphere and find it inconceivable that

119

spirit healing, which they don't understand, can succeed where medicine often fails.'

'Well, I am of the opinion that orthodox medicine, however advanced in the light of scientific discoveries, knows very little of the forces of the body,' Dr Stephanides replied. 'There seems to be a lot of things which influence the human body and which have not so far been proved or recognised. This is the reason why I would like to see full research into spirit healing so that an assessment could be made of the assistance it could render orthodox medicine.'

'So you would welcome co-operation between the medical profession and spirit doctors?'

'Yes, if I knew that a patient had tried orthodox medical treatment without success, I'd certainly be only too pleased to advise him to try spirit healing, to consult Dr Lang. And you can take it from me that I am not by any means the only doctor who believes in the vast possibilities of spirit healing. Have you read, for instance, the books on the subject by Professor Charles Richet and Dr Alexis Carrel? They were both orthodox medical practitioners, but they believed it was possible to get amazing results from spirit healing. They didn't profess to know *how* the results were obtained, but that they were obtained they were certain.'

I am grateful to Dr Stephanides for allowing me to publish his views. I only wish that more members of his profession would cultivate his attitude, if only for the reason that any form of treatment, orthodox or unorthodox, which ultimately benefits mankind, is worthy of consideration. Perhaps a more embracing interpretation of the Hippocratic Oath would help them to open the doors to those parts of their minds which remain so tightly shut.

20

A Matron's Unexpected Help

THE FOLLOWING case is different from others in as much as the details of the medical history and the spirit healing by Mr William Lang were not revealed to me by the patient, but by the Matron of the Seven Gables Nursing Home where the spirit operations and treatment were carried out. The matron is Mrs D. M. Williamson, S.R.N., S.C.M., of Winslow, and the value of her testimony is enhanced, I believe, not only because of her extensive medical knowledge, gathered during a lifetime devoted to nursing, but also the fact that she was present on every occasion Mr Lang came to visit his patient. Mrs Williamson was thus able to satisfy herself about the spirit doctor's unique abilities.

'Mrs Jo Brown, who had been transferred to us from Stoke Mandeville Hospital in early September 1958,' Mrs Williamson told me when I saw her at Winslow on 26 October 1964, 'had sustained a broken neck and other multiple injuries in an accident. She had been at Stoke Mandeville Hospital for several months but her condition was regarded as hopeless. It defeated the best that medical science could do. The patient was completely paralysed from her neck down. She was unable to lift her head off the pillow, or even turn it, and had difficulty in taking in food when being fed. There were certain functional disabilities.

'When Mrs Brown was admitted here, her husband told me that he had arranged for a Mr George Chapman of Aylesbury to call and see his wife to try and help her. He explained that Mr Chapman was the medium of the spirit doctor William Lang. Mr Brown was concerned about my reaction to the news and to pacify me and secure my help, he emphasised that his sole purpose was to try *anything* that might possibly help his wife.

'I must admit I felt somewhat lost for words. Having been so closely connected with the medical profession all my working life, it was only natural that I had never given a thought to spiritual healing or spirit doctors – to be quite frank, I did not even know that either existed. Although I was far from convinced that it could achieve any benefit, I could well understand the anxious husband being ready to try *anything* to help his wife. Knowing the doctors' verdict on this patient and her pitiable condition, I had to admit that nothing could be lost by trying spiritual healing – although it was hard to understand what could be gained. In the circumstances I told Mr Brown that I thought he was right to try.

'When Mr Chapman arrived at the Nursing Home, for a reason I cannot explain, I immediately felt that here was an honest and sincere man. Before taking him to Mrs Brown's bedroom I talked to him for a moment about her condition and explained to him that the doctors at the hospital were of the opinion she would never again walk or be able to move about. It was obvious to me, though, that he had no medical knowledge at all, and I couldn't help feeling that his visit was going to be a waste of time, and, worse, a shattering disappointment to poor Mr Brown. Not to mention his wife.

'As soon as we went into Mrs Brown's room, Mr Chapman told her in a very reassuring manner that Dr Lang would do everything possible to help her. As he sat at the bedside, I watched him closely and noticed that his eyes were closed, as though going to sleep. It seemed to me that his face changed and became older. His body too seemed to shrink. After a time he stood up, stretched out his hand in greeting to me and said: "Good morning, young lady, I am grateful to you for having allowed me to come." His voice was entirely different from Mr Chapman's. It was gruffer, the voice of an old man, and the way

122

he spoke was very cultured. It was a remarkable experience for me I assure you.

'Mr Chapman introduced himself as Dr William Lang, and walked over to Mrs Brown's bedside. While touching her head, arms and body lightly with his hands, he correctly diagnosed her condition. I was stunned. I am a trained nurse of considerable experience and I was astounded by the accuracy of his diagnosis. Incredible as it may seem, when he said he was sure he would be able to help, I half believed him. I don't know why, but I did. His warning that the process of recovery would be long increased my confidence in him because, if Mrs Brown could be helped at all, it was obvious that it could only be done step-by-step.'

Mrs Williamson remembered Mr Lang's explanation about the spirit body and the physical body, and how operating on the former would transfer its effect to the latter. 'It was a little bit much for me to digest,' she said. 'I had never before heard anything like it. He radiated so much confidence that I could not take my eyes away from him. I have had a lot of experience in the operating theatre, and the way his hands moved a little above the patient's head and body was so real as to suggest that a most delicate operation was being carried out. I tell you, I was transfixed.

'Afterwards Dr Lang told me he was quite certain the effect of his surgery would transfer from the spirit body to the physical body, and he said he would come again in two days' time to perform further operations. He asked me if I would co-operate with him, and when I assented, he told me exactly what he wanted me to do – gentle massage of the patient's neck at the site of the vertebrae.

'He then went back to his chair, and very soon I was again facing Mr Chapman. He was once more as tall and upright as when I'd first met him, his face having changed to that of a youngish man, and his voice having reverted to the normal timbre before going into trance. I was left in no doubt that I had in fact met two entirely different people.

'Dr Lang continued visiting Mrs Brown one or twice a week, and every time he performed his spirit operations I was present. During each visit he instructed me exactly on what he wished me to do, and of course I did it. He was very grateful for the co-operation. But you should have seen Mrs Brown!

'Gradually, she was able to use her fingers; then she began to lift her arm a little and also her legs; she could turn her head from side to side and make other movements. It was really marvellous the way she recovered, and all this after what the doctors had said.

'I saw to it that Dr Lang's instructions were carried out in every detail. The gentle massage on Mrs Brown's vertebrae improved the placement of that part of the spinal column and enabled the spinal fluid to flow more normally. We used to encourage her to push, move and draw her legs up, and use her hands. With help, she began to feed herself and eventually was able to do this quite comfortably. Her next victory was to comb her hair, very unsteadily at first, but with perseverance she managed. It was a case of co-operation between the spirit doctor and medicine.

'Then one marvellous day Dr Lang decided we should try and get her to stand. I remember him saying to her: "Now you really can stand up, you can do it, you are all right and you'll soon be able to walk." She was terribly nervous, but we gave her all the encouragement we could, and told her it would be all right. With a little help she stood up, very slowly and shakily, and then she straightened up and stood there, unable to believe it, trembling with excitement and her eyes shining. Afterwards, we were present at the side of her bed twice a day to give her confidence while she stood up. It took about six months until she could, with help, walk about her room.

'Three months after Dr Lang had first visited Mrs Brown, we were able to drive her to Bletchley station to meet her husband each week-end when he came to visit her. I remember the first time. We had not told Mr Brown what we intended to do, we just got her ready, put her into the car, and she was at the station waiting for him. He was so excited, he couldn't believe that it was his own wife waiting there for him.

'Mrs Brown stayed at our Nursing Home for a year, and throughout that time Dr Lang came to visit her each week. He was as pleased and thrilled with her wonderful progress as were all of us.

'When she left us, she was able to walk – with someone at her side because she was still nervous but she could stand unaided. It was just a matter of time and of gaining confidence.

'During his visits I spoke to Dr Lang in what you might call medical jargon – as I would talk in my capacity as matron to any consultant specialist visiting a patient. Over the months I came to have a great admiration for this gifted man, and having seen the results of his treatment, I found myself seeking him out whenever either myself or my daughter needed treatment of any kind.'

I asked Mrs Williamson about her own indisposition and she said:

'I had suffered for a long time with bladder trouble, and I also had trouble with my legs. I had had medical attention, but it didn't do me any good and I thought I just had to accept the situation.

'When I consulted Dr Lang he told me he would help me. It was completely painless and I am not exaggerating when I say that he indeed succeeded in curing my trouble.

'With regard to my daughter Chérie, her eyesight deteriorated considerably after an attack of measles. We first noticed it when her piano teacher told us that she was unable to read the music. She was seen by an eye specialist who tried to correct her impaired vision by prescribing spectacles for her but, even so, her eyesight remained poor. The specialist said that there was nothing else he could do for her.

'I took Chérie to see Dr Lang. He attended to her eyes and the result was that her vision improved tremendously. She no longer has any difficulty and, in fact, passed her driving test. Before she went to Dr Lang her vision would not have been good enough. From having to wear spectacles regularly she is able to take them off whenever she wants and can see quite well without them. Chérie is an actress, and this relief is quite important to her, especially when she appears on television. In fact when she has any part that calls for a girl with normal eyesight she can act it.

'We are not what you would call "convinced Spiritualists", but we take a great interest in it since we met Dr Lang. He does an excellent job in this world, and I only wish that many more members of the medical profession would work with him. By doing so, they would help him to help people who otherwise might be destined to die before their time, or are condemned to live in misery and pain.'

21

Drama on the A-41

SATURDAY, 6 SEPTEMBER 1958, started like any other ordinary working day for George Chapman. He left his house as usual in the morning to drive his car from Aylesbury to Birmingham to enable Mr Lang to keep his appointments with his patients at the Healing Centre. It was an uneventful journey – George Chapman knew the road well and drove at his customary speed so as to arrive at the Midlands town in good time.

And, as on most occasions, there were so many patients at the Centre that it was rather late in the day when the last visitor left, and George Chapman was able to become his own self again.

George was obliged to stay overnight in Birmingham, because appointments had been made for some patients to be seen on Sunday morning at Brownhills Spiritualist Church.

The return journey to Aylesbury early on Sunday afternoon was once more one of those routine trips. Chapman, travelling at a speed of about 85 m.p.h. on the straight stretches of the A-41, soon had Solihull, Warwick and Banbury behind him. If conditions remained favourable, he expected to cover the next twelve miles to Bicester in under ten minutes, and reach home within half an hour.

He was about four miles north-west of Bicester when it happened.

The nearside front tyre burst while the speedometer needle was climbing towards the nineties. The car went out of control, and then began to roll over and over. The driver of a car behind saw the whole thing. He told police

127

later that the speeding Citroën must have turned over ten times before it came to rest. His wife verified this.

When I asked George Chapman to tell me what he thought and did at the moment of accident, he replied:

'When the car became uncontrollable and started to roll over, I thought: I must get out quickly. I had my tank almost full of petrol and feared it might explode and engulf the car in flames. Almost at the same moment I could see myself lying on the rear seat as though asleep and the thought occurred to me that my spirit body was in fact examining my physical body.

'Then I saw myself suddenly standing outside the car and looking at the wreck. At that time I didn't know whether I existed in my physical or spirit body. I actually wondered if those who spoke to me were discarnate, but the feeling gradually grew upon me that I was still on earth.'

The motorist who witnessed the accident said that, almost immediately after the car stopped turning over, he and his wife saw its driver standing beside the car looking at it as it rested on its roof.

'How did you manage to get out?' I asked Chapman.

'I have no recollection of leaving the car,' he answered. 'In my dazed condition I assumed that I must have crawled out through the broken windscreen, but I couldn't have done so because it was intact, and so were the other windows.'

'Could you perhaps have crawled out through your open offside front window?'

'It was open, but only about five inches,' he said. (The police report confirms this.) 'Yet, although I don't know how I got out, I found myself outside without being seriously hurt,' he went on. 'The only injury I had was a cut on my head.'

'What about the doors?' I persisted, trying to get an explanation of how he managed to escape. 'Couldn't you have opened a door and . . . ?'

'That's no good either,' Chapman replied. 'Neither the driver behind me, nor the police and insurance surveyor, could explain how it had been possible to get out of the car. Not a window was broken but they could not be opened, and when the police patrol arrived on the scene they found that every door was still *locked from the inside!* I couldn't have opened a door and got out through it, and the windows, too, were jammed.'

The car was so badly damaged that the insurance company considered it a write-off. Yet neither the windscreen nor any of the windows were broken or even cracked!

The incident was investigated by the Bicester police (Oxfordshire Constabulary), and the facts recorded by the officers who probed the accident confirmed every word George Chapman told me. The police report stated: Doors locked from inside. Doors and windows immovable due to damage. Windscreen and windows unbroken and shut with exception of front offside window which was lowered 5 inches from top. Driver cannot explain how he left wrecked car . . .

'How do you think you got out?' I pressed.

'Well, I don't know really. All I can say is: I feel that although this incident demonstrates a good example of involuntary spirit projection, it also goes much deeper and shows that in circumstances of absolute extremity spirit power can apparently overcome physical laws. One could perhaps also say it is materialisation in reverse or something like that.'

One other unexplainable thing needs to be recorded.

'The following day, in the company of a former Superintendent of Police, I visited the scene of the accident,' Chapman recalled. 'We both carefully examined the wrecked vehicle, and then the surface of the road. We were surprised to find that it bore no signs of an accident – not even a tyre mark was to be seen.'

I should perhaps add that the cut on his head which he had sustained during the car accident was completely gone after a full day of trance healing on Monday, 8 September 1958. Mr Lang attended to his medium so perfectly that not even the slightest sign remained of a bloody wound he had carried that morning as he went into trance.

22

The End of a Twenty-year Hell

PATRICK P. CALDER of Ballinger suffered for twenty years from spondylitis. Yet, although he was under constant medical care and everything known in medicine was done for him, he found no relief from his ailment.

'I suffered with spondylitis from 1942 until 1961,' Mr Calder told me in December 1964. 'During these years I had hospital treatment for it in 1944 while I was in Italy with the Forces and again in 1948 when I was in Scotland. Later, when I came south, I received regular treatment at Lambeth Hospital in London. The orthopaedic specialist was Dr Robb, and he did everything he could to help me. I was receiving radio-therapy at regular intervals, but it didn't help.

'Ten years went by, and I had become worse. The doctors could do no more than they were doing already and made it plain that it was one of those cases in which the patient had to reconcile himself to the fact that no other alternative treatment was possible.

'My health deteriorated so alarmingly in 1958 that I became really desperate, but fortunately for me someone told me about spiritual healing, and in particular about the spirit doctor William Lang who worked through the mediumship of a Mr George Chapman in Aylesbury. I was told Dr Lang had cured many people whom doctors and hospitals had classed as incurable, and I was advised to find out if I, too, could be helped. I had nothing to lose – throughout my illness my only relief was codeine tablets – so I decided to give Mr Chapman and his spirit doctor a try.

'Well, I met Dr Lang on 27 October 1958. Although I was a little nervous – and naturally also somewhat sceptical – the elderly spirit doctor with his kindly approach and his reassuring way put me at my ease. We had a little talk and then he asked me to lie down on the healing couch.

'While he examined me, we spoke about the radiotherapy treatment I had received at Lambeth Hospital; he told me he did not approve of it as it dried up the natural fluid in the joints and left them without any natural lubricant. He told me he would operate on my spirit body and was certain he could cure me of my complaint if I was prepared to undergo treatment from him at regular intervals for a considerable time. I was willing to do anything that would help me to get rid of the spondylitis which was crippling me.

'It was a strange experience. Although he was not using visible instruments, I used to feel the inoculations as the spirit needle was inserted into my spine. It was a sensation I can hardly describe because I had a sort of champagne feeling when I got off the couch.

'Dr Lang asked me to come and see him again in six months' time for further contact healing, and asked me in the meantime to regularly report my state of health to Mr Chapman, so that contact could be maintained and I could continue to receive spirit treatment during my sleep state. I did this and began to improve slowly but surely.

'I saw Dr Lang at six-monthly intervals – in April and October every year – and at every visit he performed additional operations. After six visits – the last one was in April 1961 – my back was completely cured and I was free of it and never experience even the slightest twinge. I am a self-employed garden contractor and get through a lot of hard and rough work every day. I would certainly have been unable to do what I do but for Dr Lang.'

Apart from freeing Mr Calder from spondylitis, Mr Lang also attended to a cyst on his right wrist by means of an operation on his spirit body. This cyst had troubled Mr Calder to such an extent that he had planned to see his doctor about it. However, Mr Lang noticed it and dealt with it in his usual painless way.

Mr Calder recalled the occasion: 'The cyst on my right wrist was about the size of a pigeon's egg, very painful, and Dr Lang got rid of it without fuss or bother.

'A few days after he performed the spirit operation, a small red scar appeared on the wrist. As the days went by it disappeared, and I then noticed that something strange was taking place on top of the lump. The skin seemed to be dying and withering and then a small blister began to form between the layers of the skin.

'Then, one day when my wife and I were out in the car, my wife suddenly asked me what was on my wrist. Out of the top of the lump a clear jelly-like stuff was oozing. With the help of my wife I pressed the lump until it was free of fluid. It didn't hurt at all, and afterwards the cyst disappeared.

'All that I'm left with is a small red scar about the size of a sixpence. Actually I'm rather proud of it and show it off whenever I get the chance.'

23

The Doubting Oculist

TEN YEARS AGO, Mrs Joan D. Harris, M.A. (Oxon)
of Maidenhead, had to face up to the unpalatable fact
that she would have to wear a steel jacket. The reason for
this went back many years, to a time when a serious injury
caused a crushed disc in her spine. The back injury was
eventually remedied, but, as Mrs Harris told me in
November 1964, there was another distressing side effect.

'My sight was affected,' she said. 'Whenever I took up a
book, I could only manage to read a single page, and then
everything became terribly blurred. I was not very old and
to be unable to read was really a dreadful blow. I went to
see the ophthalmic consultant under whose care I'd been
for years, but when he examined my eyes, particularly the
left one which was the troublemaker, he asked me if I had
been accustomed to doing much fine work. I told him that
I had taken a degree in mathematics which entailed doing
a lot of fine drawing at one time. I had also done considerable embroidering. He said: "Well, there is no question of
doing any more, you must drop it, because I can't correct
your eyes. I can't do anything for you. You'll have to be
content with reading a little at a time, and when your
vision gets blurred, put the book down, look around the
room and take a break before starting again. But don't
read too much." He consoled me by saying that he didn't
think my eyesight would get any worse, and said he'd give
me some spectacles for long distance and reading. The
idea, I think, was that they would help just a little, but that
I couldn't expect any radical change for the better. He left
it at that.

'Then, fortunately for me, I was given a copy of the *Psychic News* by a friend containing an article about Dr Lang in which it was revealed that he was once a Moorfields man. I came to the opinion that I ought to see him. There was, I realised, nothing any eye specialist could do for me, and I had nothing to lose by seeking help elsewhere.

'My appointment with Dr Lang was for the early afternoon of 17 June 1959.

'When I arrived at Mr Chapman's house and his wife admitted me, I thought what a lovely atmosphere there was in the house and how charming Mrs Chapman was. Then Mr Chapman came in and I found I liked him enormously. He was a really genuine sort of man, very much interested in healing, and very kind. In meeting certain people one may have immediate reservations, even regret, but it was exactly the opposite with Mr Chapman. I trusted him at once and thought, "Everything will be all right."

'Having talked with him for some little time about ordinary things, we went into Dr Lang's consulting-room where he sat in a chair, a very healthy, virile and upright middle-aged man. And as he sat there with his eyes closed, I saw him changing – he shrank into an aged man in a most extraordinary fashion!

'When he got up a minute or two later and greeted me with "Good afternoon, Mrs Harris," his voice was entirely different. In Dr Lang's voice there is not the slightest resemblance to Mr Chapman's, none whatever. Dr Lang's voice is cultured, very old and rather tired. His choice of words and manner of speaking was most striking. Listening to Dr Lang's speech, it struck me how much faster we talk these days.

'That afternoon was perhaps one of the most astonishing occasions throughout my life. I was surprised when Dr Lang said to me: "You have come about your eyes, haven't you?" When I indicated this was so, he told me reassuringly, "Oh, we'll see to that." I had not mentioned in my letter to Mr Chapman the reason for the appointment I asked for, and when I talked with him before he went into trance, we did not discuss my disability.

'When Dr Lang told me: "There is something else, you know, that must be dealt with as well," I looked at him questioningly and thought immediately of my back. But I dismissed the thought, because everything that could be done for it had been done.

'"You know, don't you," he said, "that you look as if you are overweight? You are somewhat, but a lot of you is puffed up." I replied: "Yes I know I'm a bit plump, but I didn't realise that I was 'puffed up', as you put it." He said: "It's not so much your overweight that worries me, it's that you *are* puffed up. It must be put right. It is very bad for you."

'I looked at him in some surprise as he said: "I'll give you a diet that will put you right, but you must keep to it under my guidance for not longer than a month. You must not pass it on to anybody else, or use it again unless I tell you to do so."

'He then said: "We'll do your eye now. You needn't worry, it will be painless and all you need to do is to lie still, relax and keep your eyes shut – don't open them." Usually I don't find it easy to follow this advice, because I am very highly strung. I know this. Lying on the healing couch, however, I felt relaxed in a quite extraordinary fashion, almost as if I had been helped by someone else, rather like the feeling you have when you are given injections before surgery. I didn't open my eyes, but I think he must have seen from my expression that I was wondering what he was doing. He said: "Oh, Basil is my son and he is helping me and he knows what I mean when I click my fingers."

'The operation was completely painless, but I could feel something like cold metal above and beneath my eye. The whole thing took very little time.

'When he told me that everything was finished, Dr Lang said: "Just a moment, keep your eyes shut and rest." And as I remained lying on the couch he continued operating.

135

He explained that I should wait a month before seeing the ophthalmic consultant again and he advised me to have them tested every year. Until then I used to see the specialist every two years, but I was more than willing to take this advice.

'Before I left Dr Lang, he told me that he regretted he was unable to make my eyes well enough to dispose with spectacles altogether, but that doesn't worry me now because I can see well enough with this aid. Dr Lang said: "You will have no more trouble with your eyes. Nor will there be for the rest of your life. You will see clearly and you will not again be troubled by distorted vision."

'He asked me if by any chance I had paper and pencil with me, or a pen, because he wanted me to write down a note to my oculist. Luckily I had, but I asked him if he really wanted me to pass on a message to the oculist. I mean it does strike one as a bit odd, doesn't it?

'"Yes, I want you to tell him what I have done," Dr Lang said, and began to spell out for me the word "chemosis". "It means," he explained, "the aqueous fluid is not clear. That's why when you try to read everything looks as if it is under water." I'd never heard of "chemosis" and "aqueous liquid" before! Dr Lang continued by spelling out the words "occipito frontalis", explaining: "This means that the muscle has dropped and therefore there is pressure on the retina; these two things combined made it difficult for you to see but I have now put everything right. I want you to pass on these details to your oculist." I promised I would.

'When I returned home to Maidenhead in the late afternoon, I felt rather tired and disinclined to do anything. I decided I would not attempt to read and, in view of the operation, to give my eyes a rest. But the next morning, when I picked up the newspaper from the breakfast table, I found I could read the newsprint easily without the small letters clouding.

'It hit me all of a sudden. "Good gracious, I haven't had to look up and blink once!" You know what I'm getting at, don't you? It meant my sight was all right. And, since

136

that afternoon of 17 June 1959, when Dr Lang performed his spirit operation on my left eye, I have never had the slightest trouble.

'I carried out to the letter the instructions Dr Lang had given me regarding my diet. The regimen was severe, to say the least and normally I'd have found a great difficulty in keeping to it. For some unknown reason I took it in my stride, and the enormous puffiness just fell away from me during that month. And it disappeared for good, just like pricking a balloon. I've never put it back since and as a result I feel much better.

'I went to see the ophthalmic consultant a month after I'd seen Dr Lang. He examined my left eye and confirmed that the impossible had happened – that my eye was completely cured. I told him about Dr Lang and read out to him the message which had been dictated to me. He looked at me with raised eyebrows and said: "Well, of course you don't see mistily any more." I replied: "No, I don't," but he had nothing further to say, then or subsequently, when I've seen him each year. I've often thought it was a pity that he didn't respond in any way, because I felt Dr Lang would like to have drawn him into it.

'Four years passed, and during this time I received distant healing from Dr Lang. I have had arthritis, particularly in my hands and in my knee, and I also suffered from asthma and hayfever. I felt considerable relief from the distant healing, but last year I was in real trouble with bronchitis, asthma with hayfever, sinus, catarrh, the whole works – I was full of it. I decided to see Dr Lang again and made an appointment for 12 June 1963. Again I didn't say exactly what was wrong with me. I only wrote that I wished to come and see him.

'When I entered the consulting room, Dr Lang said: "Good afternoon, Mrs Harris, I am happy to see you again." Almost immediately he added: "You know, you are very full of catarrh, both in your head and chest." Well, I was dumbfounded, all I could say was: "That's what I have come to see you about."

'Dr Lang then asked me to lie on the healing couch and he worked on my left lung which is always the one that fills first. I could feel how the gummed-up feeling, as I call it, just went. He snapped his fingers and asked Basil for some injection – I wish I could remember what he called it – and I could almost feel the injection by the pressure. "That will relieve you a lot," he told me, and he was right. Until then I had had to breathe through my mouth and the pressure was as if I had a welt across my eyebrows from the swollen sinus, but he moved it all. It was wonderful how speedily he relieved me.

'After the spirit operation and treatment, Dr Lang explained to me that he couldn't cure asthma and hayfever, or prevent the onset of these complaints. The most he could do was to keep them under control by continuing to give me distant healing. This is being maintained and it undoubtedly helps me.

'I haven't been back to see Dr Lang since June 1963, the distant healing keeps my arthritis, asthma and hayfever at bay. However, as far as my eye and the overweight are concerned, I have never had any trouble since he performed his spirit operations during that remarkable afternoon in June 1959.'

24

The Mending of a Former Conservative M.P.

THE CASE of Mr Norman Bower, M.A. – a non-practising barrister-at-law and former Conservative Member of Parliament for Harrow West – is remarkable because he had been suffering from liver trouble and spastic colon for almost thirty-five years. It was his state of health that forced him to give up his career in Parliament. He was told about Mr Lang – at a time when he needed help most urgently, and decided to go to Aylesbury. Mr Lang performed a painless operation on his spirit body, and as a result of it and subsequent healing, Mr Bower was completely cured of his ailment within ten months.

George Chapman mentioned Mr Bower's case history to me in the summer of 1964, and told me that this ex-patient might be willing to give me full details about his experience. I contacted Mr Bower and a few days later was invited to his London flat in Mayfair. First reactions on meeting him pointed to the fact that he was a highly literate man with a lively mind and a rational way of thinking.

Norman Bower was born in 1907 in Hampstead, the son of a prosperous businessman. He was educated at Rugby and Oxford.

'From about the time I was twenty I suffered with my liver,' he told me. 'To be honest I did not know what the deuce was wrong with me until I came across a doctor in the South of France on an occasion when I was visiting my mother. She used to winter out there. Well, I was talking to this chap, telling him how I felt and all that, and he told me that my liver was enlarged and I ought to diet. I was not to eat anything fried, avoid all alcohol except claret and leave things such as eggs, pastries, chocolate, etc., alone.

'I must admit that while I observed this diet, I felt quite all right, but if I deviated from it at all, I became ill again. Of course at that age one tends to forget medical advice. I'm afraid I did, and in fact after about a year I became very lax indeed. Forgot all about it, didn't stick to the instructions at all. But by golly I paid for my stupidity. I got some really nasty attacks again.'

Mr Bower studied law and although he became a barrister, he did not take up the profession and instead went into business. His interest in politics was aroused from the time he was at Rugby and Oxford. It was a subject constantly in his mind. 'But there was the question of getting an opening, and that's not always easy. It takes time if one has no particular influence, and I had none at all. My father had no political connections and party affairs did not appeal to him. Well, I simply went about it in the only way I knew. At Oxford I took part in its various political activities with some enthusiasm, and did a certain amount of speaking at the Union and other meetings. When I came down, I went along to the Conservative Party Central Office, in London. I'd decided by this time that this was the party I wanted to belong to. I got my name put down on their list as a candidate. Eventually I was put on a short list, and I don't remember how many times I tried to get adopted. I used to go all over the country, trying various constituencies, and I got turned down times out of number.

'At long last I got the opportunity to fight a more or less hopeless seat in the General Election of 1931. I was defeated, and again in 1935 in similar circumstances. But I hadn't done too badly, not badly at all.'

When the Second World War broke out, intensified political campaigns came to an end. The outbreak of war also brought about the closing down of Mr Bower's successful business venture and he joined the army.

'I practically put politics out of my mind then,' Mr

Bower continued. 'Then, by an extraordinary chance, a by-election occurred in Harrow during the war, and my application for adoption was accepted. My political luck had turned. I had the experience of course, and having fought previous seats, I had a good deal of political knowledge and acumen, and that happened to appeal to them. And I was the right age – thirty-four. They quite liked the idea of having someone from the army. So there it was, I became an M.P.'

Mr Bower's activities as a Conservative Member of Parliament for Harrow West seemed to mark him out for a prominent political career. He was not only liked and respected by his colleagues in the House, but became also fairly well acquainted with Winston Churchill. But Norman Bower's assent to political prominence was prematurely cut short.

'It was the spastic colon that finally compelled me to give up my political career,' Mr Bower recalled regretfully. 'This unpleasant and serious condition so affected my health that both my doctor and my specialist warned me that I was unlikely to recover unless I led a less strenuous existence. And the specialist warned me that my illness was partly accentuated by a nervous condition and it was imperative for me to lead a very quiet life if I wanted to avoid still greater trouble. So I had no other alternative but to give up my seat in the House of Commons.'

Neither antibiotics nor any other treatment improved Norman Bower's health, and towards the end of 1961 he began to suffer from a distressing type of distension after meals. Fearing that it might be a growth or some other serious condition, he consulted his doctor and was advised that until an X-ray was made no diagnosis was possible. Before this took place, the doctor decided to try a course of tablets but they were of no help.

Mr Bower viewed the forthcoming test with some apprehension. He had had previous experience of barium – the sulphate powder that the patient has to take in liquefied form prior to an internal X-ray.

'It is terrible stuff,' Mr Bower recalled. 'And I was afraid it might make me ten times worse. I was terrified.

'Fortunately Miss Yeatman of the College of Psychic Science had in the meantime told me about Dr Lang and Mr Chapman, and I thought I would like to go and see him. I was pretty desperate and had great hopes that spiritual healing might help me.'

On February 20, 1962, Mr Bower wrote to George Chapman, requesting a consultation with Mr Lang. He was particularly careful not to disclose any details about his condition and just stated: 'I feel very unwell. My doctor suggests a form of examination which I am anxious to avoid. Due to my serious condition, I should be obliged if an early appointment could be arranged.' George Chapman arranged for Mr Bower to see Mr Lang on 27 February. This was how Mr Bower described his visit to Aylesbury:

'When I went into the consulting room, I wasn't prepared for what I encountered. I anticipated seeing Mr Chapman to begin with, and was surprised to find he was already in trance. I thought it very strange. I had seen his photograph and he didn't resemble it in the slightest way. I knew that Mr Chapman was about forty but the gentleman I faced was unmistakably an elderly man.

'It only dawned on me then that I was meeting Dr Lang. He greeted me and introduced himself. He talked to me about the Middlesex Hospital and Moorfields, and he spoke in a way I imagine a Victorian or Edwardian doctor would speak. I was staggered, really.

'I saw that his eyes were closed and that seemed to me to be peculiar. Nevertheless, he was capable of walking about the room without any difficulty and was able to avoid anything in his way. He asked me how old I was, and when I told him, he remarked that I looked younger.

'He told me a number of things about himself and his son Basil who had also been a surgeon. He said Basil was now helping him with his spirit operations. Then he started examining my spectacles and remarked, "My goodness, don't they make them big these days." In his days, I imagine, spectacles were either rimless or had thin silver or gold frames.

'He passed his hands over my eyes – gently, without really touching – and told me at once that the fluid at the back of my eyes had become disturbed some years ago when I had suddenly lifted some heavy weight, and that ever since I had periodically seen little black spots floating across my vision. They didn't actually impair my sight. *I* knew this of course. But how did he? I don't think it could have been through telepathy because nothing was further from my mind. I had come for help for another reason and was certainly not worried about my eyes.

'Then he passed his hands all the way down my fully clothed body, and almost immediately started telling me about my illness. He mentioned the various symptoms I had and explained how they affected each organ. These symptoms were of course familiar to me and I wondered if his knowledge of them could have been obtained through telepathy. But there was one thing which finally convinced me that it had *not* been telepathy. These were the terms "intestinal diverticulum" and "diverticulosis", which he went to the trouble of spelling out for me. I can absolutely swear that I'd never heard them before and, consequently, they could not have been in my mind. Later, I asked a doctor if he had heard of these terms and he confirmed that he knew them.

'I told Dr Lang that my doctor wanted me to have an examination which I was anxious to avoid, and he replied, "Well, the X-rays would not have shown anything, because what you are suffering from would not reveal itself in this way. No doubt they would then want to carry out an exploratory operation. It is just as well that you didn't have it." I accepted all he said as reasonable.

'Dr Lang then told me that in the past I had had an enlarged liver and this was now causing inflammation. He said he would perform a spirit operation.

'While I lay on the couch, he told me: "I've got my son Basil here – he's going to assist me," and then he called for various instruments. And each time he used one he flicked his fingers. I imagined that when he did this he was using the instrument in a certain way, but I didn't feel anything, not a thing. After about five minutes, he went through the motions of sewing up.

'He then told me that it was all over, and asked me to sit up again in the chair. He told me that he would give me distant healing, but he said that he felt that my condition would improve only gradually. "I think you'll be quite all right," he said. "It won't be an instantaneous cure, but I feel confident that you are on the right road and you'll find that there will be a steady improvement."

'He instructed me what I was to do so far as diet was concerned, and what he advised was much the same regimen as my French doctor had suggested many years ago. He asked me to write once a month about my state of health.

'When I left Dr Lang's, or Mr Chapman's, consulting-room, I felt I must not be hostile, or sceptical, but rather to take it for what it was, because only later would I be able to judge by the results. Should these prove successful, I'd have proof of the unique power of spiritual healing. I ought to say, however, that I was very hopeful of the results, and in a sense thankful – whatever the explanation of this phenomenon – I had been given the chance of recovery.

'The more I thought about my visit to Aylesbury – and cogitated on the possibility of Dr Lang really being a secondary personality of Mr Chapman the firmer grew my conviction that I had indeed met the old doctor. I was sure I would have liked him as my medical adviser. He was very forthright and kindly and had a great store of medical knowledge and experience.

'I went home and the same night, after dinner, I felt there was a slight improvement. I could feel the trouble in some way resolving itself in the form of wind which I was able to get rid of. And the distension began to lessen. It was less painful than it had been for some months past.'

Mr Lang continued giving Mr Bower distant healing, and four months after his visit to Aylesbury, on 25 June, the patient was able to write the following letter:

'I am glad to report a further very pronounced improvement in my condition during the past month. I have since been pretty well one hundred per cent normal – better than at any time since the start of the trouble last October. I feel that provided I continue to be careful about my diet, which is clearly very important, my recovery is now so well established that no further distant healing is necessary.'

Complying with Mr Bower's wish, distant healing was discontinued, but the result was the following letter which the patient wrote to George Chapman the following month:

'I think perhaps that the distant healing I had received was terminated prematurely, before my recovery was properly consolidated, as I have not been feeling so well this month. I have again been getting intermittent attacks of intestinal inflammation causing a certain amount of pain and distension, though they are not nearly as bad as they were when I visited Dr Lang in February.

'Do you think a resumption of distant healing for a further period of say, a month or two might be beneficial, or is a complete and absolute recovery from this sort of condition too much to hope for? I should be most grateful if it is possible for you to obtain Dr Lang's opinion on this point.'

William Lang's opinion was: 'This condition can be cured completely', and he recommended distant healing. Mr Bower's next letter to George Chapman, written on 26 August, 1962, read as follows:

'I am glad to say that I have been considerably better again during the past month. Much of the time I feel quite well, but I still get occasional setbacks if there is any irregularity in the action of the bowels, which is sometimes hard to avoid. However, they are almost invariably short-lived, and the symptoms are very much less severe than they used to be.

'I feel that perhaps one more month of distant healing should bring me to the point where it can be permanently discontinued without my suffering any further setbacks of a major character. I am indeed thankful for the great improvement which has taken place in my condition since I visited Dr Lang, when I was almost in despair.'

Another month later, on 23 September, Mr Bower wrote again to George Chapman:

'I am pleased to be able to tell you that there has again been a great improvement in my health during the past month. Almost from the day I last wrote to you, my bowels have been acting with much greater ease and regularity than for years past, with the result that I have been able to avoid even the mildest aperient and have consequently experienced no further distension or any other form of intestinal discomfort.

'In fact, I appear to be right back to normal again now. Let me say over again how very grateful I am for all Dr Lang has been able to do for me from the moment of his remarkable diagnosis to the truly wonderful effects of the distant healing. It would seem that the time has now come for the healing to be discontinued, but I prefer to leave this decision to you.'

Mr Lang, advised by George Chapman about Mr Bower's report, decided: 'His ailment responded wonderfully well but I'd like to keep an eye on him for three months longer.' Mr Bower, however, was not advised about Mr Lang's decision and believed that the distant healing was no longer given. Indeed, when I spoke to him some two and half years after his visit to Mr Lang, he told me:

'Despite the fact that distant healing was stopped in the early autumn of 1962, I was completely all right after another three months. My illness cleared up and I've never had any more trouble.'

Mr Bower is genuinely grateful to Mr Lang and George Chapman for the painless and complete cure. He says that if ever he becomes ill again, he will immediately turn to George Chapman and his spirit control, William Lang.

25

A Surgeon Here and a Surgeon There

MANY OF those who dismiss out of hand the entire concept of spirit healing, do so from a basis of the sketchiest knowledge of the extent of its significance. Prejudice is perhaps the commonest of human failings, as much in this century as in earlier times, and an open mind a rare virtue.

How refreshing is it then to come across an example of clear judgment free of all bias among a profession which has its share of Philistines and closed minds. This story concerns a nurse and a Harley Street surgeon. It is true in every detail and can be verified.

The nurse is Miss Evelyn B. Habershon of Lindfield, Sussex, the surgeon Mr Vincent Nesfield, F.R.C.S. Eng.; L.R.C.P. Lond.; Major L.M.S. retired.

Evelyn Habershon was born an astigmatic with a blind spot in her left eye. At one time it appeared that her future would be imperilled because of deficient sight, but with the help of spectacles she was able to pursue her studies and eventually qualify as a nurse. Then, in 1958, her vision deteriorated alarmingly. A well-known ophthalmic surgeon told her: 'You have got a cataract which will have to be operated at some time in the future.' This prospect was four years in coming, but in 1962 Evelyn Habershon's sight became so poor that she knew something would have to be done quickly.

'I tried to make an appointment to see the ophthalmic surgeon late in 1962,' she told me, 'but I was told that the earliest date he could see me was the beginning of the following year.

147

'I already knew Mr Nesfield's name as an eminent ophthalmologist, and I telephoned him and arranged to see him on 15 November 1962. When he examined me, he confirmed that I was astigmatic, had a blind spot in my left eye, and added: "You have an advanced cataract in the right eye and traces of one in the left. An operation is necessary. I can do it for you at the end of December. Would that suit you?"

'Mr Nesfield must have known how greatly I feared the operation because, when I saw him again in December and he again examined me, he said: "There's no immediate hurry for this you know. I'm going away at the end of January so suppose we leave it until some time in March or April, when the weather is warmer? I'll let you know. Meanwhile, there's no need to worry." And he left it at that. Needless to say, I was very happy with the unexpected reprieve.

'During Mr Nesfield's absence I had spiritual healing from Mrs Catherine Sheppard, a psychic healer, at her sanctuary. In the first week of April 1963 I knew that the cataract had suddenly begun to separate and, as I hadn't heard from Mr Nesfield, I wrote to him and asked if I could see him because I thought the cataract was separating. Rightly or wrongly I was sure that it was due to my having received spiritual healing. Mr Nesfield had told me it was an advanced cataract. As a nurse I knew something about these things, and I was certain that a cataract doesn't begin to separate just like that, on its own.

'Mr Nesfield arranged an appointment for me, and after he looked at my eyes he said that the cataract was indeed separated. He said, simply, "The improvement of your eyes is due to divine healing." I hadn't told him that I had been receiving spiritual healing. And yet he made this observation unhesitatingly.

'Shortly afterwards I heard through the *Psychic News* about the spirit doctor William Lang who had been an outstanding ophthalmic surgeon during his lifetime. I felt that he might be able to help me even more than Catherine Sheppard who, at that time, was very ill. I wrote to

Mr Chapman for an appointment to see Mr Lang, and went to Aylesbury on 28 May 1963.

'Mr Lang immediately diagnosed precisely what my trouble was by touching my eyes lightly with his fingers. "A physical operation is not for you, young lady," he said. "I'll perform a spirit operation now," which was what he did. I could hear him asking for scalpels and other instruments, talking with someone he called Basil. After the operation Mr Lang asked me if I would be returning to Lindfield that same day. I told him I would stay overnight at a hotel in Aylesbury because I was afraid the long train journey back might prove too great a strain for me and undo what God had done for me, working through the doctor. You see, after the operation I felt desperately tired. Mr Lang was very pleased to hear of my intentions and said: "Go to bed at nine o'clock after a light meal, and I'll come to visit during your sleep state to see whether anything needs clearing up."

'When I left Mr Chapman's house, I was astonished at the extent of the improvement the spirit operation had brought about. I had only been able to get about in taxis because of the mist that always swam before my eyes. But now I could suddenly see things around me. I felt I would be able to resume my usual life using a stick as before. Of course I used common sense, I had to be careful of steps, but I *could* see. After that I even started going up to London on my own.

'In June – three weeks after going to Mr Lang, I went to see Mr Nesfield. I admitted to him that I had had a spirit operation, and he seemed very interested. He tested my eyes and said he found an enormous improvement, though the centre, the lenses, were not clear yet. But he repeated that part of the cataract was much improved. He knew of course that I hadn't had any physical operation and repeated what he had said two months earlier: "The improvement of your eyes is due to divine healing." He also added: "You have additional sight developed in your left eye." I was so grateful to him for not being annoyed with me for having undergone spirit surgery and treatment, and very moved by his desire to help his patients in every way – even if someone went behind his back to a spirit doctor to seek additional help.'

Miss Habershon saw Mr Lang again in July 1963, when he performed further operations on her spirit body. There was again an improvement in her vision, and when she went to see Mr Nesfield afterwards, he confirmed this fact.

These alternate visits to the spirit doctor and the eminent Harley Street specialist continued.

'When I saw Mr Lang again last July,' Miss Habershon told me in November 1964, 'he told me that my eyes had improved to a quite remarkable degree and were now requiring different glasses. "You can now ask Mr Nesfield to prescribe glasses for distance," he said, and asked me to give his "colleague", of whom he thought so much, a message: "Tell Mr Nesfield when he gives you the glasses to have special regard for the macabus muscle." (As I had never heard the term before, or knew what its function was, it is unlikely that I could have made up the message.)

'Now put yourself in my position – a *nurse* was to give an *eminent surgeon* a message from a spirit doctor what to do! I felt very uneasy about it but I knew I must pass on the message. When I saw Mr Nesfield, I said somewhat uneasily, "I have a message from the spirit doctor William Lang to give you. I can only pass it on, Mr Nesfield." He was quite marvellous, honestly. He said that those who are in spirit know more than we do. "The surgeons won't accept the fact that there are more things than man understands – they may know it but they will not accept it," he said. And when he tested my eyes and wrote out the prescription for the new glasses for me, he said that Mr Lang's message made sense and that he was paying attention to it.

'When I saw Mr Lang again in September, he told me how very pleased he was with the progress I had made and he asked me to tender his congratulations to Mr Nesfield on the spectacles he had prescribed. Mr Nesfield, however, was away, so I had to tell Mr Lang, when I saw him again in October, that I would do it when I saw Mr Nesfield in November. I enquired from Mr Lang whether

I could now have reading glasses. "No, I don't want you to have them yet because for the present it may lead to strain," he said. "Ask Mr Nesfield what he thinks about the idea. But don't worry, young lady, you won't have to wear those you now have very much longer, you'll get ordinary ones when the time is suitable."

'When I saw Mr Nesfield, on 13 November 1964, I gave him at long last, Mr Lang's message about the very good work he'd done with my glasses. He smiled in acknowledgment and, after having examined me thoroughly, he said he was very pleased with my condition which had greatly improved since he last saw me. He endorsed all that Mr Lang had said. I still haven't got reading glasses. But I'm not worried. I know I'll get them when the time is right.

'Words can hardly express my gratitude to the power of God and to the two distinguished ophthalmic surgeons who have helped me to see again – which means that I am alive once more. And although I know that Mr Lang gave me back my vision by his numerous operations on my spirit body, I am equally aware of how important to my recovery was Mr Nesfield's skill and understanding. It was he who prescribed the right glasses for me and co-operated with his spirit doctor "colleague", William Lang.'

26

An Unexpected Reunion

Mrs Ethel J. Bailey of Streatham Hill knew Mr William Lang in his days as ophthalmic consultant at Moorfields. And when she went to see the spirit doctor William Lang in the autumn of 1963 at Aylesbury, she was left in no doubt but that she was facing the same specialist.

Here are Mrs Bailey's personal recollections.

'My right eyelid has been completely closed since birth, and every doctor my mother took me to said that it might right itself as I grew up or, failing that a small operation could be performed in later years to correct it.

'In 1915, when I was twenty-one, I went with my mother to Moorfields in the hope that the time had now come for the long-awaited operation. I was engaged to be married and anxious to be given normal sight before my wedding.

'I was seen by Mr Lang and, after he'd examined me, his verdict was that he couldn't do much for the "child's" eyelid (he called me "child") because, as he explained, if he operated, the eyelid would remain permanently open. We decided to think matters over before deciding whether or not to go on with the operation. I did not want to have to make my own decision, and therefore wrote to my fiancé, who was in the trenches in France, and asked what he thought about it. I shall always cherish the letter he wrote to me in reply. It ended by saying: "Remember Ethel, I chose you as you are, so leave things well alone." I did. I had nothing at all done and was happy that is what he wanted.

'Years later I became interested in Spiritualism and divine healing. Then I had a car accident and so seriously injured my back and legs that, for a time, the doctors doubted if I would ever walk normally again. I had always been very active, and suddenly finding I was unable to get out and about, and suffering pain most of the time, my health began to go. Prior to my accident, I had been a patient of Mr J. J. Thomas, a spiritual trance healer, but he had moved to Brighton, and in view of my condition further visits were out of the question. Fortunately a friend suggested I should visit Mrs Durrant – Mr Harry Edward's sister – who lived near me in Streatham. I couldn't walk, and had to have a taxi wherever I went, so, as you can imagine, it cost me quite a bit getting there and back. But it was worth it, because after a time I was actually able to walk again.

'It seemed strange to me though that no one ever spoke about my "lazy" eye and permanently closed lid, or that the spirit guides had not thought it right to help me with this. But one day in 1963, I read about a Dr Lang who worked through the mediumship of a Mr George Chapman. I thought that this Dr Lang must be the late Archbishop of Canterbury and might perhaps be a brother of *my* Mr Lang from Moorfields, so I decided that if indeed he belonged to the Lang family, I'd like to meet him and wrote to Mr Chapman for an appointment.

'When I arrived at Aylesbury and went into the surgery, Mr Chapman, who was Dr Lang of course, greeted me by saying: "Oh, come along my child, we have met before."

'I recognised his voice immediately and said: "Yes, sir, we have met. I came to Moorfields in 1915 and you told me you couldn't do very much for my closed eyelid. It was the last time I saw you."

'He put his arm around my shoulder and said: "Oh, how big you are now. You were such a little thing and very frail when we met. What were you then – twenty-one, twenty-two?"

'I said: "Twenty-one."

'"You were about seven stone two or three, weren't you?"

'I said: "Well, I was about that in those days, but I've got stouter since I had a family."

'The longer I talked with Mr Lang the more certain I was that he was the same person I had gone to see with my mother at Moorfields. I would have recognised him if only for the way he spoke. And when he showed me around the room, pointing at photographs of himself, his son Basil (who was of course alive in those days) and his colleagues, I had a peculiar feeling that time had been put back and I was again at Moorfields talking to him.

'Mr Lang then told me to lie on his healing couch so that he could perform an operation on my spirit body which, he said, would put my eyelid right. He called Basil to assist him, asked him for instruments, and I had the odd notion that I was not even present although something marvellous was being done for me. And I didn't feel a thing. I just lay there and said a prayer, I think.

'When he told me that he had finished spirit surgery and that my eyelid was all right now, I prepared to get up from the couch, but he held me back and said: "Oh no, you stay where you are, we've something further to do for you." And then he did another operation – on my liver this time. When it was all over he asked me to get up and rest for a while in the chair. And while I sat opposite him, he described my dress in detail, the colour, pattern and even the large buttons, and then talked about all sorts of things. I just sat there thinking how wonderful it was meeting him again after forty-eight years and still remembering him so vividly.

'When I went out to my husband, who'd been waiting for me, I said to him: "Well, how do I look?" He stared at me but was unable to say a word. But our friend Frank Hill, who'd been kind enough to drive us to Aylesbury in his car, said: "Thank God, oh thank God!" You see, my eyelid was open. Remember it had been closed permanently all my life – for sixty-nine years! Yet, from the moment Mr Lang performed his spirit operation, I was able to open and shut my eyelid as easily as I can now – as if nothing had ever been wrong with it.

'This in itself would have been a miraculous thing, and I'd have been more than thankful. But Mr Lang did very much more for me. You see, due to the fact that my eyelid had been permanently closed all my life, I had very little vision in my right eye – it was what they call a "lazy eye". But Mr Lang didn't just operate on my eyelid alone, he also attended to the sight.'

Mrs Bailey visited Mr Lang again for a check-up in the late Spring of 1964.

'Mr Lang was very pleased with the progress I had made. He decided an additional operation was necessary to improve the vision of the right eye still further and I am happy to say he was able to accomplish this.

'Afterwards he discovered that a bone in my thumb was displaced. It had been painful for some time but I hadn't mentioned it to him because I didn't want to take up too much of his precious time, especially as I thought it was nothing serious and would eventually right itself. Anyhow Mr Lang operated on it and stitched the joint. Afterwards he asked me to grip his hand to prove all was well. From that time domestic chores such as polishing and ironing were done more comfortably.'

Mrs Bailey told me that she was due to see Mr Lang again on 20 November 1964. I got in touch with her after her visit to Aylesbury and she explained:

'When I saw Mr Lang a fortnight ago, he was very pleased with the progress I had made since last visit and again performed some operations on my once "lazy" eye.

'I can say my vision is much better for it – in fact I can read your manuscript. When one considers that I had practically no vision in this eye, I think you'll agree that what Mr Lang did for me was quite wonderful.'

27

A Man from West Germany

IT WOULD be wrong to think that those who come to Aylesbury seeking help do so from near-by counties. While working on this book, I came across a distinctly German name in George Chapman's files. As much out of curiosity as anything, I traced the address, and though I found the case was far from finished, I decided it deserved a mention here if only to show that the spirit doctor's fame has spread far from the shores of Britain.

In 1938, when he was eighteen, Alfred Prehl, a West German clerk of Würzburg, noticed that an alarming tremor had developed in his right arm. It had come on without warning and grew worse with time. At the end of five years he had lost almost entirely the use of his main muscles.

During this period Herr Prehl consulted doctor after doctor. He was seen by distinguished specialists at the University Clinics at Würzburg and Freiburg, but none of them was able to help him. They were unable to comprehend the nature of his illness.

'Take medicaments containing belladonna and keep to a strict raw-food diet' – this was the sum total of the advice he received. But it had no effect and he became worse. As the years wore on, Alfred Prehl's loss of muscle control became pitiful. The Second World War had ended, and everywhere in Germany the ravages of war were being obliterated. But Alfred Prehl slipped further into misery. He was forty-five-years old when a specialist told him bluntly: 'As a normal man, you are finished. You'll never walk normally again.'

Further complications appeared in the autumn of 1963. Herr Prehl began to suffer from intense pain in the lower part of his body and to pass blood. In April 1964 the pain increased to such a degree that a specialist had him admitted to the Urological Clinic, where X-rays revealed a stone in the kidney. He was given the orthodox treatment for his condition, salines and infusions, and a loop was also fixed. He failed to respond, however, and the persistence of renal colic became so distressing that he was given drugs to alleviate the pain.

During this time, Herr Prehl read in *Die Andere Welt*, a German magazine, an account of the activities of George Chapman and his spirit control, Dr Lang. He was impressed and began to consider the possibility of consulting the spirit doctor. But, he asked himself, would he be justified in spending so much money on a journey which might prove futile? What made matters still more difficult was the fact that for the past twenty-five years his illness had prevented him from working and was unable to travel anywhere without his wife accompanying him. Eventually, Herr and Frau Prehl decided to undertake the journey together and, on 15 September 1964, travelled by air from West Germany to England.

When I heard about Herr and Frau Prehl's visit to Aylesbury, I was anxious to find out what had given them the confidence to assume that Mr Lang might be able to help them. Consequently I contacted Herr Prehl at his home in Würzburg, and he kindly gave me the information I had asked for.*

'I knew that no practising doctor could help me, so when I read about Dr Lang and Mr Chapman, I felt an overwhelming desire to find out whether these gentlemen could do for me what it was said they had done for others,' Herr Prehl told me.

'I worked out that the air journey and the stay in England would cost about a thousand West German

* All questions and answers were put in the German language and are a true translation.

Marks – an enormous amount of money for someone in my position. You see, due to my illness, I have been unable to follow my occupation as a clerk, and we live on the earnings of my wife who is a nursing sister at a hospital. But what wouldn't a man do to regain his lost health, even partially? My wife showed great understanding and that made my decision to travel to Aylesbury easier.

'We arrived at Mr Chapman's house on 15 September and at the moment when another patient was just leaving by car. As we had come on the off-chance, having no appointment, my visit came as a surprise to Mr Chapman who had just come out of trance because he thought he had finished for the day. Nevertheless he was willing to accept me as a patient and invited us in in the friendliest manner.

'After a brief conversation in the consulting room, he told us he would now go into trance. Sitting comfortably in the chair opposite me, his eyes were closed, and, resting his head as if going to sleep, he remained in this state for a time. Then he introduced himself as Dr Lang. His way of speech was now more difficult for me to understand than when he had been in a waking state before. I think I ought to point out that my knowledge of the English language is rather limited and, naturally, I did not understand every word he said.

'When he started talking with my wife and I told him that she worked as a nursing sister at the hospital, Dr Lang, in the person of Mr Chapman, seemed very pleased to meet her and he went across to her and welcomed her cordially. His behaviour was very different from what Mr Chapman's had been during his wake state, older, more deliberate, and old-fashioned.

'Dr Lang examined me and gave me his diagnosis. I am not a medical man, and my knowledge of the English language is insufficient to understand everything correctly. But because I considered his diagnosis of great importance, I asked him if he could confirm his findings to me in writing so that I was sure I had it right. He agreed, went to the dictaphone which stood at his desk, and recorded exactly what he thought was wrong with me and the reason for it. His diagnosis, which Mr Chapman sent me three weeks later, was as follows: "Virus infection at an early age. This caused a condition of slowly spreading disseminated sclerosis which is scattered in patches of degeneration in the white matter of the brain."

'Still in trance, Mr Chapman asked me to lie on the couch which stood by the wall so that he could start giving me treatment. For about fifteen minutes he attended to me. Mr Chapman's hands hovered along my body from feet to head. He came back several times to attend to my abdomen because he obviously felt that here additional treatment was required.

'This was indeed perplexing, because he kept coming back to that part of the body where I had had the most violent and painful colics. I hadn't spoken about these pains at all, nor had my wife. The fact is, we considered them to be of far less importance than the other complaint I was suffering from, and which had been the reason for our flight to England. So, as I say, nothing about those pains was mentioned to Mr Chapman.

'When he had finished treating my body, Dr Lang asked me to sit on the couch, and he attended to my spine in the same manner as I described before – again never really touching me. I was told later that he had performed an operation on my spirit body. I did not feel a thing, but then, I must add, due to paralysis, my body is rather unreceptive to all feeling.

'And I can't claim to have felt an immediate improvement when I left the surgery that day. But within a few hours, the difference was appreciable. I was able to walk with greater confidence and with more strength than at any time during the past twelve months or so. And after our return to Germany, the improvement continued. But ten days after my visit to Aylesbury, I became subjected to a sudden and violent colic, caused by the kidney stone and I wrote at once to Mr Chapman, asking him to inform Dr Lang of my unexpected trouble. A few days later the stone left the ureter and entered the bladder!

'Now, I thought, as did my doctor, that a kidney stone in the bladder would not cause any further trouble, and that I would eventually be rid of it. But this particular kidney stone was probably too big for the bladder to eject without trouble. As a result every time I urinated, I suffered acute pain.

'A fortnight later, I wrote again to Mr Chapman and informed him about this condition. Within a few days the kidney stone promptly left the bladder! We were astonished at the size and shape – it is approximately fifteen by five millimetres big and has sharp edges. I keep it as a souvenir! The steady improvement of my major disease continues to this present day.'

Only three months had elapsed from the time Herr Prehl first received spirit treatment from Mr Lang to the time he gave me the information I had asked for. In view of the serious nature of his illness, and the fact that at the time of writing this book he has been under Mr Lang's care for so brief a period, albeit successfully, I kept in touch with Herr Prehl. His frequent reports recorded an uninterrupted chain of success – his health improved steadily, though he was still far from being a healthy man.

A year after he had performed the first series of operations on Herr Prehl's spirit body, Mr Lang considered that the time had come for the patient to undergo further contact healing at Aylesbury. Though this meant another £100 or so travelling expenses (which Herr Prehl could ill afford) the German and his wife nevertheless decided to fly to England. The improvement of Herr Prehl's overall condition had been so marked that they believed additional spirit operations could only mean further considerable progress. And when Herr Prehl informed me about his decision to see Mr Lang, he asked whether I could be present – to see for myself what was taking place and to act at the same time as interpreter. Herr Prehl's knowledge of English was still poor and naturally he wanted to know *everything* Mr Lang had to say.

On 29 November 1965, I met Herr and Frau Prehl at George Chapman's house in Aylesbury. Alfred Prehl was still a wreck. His speech was only a little less impaired than a year earlier, his hand was still unable to grip mine firmly as he greeted me, and he walked weakly. From his written reports to me I had imagined that his state of health was much better than in fact it turned out to be. Knowing his financial state, I remarked: 'I'm surprised that you undertook the costly and strenuous journey to England.'

'I don't quite understand,' he said.

'Well, it doesn't look to me as though your improvement is as great as all that. . . .'

'But *it is!*' he said emphatically. 'It may seem to an outside observer that there isn't much improvement because I still look an invalid, but *I* know how very much more strength I've built up during this past year. And if Dr Lang succeeds in bringing about a similar additional improvement, then all the expense and physical strain of our journey will be more than worth it.'

When we entered Mr Lang's consulting room, he greeted all of us with his usual cordiality. He quickly got down to examining Herr Prehl, and within minutes was saying: 'I am very pleased with the progress you've made, young man. You have reacted admirably to treatment.'

He then performed, with his unseen colleagues and assistants, a number of operations on Herr Prehl's spirit body, keeping Frau Prehl, the hospital sister, and myself informed about what he was doing.

'Do you think I'll ever get better, Dr Lang?' Herr Prehl said when the last operation was concluded.

'You *will* be cured,' the spirit doctor replied with firm conviction. 'Due to the very serious nature of your complaint and the fact that you consulted me rather late, it will take some considerable time before you are cured of your disease, but I can promise you that you *will* regain normality – provided you *don't* give up and that you *do* continue co-operating with me.'

Tears of gratefulness and happiness streamed down Prehl's cheeks. 'You can be sure that I'll never give up,' he whispered.

Mr Lang then demonstrated how and where Frau Prehl should massage her husband, the kind of exercises Herr Prehl should do daily, and told him what food to eat.

'He hardly eats any food,' Frau Prehl cut in. 'He doesn't listen to me when I tell him he must have proper meals, and insists that he can't eat anything else but a few slices of dry bread a day. . . .'

'It is imperative that your physical body is kept well nourished,' Lang told him, 'because, if this is not done, the strength which I am putting into your spirit body cannot transfer efficiently into your physical body. You must realise this and comply with my advice if you wish to be cured.'

'Oh, I will, I will,' Prehl muttered.

'I promise you, Dr Lang, I will see to it my husband will do *everything* you want him to do,' Frau Prehl pledged.

'I shall continue visiting during your sleep state, young man, and you will find that in a month you will experience further improvement,' Mr Lang said at the end of the consultation. 'I hope you'll have a pleasant journey to Germany – actually, I know you'll have a good journey home.'

Ten days after his visit to Aylesbury, Herr Prehl contacted me and said he had already experienced a very marked improvement. At the time this book was in proof form and ready to be printed (in January 1966), he gave me the latest up-to-date details about himself:

'My wife complies religiously with Dr Lang's instructions and massages my spine exactly as he showed her; I do all the exercises Dr Lang asked me to do; I am also eating regular nourishing meals.

'The improvement of my condition during the past two months is very much greater than the improvement was which I experienced during the year between my two consultations with Dr Lang. I feel very much stronger and am able to use my limbs much better than when we met at Aylesbury on 29 November 1965. My own and my wife's gratitude to Dr Lang and Mr George Chapman is too great and overwhelming to be expressed adequately in words. This good spirit doctor has pulled off a miracle because he has already enabled me to get about, whereas all the other doctors and specialists under whose care I was made it abundantly clear that I was beyond help.'

28

'. . . And There Shall Be No More Death, Neither Sorrow, Nor Crying . . .'*

JONATHAN BELL was five years old and as lively as any child of that age. The family lived in Worksop and to Mr and Mrs Bell, though they would only say it to one another, there never was a child like Jonathan.

They would catch a glimpse of him playing with his friends, or see his grubby face impish and mischievous after some prank, and look meaningfully at each other. They had watched him grow from babyhood, had marvelled at the arrival of his first tooth which stood out from his gums like a tiny white tombstone and they hugged and cuddled him the day he took his first steps. And as he developed into a little harum-scarum boy, they stood by, the proud and protective onlookers. The rare happiness that only children can bring belonged to the Bells, until late in the summer of 1964.

It was then they began to become a little uneasy but not alarmed. At that time it was difficult to sense the change slowly taking place in their little boy. He played a little less vigorously one day than he had on other occasions. But children were creatures of mood and whim. Perhaps he was over-tired in the way children exhaust themselves.

The next day Jonathan Bell was still tired. But you never can tell with children. In a day or two he would be his old self again.

Jonathan did not regain his high spirits. He didn't want to go out and play, he just wanted to rest. The day the

* Revelation of St John.

164

child's face began to puff up, his parents decided to call in a doctor. After the examination he turned to the parents and said:

'I'm afraid, Mr and Mrs Bell, that Jonathan is suffering from advanced leukaemia.'

What he told afterwards they scarcely heard. They knew enough about leukaemia to realise that anyone who contracted it was in the grip of a fatal disease. They had, from time to time, read the heart-rending accounts of children who had been 'condemned to death' by it. And, now, it had struck at themselves, the Bells, and their little boy Jonathan.

The doctor wanted to be certain of his diagnosis and arranged for a blood test and a second opinion by a specialist.

The boy was taken to Kilton Hill Hospital, Worksop, where the doctor's diagnosis was confirmed. It was leukaemia. The disease was particularly rife in the spinal fluid and was so advanced that the little chap was given only about two months to live.

Mr and Mrs Bell became desperate and refused to accept the sentence of death on their little boy. Mistakes had occurred before in hospitals and they told themselves that the diagnosis could be wrong. Why should Jonathan have to die? He'd always been so healthy and full of life. It was unthinkable that he could be taken from them now. They had heard of the famous Hospital for Sick Children at Great Ormond Street in London. There, they hoped, perhaps the doctors might prove the local hospital wrong. Or, if the boy did have leukaemia, maybe they'd find it was only in the early stages and be able to cure it.

Jonathan was taken to the famous hospital. But the verdict was the same:

Advanced leukaemia.

Mr and Mrs Bell were given tablets which Jonathan had to take daily, and the family returned to Worksop. Arrangements were made for the child to be seen again.

Back home, the parents cherished their dying child. The few weeks of his life that remained, they knew, would see

165

the ebbing away of his strength, and they wanted to be with him for every precious hour that was left to them. If there was anything the child wanted, they would do everything within their power to give to him.

In their desperation they went through periods when they rejected the cruel truth and hoped that the tragedy which had invaded their home might remit itself. They prayed for a miracle. Was it too much to ask for? That one small life be spared. But when further visits to the London hospital convinced the parents that nothing could be done for Jonathan they decided that all that was left to them was to try and keep him happy – until the end.

This then was the situation when Mr and Mrs Rose, Birmingham friends of the Bells, made a hesitant suggestion to them. Mr and Mrs Rose were deeply moved by the grief of their friends at Worksop, and the thought of what yet lay before them. The Roses themselves knew of William Lang and his medium George Chapman. They were aware of some of the startling successful cures that had been brought about in the house called St Brides and at the Birmingham Healing Centre, and yet it was with reluctance that they suggested to the Bells that Jonathan might yet be saved by the spirit doctor. It was a reluctance born out of knowledge of the distrust felt by so many people towards anything connected with spirit healing. Under *ordinary* circumstances the Bells would hardly have consented to go near a spirit doctor. They were far from convinced that anything other than medical skill could be of any value; but what was there to lose? Their son was dying. This was the brutal truth. On Saturday, 19 December 1964, Mr Rose took Jonathan to see William Lang at the Healing Centre. The boy, of course, was too young to know the purpose of this visit. As far as he was concerned he was going to see another doctor, one of the many who had examined him, looked serious, jotted down notes and talked quietly to his Mum and Dad.

When Lang examined Jonathan, he confirmed that he had advanced leukaemia, and said it was particularly heavy in the spinal fluid. He then told Mr Rose that he needed to operate in order to help the boy.

166

William Lang operated on Jonathan's liver and opened up the heart valve to increase its blood count. It was all very mysterious and strange to the child who felt nothing and wondered why this man in a white coat with his eyes closed, talked to people who weren't there. Then there was the funny business of this doctor washing his hands even though Jonathan had not seen him do anything to soil them. But he liked the way the funny man did those things with his hands and fingers. It was, he thought, a curious game, but was amusing.

Mr and Mrs Rose watched William Lang attending to the boy. The minute hand of the clock moved round with agonising slowness. Was there any hope? Even a shred? They hardly exchanged a whispered word. There was so much to say, and yet so little that could be put into words. What was happening? Anything? And then there was Lang standing up, his operations finished. Jonathan got up from the couch and was quietly, calmly smiling. And as Mrs Rose led the child out of earshot, her husband faced the man in the white coat.

'Well,' Mr Rose said, 'do you think there is any chance of doing anything?'

'Oh, yes,' Lang answered. 'Quite a good chance. I want to see Jonathan again in six weeks' time, and then I'll be able to tell you more. To what extent the operations were successful and so forth. But I can tell you *now* that there's nothing much to worry about. We are doing all we can for the boy and I'll be visiting him during his sleep state to give him additional treatment.'

Mr Rose spent a few minutes talking with Lang, asking many questions and trying desperately to establish some sort of basis for confidence from which he and his wife could draw and transmit to the boy's parents. There was much that was consoling in what Lang said, but at the same time Rose knew the Bell's fears were now so deep-rooted, and their suspicions of spirit healing so strong, that he hardly knew how to convince them that there was hope for Jonathan.

Within three weeks after Lang's operations, Jonathan

was due at Kilton Hill Hospital for the customary blood test. But within *two* weeks, the boy had improved so much that his parents could scarcely believe it. The doctors were amazed at his blood count.

Five weeks after Lang's operations, Jonathan kept his appointment at Great Ormond Street Hospital. The examination tests established that the spinal fluid was clear of leukaemia. The medical staff appeared astonished and said quite frankly that they didn't know how the change could have happened.

Six weeks after Lang's operations, Jonathan had his second appointment with the spirit doctor. It was at the Birmingham Healing Centre. The date was Saturday, 30 January 1965. Lang was very pleased with the progress the boy had made since he had first seen him. He told Mr Rose that the operations on the spirit body had been successful. 'Jonathan is going to be perfectly healthy again – now there's nothing to worry about any longer,' he explained. He requested that the boy be brought to him again in three weeks.

The third appointment with the spirit doctor – on Saturday, 20 February 1965 – was of course kept. William Lang was delighted with how well his young patient reacted to treatment and confirmed: 'Everything is now working perfectly, the spinal fluid is clear and there remains only a slight trace in the bloodstream, but this will clear. Jonathan will be a perfectly healthy little boy again, but treatment must be continued for some time.'

The improvement in Jonathan's health condition was remarkable. He felt well, was full of energy, and had lost all blown-up appearance about his face.

Any small doubt that may have lingered in the minds of the boy's parents was stamped out of existence. At the beginning they were of course keenly aware that in many instances a seeming improvement comes before deterioration and death; indeed the first months added up to a time of almost unbearable breath-holding.

But, bit by bit, stage by stage the signs of improvement came, were consolidated, remained. The visits to William

Lang's Birmingham Healing Centre were maintained, and the young body of Jonathan Bell became stronger as the days went by. There came a day when it was felt he could return to school, then another day when the most rigorous blood test showed that the child was free from leukaemia. Today (in November 1965) he runs and jumps and shouts and plays pranks like any other schoolboy. And his progress at school is enough to cause small stirrings of pride in the breasts of two people who thought his school days were over.

On 29 November 1965, I spoke to William Lang about Jonathan Bell. The face of the old man smiled with inner contentment. After a while he said: 'Thank God he was brought to me just in time.'

And the parents who were stalked by tragedy no longer look grey with sorrow. The shadow of death has gone from their home and they are able to marvel at a reprieve that has given them back their little son and richly restored their faith in the future.

29

More Things in Heaven and Earth

DURING THE extensive research I carried out into every aspect of Mr Lang's spirit healing, I decided to discuss his cures with an eminent physician who was a senior member of a famous London hospital.

The doctor in question agreed to meet me, on the strict understanding that under no circumstances would I disclose his identity or the name of the hospital. He explained that he had no desire to get into trouble with the British Medical Association for 'co-operating with an unregistered practitioner', or lay himself open to a charge of 'unprofessional conduct'. I gave him this undertaking, indeed I could not do otherwise, but I can assure those who read this book that the account of this interview is genuine and based on a verbatim transcription of a meeting which took place in the late autumn of 1964.

I had brought along a number of Mr Lang's most striking case histories together with particulars of evidence from doctors, hospital authorities and distinguished specialists who confirmed that the patients in question had not reacted to the treatment that had been given them; that in their opinion there was nothing further medical science could do for them; and that they were incurable.

As against this was the evidence that these incurables had *not* died and had, in fact, got better after treatment from William Lang. And their improvement and cures were verified by those same doctors who had previously had them under their care, indeed in some cases had written them off.

This, perhaps, was the most valuable evidence of all. After having examined the patients most thoroughly and subjected them to all forms of clinical tests, these medical experts had confirmed that the diseases had been cured completely, and that no trace of any hidden or dormant signs could be found.

When I presented the physician with this well-authenticated evidence and asked him for his comments, he examined the papers very carefully and after much thought replied:

'Well, speaking from a strictly medical point of view, I have no explanation to offer on how it is possible for patients, who are found to be beyond hope, to recover from time to time. If cures of this kind happen, it is usually assumed that nature itself somehow brings about what is otherwise inexplicable. On more than one occasion I've heard eminent physicians and surgeons say that "a miracle has happened". They are of course right in one sense, because with some incurable diseases it is quite evident that only a miracle – something beyond our comprehension – could have brought about the cure of a patient, regarded from the viewpoint of orthodox treatment, as beyond hope of recovery. One finds in a quite a few medical institutions the inscription, "We dress the wound, God heals it", which is benevolently tolerated by our very strict association. But I think in reality an awful lot of us accept the truth of that inscription.'

'Having examined the evidence of Mr Lang's successes in curing incurable people, would you agree that they were the result of his spirit operations and other forms of healing?' I enquired.

'Well, the evidence you have presented is certainly most convincing. What else can I say?' He paused for a moment, and added: 'If I were to consider these cases simply in the light of the medical code we observe, I'd be forced to dismiss any possibility of spirit operations and healing being able to achieve *anything*. According to our way of thinking, only qualified medical practitioners and medically trained staff are able to treat patients properly.

But . . . well, I personally am not so sure about this tenet.' He paused again, and after a while said: 'But to answer your question. Yes, I believe that the complete and confirmed cures of the patients whose case histories you've shown me *are* due to spiritual help – to Mr Lang's spiritual operations and treatment, I should really say.'

'You accept then that by performing invisible and painless operations on the spirit body of a patient Mr Lang is able to bring about a corresponding effect on the physical body?'

'I did not say that,' the physician asserted. 'You see, I'm not at all convinced that there is such a thing as a "spirit body", and therefore I cannot accept that treating a so-called "spirit body" brings about *any* effect on a patient's physical body. I may of course be wrong – perhaps there is such a thing after all – but I haven't come across it during the many years I've practised medicine.

'But don't let's argue as to whether there is or isn't a "spirit body", because neither of us can furnish conclusive proof of our beliefs. Let us instead consider the issue of spiritual help objectively and rationally. As far as I am concerned, I do not really care *how* Mr Lang cures his patients; the significant thing to me is that he *does* cure them. I am prepared to say I accept this.'

When the question of distant healing was mentioned I regretted not having brought along the documentary evidence of the successes achieved by Dr Lang with many patients, but I was able to tell him about a number of cases I had investigated. The physician heard me out, his eyebrows rising occasionally, but he made no comment until I had finished.

'Well, I am not suggesting that what you've told me is incorrect or exaggerated,' he said. 'But it is difficult for me to believe that healing from a distance, just by means of letter-writing produced the results you have suggested. Although I don't know exactly how spiritual contact healing can work, as it apparently does, I still believe that something happens, and extraordinary things take place. Maybe by actually touching a patient's body and establishing direct physical contact, Mr Lang somehow succeeds in harnessing some kind of spiritual power, I don't know. Healing rays maybe. To accept, however, that the same thing is possible from a distance, through a sort of correspondence course, is really too much to expect from a member of the medical profession.'

'Would you like me to offer you the same kind of evidence of Mr Lang's achievements as I have given you in regard to his contact healing?' I asked.

'Well, yes, I would be most interested,' he replied. 'But don't send it to me care of the hospital. I don't want to risk having the letter opened by mistake. Send it to my private address please.'

I kept my promise.

A few days later the physician returned the case histories relating to distant healing. He did not say what he thought of the evidence and his letter consisted only of the following lines written in a determined hand:

'It is astonishing, to say the least!

'I hope you don't consider me banal quoting William Shakespeare but, as usual, he said the most appropriate thing to fit the situation: "There are more things in heaven and earth, Horatio, than are dreamt of in your philosophy."'

30

How Effective is Distant Healing?

THIS QUESTION is best answered by recording some of the many cases of distant healing which I picked out at random from George Chapman's bulky filing cabinets.

Mrs Marjory Hemsworth of Hull requested distant healing from Mr Lang and wrote to George Chapman in March 1959:

'Will you please help me with my throat? My doctor says it is a nervous one, but I am constantly having to clear my throat every few seconds. I may add that I have been troubled with this condition for over five years.'

Distant healing commenced on receipt of the letter, and two weeks later Mrs Hemsworth reported:

'I am very puzzled; at about 11 a.m. I went to make the beds, and on nearing the top of the stairs, I could smell violets; on reaching the small landing and front bedroom it was overpowering, it was a lovely smell. I sat on the bed wondering where it was coming from; after a few seconds it gradually faded leaving me with a wonderful feeling I can't explain. I only wish someone had been there to share the experience with me.'

Seven weeks after distant healing commenced, Mrs Hemsworth was cured. On April 29, 1959, she wrote to George Chapman:

'I should like to say how well I am feeling now. My throat condition has completely cleared up.'

Mr Lang's cure was a lasting one. I ascertained this when I contacted Mrs Hemsworth in December 1964.

Marjory's husband, George Hemsworth, also became a

patient of William Lang and gave me the following account of his own experiences.

'My wife wrote for distant healing for me in December 1962,' he told me. 'I had developed cataracts in both eyes, and as I had heard of people sometimes having to wait a very long time before it was deemed advisable to operate, I was naturally worried. I gave up my driving job in November 1962, and by the end of August 1963 both eyes were so bad that I had to be led about.

'One cataract was removed in October 1963, and the other in May 1964, and although I wear thick spectacles I now have splendid vision. In fact my optician says I have better eyesight than he has!'

I enquired from Mr Lang about the type of distant healing he had given to Mr Hemsworth, and he explained: 'It is true that it would have taken many years for the cataracts to grow sufficiently to be removed successfully, so my spirit helpers and I accelerated the growth to enable the patient to have his operation at the hospital as speedily as possible.' William Lang could have brought about a complete detachment of the cataract, he explained, but this would have necessitated contact healing and would have been a lengthier process than if the cataract was operated on in hospital. Consequently he had decided to concentrate on forcing the cataract to grow speedily to be ready for removal.

In February 1962, Mr Joseph C. Manuel of Hoylake suffered from pain in the rectum and consulted his doctor who diagnosed external piles. He prescribed the known treatment, but the condition slowly got worse. He then sent the patient to a specialist who diagnosed a fistula in the rectum, and at the end of April 1962 Mr Manuel went into hospital for an operation for its removal. This was done, but the wound would not heal and the whole area became inflamed and swollen to such an extent that the patient could not sit down and could only lie on his side.

'I went back time and again to the hospital to see the specialist but the pain and discomfort persisted,' Mr

Manuel stated. 'I felt sure that they had not got to the root of the trouble in the first place. I became more and more depressed and it seemed as if I should never be rid of the condition.'

In September 1962 Mr Manuel learned about George Chapman and his spirit doctor Lang and, hoping spirit healing might possibly help him as much as it had done in a case of which he had heard he decided to 'give it a try'. So he wrote the following letter to George Chapman:

'I am writing to ask you if you would be good enough to give me distant healing for the rectal trouble from which I am suffering. The doctors diagnosed it as a form of fistula and have, following an operation, been treating me for the past six months without success. They have now told me there is nothing more they can do. As the condition appears to be getting much worse, I wonder if you can help me.'

Distant healing commenced on 25 September 1962, and a week later, Mr Manuel sent the following report to George Chapman:

'I am pleased to say that in the last three days there has been an improvement in my condition. I have had far less pain and irritation, and I am hoping it will continue to improve.'

Then, on 26 November 1962, the patient wrote again:

'I should like to say that you and your spirit control (Dr Lang) have done a wonderful job of healing in my case, as I am sure you have done for many others. Thank you, Mr Chapman, for your marvellous work.'

Mr Manuel's last report, which he sent the following month, stated:

'I am very glad to say that all the pain has now gone, and that the swelling and irritation have disappeared. I am most grateful to Dr Lang and yourself, Mr Chapman, and I wish every success in the future to you both.'

Exactly two years later – on 5 December, 1964 – I contacted Mr Lang's ex-patient to find out from him his present state of health. He kindly told me the following about himself:

'I am glad to say there has been no recurrence of the trouble and I should like to say once more how grateful I am to Dr Lang and George Chapman for the healing I received from them which completely cured me.'

William Lang's successful healing activities in the Hutton household were not confined to myself. What was accomplished for my twelve-year-old son Harold was, from a medical point of view, insignificant. But who can tell with certainty what is important or of little account? To some people the slightest feeling of illness causes concern; others, suffering from a serious ailment, often try to convince themselves it is not half as bad as it appears.

But let me tell you about Harold.

For many months my son had looked forward eagerly to mid-December 1964, when he was to go on a cruise to the Holy Land for Christmas with some of his class-mates. If the prospect of visiting Jerusalem and other places was truly exciting so, too, was the idea of a cruise – the first in his young life. The voyage would take him to Italy and Greece as well as the Holy Land, and being the youngest member of the grammar school party, he was, perhaps, more keyed up than most.

The party was to leave Worthing on the morning of 16 December, a Wednesday. But on the Sunday evening before, Harold suddenly developed a very heavy cold with severe bouts of coughing and a temperature of 101.3°.

In the past, similar attacks had always developed into bronchitis or influenza which dragged on for a week or two before he was passed fit by the doctor to return to school. It became quite obvious that Harold would be confined to bed until some time after the departure of the school party and he became very dejected. We knew only too well how much the holiday meant to him, and some of his depression rubbed off on Pearl and I.

What could we do to help our son? It was Sunday evening and there was no point in dragging out the doctor because, as we knew from past experience, he could do no more at this stage than advise keeping him in bed until it could be seen what course the illness would take. As night approached, however, Harold's temperature rose still higher, his cough became more persistent and breathing became difficult for him.

Lying awake in bed and listening to the spasmodic bouts of coughing coming from Harold's bedroom across the landing, it suddenly occurred to me to ask William Lang for help. From my many interviews with the spirit doctor I knew what to do – just send out positive thoughts to him, telling him what was wrong with my son and requesting him, or one of his colleagues, for assistance. I sent out a thought message to William Lang – without the boy's knowledge of course.

The alarm clock at my bedside table continued ticking the minutes away but no help came. The boy continued to cough, chokingly, and it seemed to me that, if anything, he was worse.

When almost ten minutes had gone by since I had first sent out my thought message to William Lang, I began to wonder if for some reason or another he had not received it. As I lay there trying to decide whether to make a further attempt I sensed the presence of someone at my bedside. I strained my eyes in the semi-darkness but could not see anyone. Then, almost immediately, I distinctly felt a soothing cool hand stroke my forehead. But there was no one there, at least no one I could see! A moment after the invisible hand had touched my forehead, the alarm clock was picked up by an unseen hand and gently put face down. Then it flashed through my mind that this was meant to be some sort of proof that William Lang or one of his spirit colleagues had received my thought message and that my call for help was being answered.

Minutes later Harold stopped coughing. He had no more difficulty with his breathing. I got up and went to his room. He was sleeping soundly and breathing easily and his temperature had dropped.

Next morning the boy was perfectly normal. His temperature was down and there was not the slightest trace left of the cough. On Tuesday he returned to school and, as planned, left Worthing with his school party on Wednesday morning for the cruise.

It may of course be argued that the sudden improvement of his condition could have been brought about by mere laws of nature. Well, everyone is entitled to his own opinion, but both my wife and I are convinced that this unexpected recovery was brought about with the help of William Lang or one of his colleagues. The connection between the phenomenon that I had experienced while fully awake and the immediate improvement in Harold's condition was too striking to induce us to seek any other explanation.

An 'insignificant' case? Perhaps. To Harold, and us, it was most significant. It enabled the boy to fulfil his dearest wish, and it gave us at first-hand an insight into the healing power that can be exercised unseen by spirit doctors.

31

Saved From a Wheelchair

IN THE realm of spirit healing are to be discovered many diverse groups of people. So far I have given accounts of most of them, from the scoffer to the sceptic, to those prepared to take a last chance and those who avow a willingness to try anything. One group, however, which I have hardly dealt with are the confirmed believers, those people who embrace fully all the faith and its tenets, its rituals and teachings.

Mrs Barbara Haines, a State Registered Nurse from Canterbury, is a confirmed Spiritualist. So is her husband. On 27 April, 1960, Mrs Haines wrote to George Chapman as follows:

'Four years ago, in the playground at school, my daughter Janet fell and her leg was fractured at the neck of the femur.

'The orthopaedic surgeon who examined her every six months since he put a pin through the neck of the femur, tells me that he will have to operate again to make the hip a fixture. As Janet has suffered so much pain and handicap during the last four years, I am very reluctant to agree to this operation.

'Neither my husband nor I approve of the treatment Janet has received. I am a S.R.N. and know just how much some specialists care for their patients these days. No more are they treated as individuals but as a number on a card, herded into waiting-rooms to be earmarked like a lot of cattle.

'We believe in spiritual healing and I have read so much about the wonderful work done by Dr Lang through your hands that I feel sure that with your help he would spiritually guide me into making the right decision, which is such an important one because it can affect the whole of the child's future, this child of God's. It is such a serious step for us to take alone, especially as my husband and I feel that through your help and our prayers it may not be necessary in six months' time for this operation to be done.

'The specialist wishes to fix the hip because, he says, the blood supply to the head of the femur has been severed. Please advise me what to do.'

Mr Lang requested George Chapman to inform Mrs Haines that distant healing for Janet had commenced on receipt of her letter and that he would be visiting the child during her sleep state, and hoped to help her sufficiently so that the planned operation would not be necessary. In the following month Mrs Haines wrote again to George Chapman:

'Many thanks for your letter of instructions and I feel now that something will be achieved in six months' time and Janet will not have to have the operation performed.

'Each night at ten o'clock my husband and I stand in meditation beside the child's bed, so as to link up with Dr Lang. Since distant healing from Dr Lang began, we have felt the spirit presence round us and I have placed my hands on Janet's hip and leg as well. I feel the glow of spirit power all tingling, and warmth flows through my arms and into my hands, and a great power presses down on my head. It brings great peace with it too.

'Janet says the pain in the hip is much better and the hip does not fix now like it used to when she stood on it for too long. She used to have great difficulty in sitting or standing if she stayed too long in one position. She can also bend more easily. To me there does not seem so much deformity and the leg itself looks better. Thank God.

'Please convey my heartfelt thanks to Dr Lang for visiting us, and to all the spirit helpers that come also, for everything that is being done for my child. We know that with God's help and power – if it be His will – all things are possible.'

Distant healing was given by Mr Lang regularly and he and his assistants visited Janet during her sleep state so as to attend to her spirit body and eventually bring about a corresponding effect on her physical body. Mrs Haines wrote about one of these spirit visits: 'My husband and my daughter Janet have both seen Dr Lang and his band of spirit helpers round her bed. Janet received a most re-markable spirit operation during which her spirit body was completely detached from her physical body and her physical body was to all who saw it, materially, "dead", *no* pulse, *no* heart-beat, *nor* breathing – and I, with twenty-five years' nursing behind me, can vouch for that.

'From that night onwards, Janet's condition improved rapidly. The pain in her leg has greatly diminished and she can stand up or sit for much of the time without get-ting pain in the hip. I hope I am not too optimistic if I hope that the dreaded operation will not be necessary after all. I know of course the surgeon's verdict that un-less I allow this child to have a fixation done to the hip she will be in constant pain, and become progressively worse as she gets older and eventually end up in a wheel-chair; but I also know that if it is God's will, spirit power will help her to recover.'

Then, in November of the same year, Mrs Haines wrote once more to George Chapman:

'Last week I took Janet to the specialist for the six-monthly check-up at the hospital. Before he examined her he said she would have to go into hospital to have the fixation of the hip performed, and he repeated that he could see no other way of the bone building up because of the blood supply being severed. This meant that the bone was gradually wearing away at the neck of the femur, causing the pain she was getting. I let him talk because I somehow knew I would not have to make the decision – in fact I felt at peace with the whole world.

'Then, when the specialist examined Janet, he was quite astonished at the amount of mobility he was able to secure without any pain. He scratched his head in amazement and eventually said: "This is not possible, I must get it X-rayed." The X-ray showed that the pin had moved out and seemed to be floating in the fleshy part of the leg while the bone itself appeared to have started to build up again. Previously X-rays showed the pin in position and the bone tissues deteriorating.

'This latest X-ray completely baffled the specialist. I suppose he was on the defensive. In the end he said: "I don't know what has happened here; I'll have her in to see." I explained that we believed it was spiritual healing that had brought about the improvement. He pooh-poohed spiritual healing and said that he didn't wish to see her again till I decided to let him open up the leg. There we left him and Janet did not return to the hospital again.'

Four years later I discovered Janet's case history in George Chapman's records, but there was no further or recent report about her state of health. Had the surgeon been right after all, had an operation in hospital been performed since Mrs Haines' last letter? I got in touch with the mother, and on 12 December 1964, she gave me the following answers:

'No operation was performed at the hospital after my last letter to Mr Chapman in November 1960. In fact because of the specialist's attitude four years ago we haven't contacted him or the hospital authorities since. Janet has made remarkable progress. Apart from a slight shortening of the leg, and a little stiffness at times, neither of which worry her in any way, she is fine. She enjoys good health and a happy life. She can walk, dance, and do most things that other children do.

'We know that Dr Lang and Mr Chapman are still in spiritual contact with us, and with God's help Janet will be protected throughout the rest of her earthly life, living it normally and able to do as others do. One of the consequences of Dr Lang's miraculous healing is that the child's whole personality has changed. She is loved by all who come in contact with her – some power emanates from her which we say is the Love of God who answered our prayers. She is always ready and willing to do *anyone* a kindness or favour and is a happy, lovable child, learning to live with the slight shortening of her leg, knowing she is in God's hands and still in the capable care of Dr Lang.

'We have so much to thank them for, and once again I say: *If* it is God's will *all* things are possible.'

32

'Please Help My Little Sister!'

M RS PAULINE PERRY, a laboratory technician of Swansea, was terribly worried. Not about herself or her own well-being, but because the life of Gwynneth, her thirteen-year-old sister, was in danger. She loved the child whose sweet personality enchanted everybody. Gwynneth was doomed to an early grave, and Pauline Perry was in despair. Anger too flooded through her – anger at the inability of medical science to save her young sister.

When things look their blackest, Pauline heard about the spirit doctor William Lang. What she was told appeared fantastic. As someone engaged in a profession in which everything had to be proved, she couldn't accept the startling claims that were made. But what was there to lose? Her sister's life was slipping away in hospital, so why not try spirit distant healing even if it *was* something a good many people just brushed aside or scoffed at?

Pauline wrote at once to George Chapman. I quote her letters exactly as she wrote them, for they provide full details of a case that illustrates the remarkable success of yet another case of distant healing.

'Please help my little sister!' Mrs Perry wrote on 30 March 1962. 'I hope you can give the child back her health although I cannot bring her to see you personally.

'My parents do not believe in these things and I have not told them about your healing powers, but it would be a wonderful triumph if Gwynneth could be healed. She is thirteen years of age and is at the moment at Morriston Hospital (Ward 2), Swansea, where she was taken after the collapse of a lung which has affected her heart.

'Since very early childhood, Gwynneth has suffered

from severe attacks of asthma, and this, coupled with continual bronchitis, has now proved to be too much for her. My little sister has suffered so much pain and discomfort that she no longer wishes to live, which is an alarming and horrifying statement to hear from a child.

'*Please* will you work the miracle and give Gwynneth the gift of health that she may be as other children. She is too bright, normally a gay little chatterbox, frail and thin but exceptionally pretty. How empty the home is without her! My parents are heartbroken, especially my mother who is on the verge of a nervous breakdown through so many weary nights spent nursing Gwynneth.

'Mother's health is generally poor, blood pressure extremely low, and she is literally living on injections from the doctor, to stimulate her circulation. She is forty years of age, her whole system is fast wearing out, and her resistance and will to carry on are pathetically low. She is a broken and exhausted woman who seems to be shrinking before my very eyes.

'Please do something for them! I know that there are so many others much worse off, but these are my flesh and blood and I love them.'

On receipt of this letter, George Chapman immediately communicated its contents to Mr Lang and distant healing commenced almost instantly. Mrs Perry was asked to send a report regularly on the health of her mother and sister. In the following month she wrote:

'Here is the first report on the progress of my mother and my sister Gwynneth.

'My mother appears to be considerably improved, but puts this down to the fact that she has had two injections from the doctor. She is given them every month as a kind of energiser, but due to her anxiety for Gwynneth the doctor gave her two instead of the customary one.

'Gwynneth, according to the medical report, is improving slowly, but has developed a heavy cold. However, she is in high spirits and longing to leave the hospital. We have been told that the lung has collapsed again.

'You will, I am sure, be interested to hear that my parents now know of the treatment you have commenced, although, naturally, my young sister does not, and they are intensely curious.

'I had to tell them, due to the phenomenon of last Saturday night.

'Completely unaware of what was happening to both Gwynneth and my mother, the family went to bed as usual. They are solid folk, not given to flights of imagination and extremely wary of having anything to do with the world of spirits.

'My other sister, Janet, sleeping alone in the room which Gwynneth had previously shared, was getting into bed when she heard voices whispering at the foot of it. (She is nineteen years old and very straightforward.) Finding difficulty in putting her feet under the bed-clothes, she thought someone was sitting on the bed, and nervously switched on the light. The whispering stopped and she saw no one.

'About the same time, my mother, who sleeps in her own bed in the same room as my father, was trying to sleep, when she felt someone sit on the bed. There was a definite pressure and the bed subsided as though bearing extra weight. Then, as she lay there, she felt a hand, cool and gentle, touch her shoulder lightly, and then move to her head.

'Rather shaken, mother told father, and then Janet came into the room in a state of anxiety to explain her own experience.

'There are no animals in the house, and the family had not watched or heard anything morbid or unpalatable on the television or the radio. Thus, I told them about you, and they are greatly interested as to a possible link between the happenings I have described and the spirit doctors.

'Thank you for everything you are doing and I shall try my utmost to carry out your instructions.'

When I interviewed Mr Lang about distant healing, I asked him if he had been concerned with the events at Swansea and he said: 'I wasn't there myself, but Basil and a colleague of his visited the house.' And how considerable the result of this visit by the spirit doctors turned out is revealed in a further letter from Mrs Perry later that month.

'I am thrilled to tell you that Gwynneth seems to have been completely healed!' she reported. 'Since leaving hospital, she has had no more attacks and has never needed an oxygen cylinder beside her bed. She is livelier in spirit, happy, and although still painfully thin, abounding with energy.

'My mother still cannot sleep without the aid of sedatives, but she appears more restful in spirit and much calmer and happier. She has not had any more injections from the doctor, but nevertheless seems to be far healthier.'

A fortnight later, on 6 May, Mrs Perry sent the following letter:

'Let me thank you again for your wonderful help in curing my young sister Gwynneth. She continues to improve and becomes stronger every day. The fluid in her lungs has dried up completely, much to the bafflement of doctors and hospital staff. Indeed, she is now riding her bicycle around and eating quite well. My sincere thanks to you and Dr Lang.

'My mother looks a great deal healthier, but still takes her sleeping tablets through sheer habit. However, she has had no injections of late to tone up her circulation and pacify her nerves which is indeed a good sign.'

Then, on 20 June 1962, Mrs Pauline Perry wrote this final communication to George Chapman:

'I think this will be my last letter of thanks to you, together with the medical report on my mother and sister.

'The two patients in question have progressed so amazingly that I think all will be well with them from now on, and it only remains for me to say once more that you have my deepest gratitude for your wonderful help.

'I do hope that you are as well as your ex-patient, my young sister Gwynneth. Thanks to you, she has not been troubled with asthma or any pulmonary complications since. May God abundantly bless you and thank Dr Lang for working a miracle.'

This last letter was received nearly two and a half years ago and as far as I could tell the case was closed. But, was it not perhaps possible that there had been a relapse and Mrs Perry had not written about it? It was imperative for me to find out the *present* state of health of Mrs Perry's mother and sister, so I got in touch with her in December 1964.

'My mother's health has improved since she received distant healing,' Mrs Perry told me. 'She has never been a robustly healthy person, but compared to what she was, I would say she is now in "much better shape".

'Gwynneth is now remarkably healthy and full of energy. Her zest for living is quite remarkable. Occasionally she has a "tightness" in her chest, but those dreadful bouts of choking asthma are gone.

'She is always under medical care really, because of what happened to her in 1962, and her doctor is obviously ready for another attack. However, I am glad to say that he is still waiting! The fact remains that my young sister is healed, and no one can dispute that fact.'

33

The Intricacy of Spirit Healing

HAVING QUESTIONED a considerable number of Mr Lang's patients about their illnesses and experiences with the spirit doctor, and then tested their evidence, it was only natural that I should want to know exactly *how* spirit operations are performed and how the patient's spirit body is treated. I questioned Mr Lang at length about it.

'The simplest answer to your question of how spirit healing actually works is: Spirit healing is healing from the spirit world and is given to a patient by spirit doctors,' Mr Lang replied. 'The healing takes place upon the patient's spirit body which brings about a change in the physical body for the better. It is as simple as that.

'If I went into all the technical details you just would not be able to comprehend it – no one could *fully* conceive the intricacies of spirit surgery and treatment until he is in the spirit world himself and endowed with the understanding of spirit. Even then, unless one becomes a spirit doctor, one couldn't understand all the complex methods and techniques. So, I think, the best and easiest way to answer your question is to reiterate what I said a moment ago – spirit healing is healing *from* spirit, *through* spirit, *to* the spirit body of the patient, and thence to the physical body of the patient.'

'I agree that I would be unable to understand fully the intricacies of spirit surgery techniques, since I am an author and not a doctor,' I said. 'But couldn't you explain it in a way which would be understood by ordinary people?'

190

'I'll try,' Mr Lang consented. After a moment's thought, he said: 'I think the best way to explain the *basic* conception of spirit healing is by making it clear that the healing vibrations that are used in spirit healing are of divine source – coming direct from God. They are precisely the same vibrations as were used by Jesus Christ – the greatest healer that ever lived! – and later by His disciples in the performance of healing miracles. These same vibrations were also used in the early days by the Sovereigns of this country when they exercised their divine power of healing but, as medical knowledge grew, the power reposing in them became dormant. To this day, exactly the same vibrations are being used by some clergymen of all denominations and religions and frequently bring about successful cures or improvements of various diseases. These clergymen, however, attribute their healing achievements to religion and do their utmost to conceal the fact that their successes are due actually to spirit healing.

'The use of healing vibrations to cure the sick is a science and not a religion. They form part of the natural laws of the Universe and should, in consequence, be used accordingly.

'When I – or any other spirit doctor – attend to a patient, I make full use of these healing vibrations. I draw healing power from spirit and this power passes through me to the spirit body of the ailing patient and thence to his physical body.'

'When I discussed your spirit operations with various people, and particularly with a doctor, I found that they refuse to accept the existence of an unseen spirit body even though they acknowledge your successes in overcoming incurable diseases,' I said.

'Well, I know that a good many people – and especially members of the medical profession – just will not accept the fact that there is a spirit body,' Mr Lang said. 'People with a materialistic outlook cannot get it into their heads that besides having a physical body which they can see, they also have a spirit body which they can't see. But each and every person has a spirit body, this is undeniable.

'It would be easier for them to accept and understand if they could say: "When my life on earth is finished, I pass into the spirit world, and when I do so, I live in my spirit body which is the same as I inhabited on earth; and the only difference is the texture, and the fact that the physical body is mortal while the spirit body lives on after death." And if they advanced a step further and said: "I have a spirit body that the spirit doctor can either operate on or apply treatment to bring about changes; these changes will in due course transfer to my physical body and improve my physical condition," they would understand the overall working of spirit healing.

'I see for myself only too often how very difficult it is for some people – and particularly medical men – to really accept these things. For example, if I talk with some doctors who come to consult me – or with other intelligent and knowledgeable patients – about, say the brain, and say: "Well, you've got a brain, you have eight cranio* bones, we can part these and remove the tumour", they know what I'm talking about. But if I say: "You have a spirit body here which you can't see and I am going to perform an invisible and painless operation on it, remove the tumour, and by removing it from your spirit body, bring about a satisfactory change in your physical body", it's beyond them. They just say "yes" but don't really understand what I am saying. So, you see, one has to express one's self in simple terms.'

'Can you tell me how it is that you are able to give such a precise diagnosis of a patient's ailment, and how you operate on the spirit body?' was my next question.

'Well, as a preamble I should perhaps tell you that as a spirit doctor, I can see the spirit body which is invisible to you and most people. Thus, when I look upon a patient, I can see both his bodies – the physical and spirit

* Cranio (kranion) = combining form denoting the cranium, the foetal head; cranial.

body – simultaneously, I can also see the person's aura,* or reflected light, which is constantly moving and changing colour, and exists about two inches from the body. The aura consists of colour vibrations reflected by the organs of the body, which are constantly changing according to the state of their health. Each organ, when healthy, reflects a definite colour in the aura, but when the organ becomes diseased, or its condition deteriorates, the reflection changes colour. So, you see, by looking at a patient's aura, I know immediately the *overall* state of health which is of course of some diagnostic help.

'However, to diagnose a patient's trouble *precisely*, it is necessary to examine the body, because the reflection of the aura, as I said before, gives only an overall picture. Now, how I examine patients I needn't describe to you because you know this from your own experience, and you also know that I always examine the patient's *spirit* body. The reason I am able to give a precise diagnosis and detect conditions which earthly doctors and specialists cannot discover by physical examination, is due to my ability to examine the spirit body.

'But don't let it ever enter your head the reason for doctors and specialists sometimes being unable to diagnose correctly, or cure, some difficult disease is that they are incompetent or just don't care about their patients! The medical profession is a noble one and not to be needlessly attacked or criticised. It is my own profession and one which, after all, provided me with my education and knowledge. It was my passport for my return to earth as a spirit doctor working through my medium.

'The reason why some doctors are unable to diagnose, or cure, certain diseases is that earthly conditions, which govern the physical body, often hinder them in their sincere desire to heal. As a spirit doctor, I am in a

* The human aura was demonstrated and photographed by Dr Kilner in 1913. Apart from spirit doctors (and other spirits) the aura can also be seen by people with very well-developed psychic faculties.

privileged position, because earthly conditions do not interfere with my work. Attending to the spirit body, I can examine each organ with ease and am not handicapped by the skin and other tissues that cover the organs of the physical body. I am able to see and recognise at once what is wrong.

'This, I think, answers your question on how I diagnose. Now as to the next one – how I operate on the spirit body and so forth.

'If I need to operate on the spirit body, or give it any other form of treatment, I must draw it slightly away from the physical body so as to establish the healing vibrations with the spirit world – draw on the spirit power – so that the spirit body is in a proper condition to be attended to.

'Now, people – and perhaps you are one of them – don't really have a complete picture of the spirit body, and those who accept the fact that there is such a thing as an unseen spirit body, usually assume that it is within the physical body. This is, however, not so – the spirit body is, in fact, outside the physical body, wrapped round it, as it were, yet it can also contract into the physical body. But, although the spirit body is outside, it is essential to draw it forward slightly so that I can create the vibrations whereby it becomes "alive". You see, when the spirit body becomes "alive", those organs which were previously tiny, assume their right size, and we are able to operate or provide what treatment is advisable.

'I am not *always* performing operations. If I find, for instance, that a patient has a liver complaint which I can cure by giving him injections, I use an astra fluid which I inject into the organ of the spirit body. Such activities as I have so far described are all carried out, one must not forget, by Basil and my colleagues and assistants.'

'Are operations on the spirit body similar to those performed by surgeons in hospital?' I enquired.

'Well, yes, on the whole there is a similarity as far as the actual surgery is concerned,' Mr Lang explained. 'Most of the spirit instruments are identical with those used in hospitals, but we use fewer instruments because the texture of the spirit body is different, and we are thus able to reach the site of the operation very quickly. A surgeon or theatre sister who watches me perform an operation knows what I am doing from the instruments I ask for and how I am using them, although they can't see the actual operation.'

I knew that this was so because several people with medical training had told me exactly the same when I interviewed them about their own cases; or cases which they had observed in Mr Lang's consulting room.

I next asked Mr Lang how it was that he, a noted *ophthalmic* surgeon during his lifetime, was now able to perform highly specialised operations in different fields of surgery?

'Oh, I am able to perform most operations because, you see, although I specialised in ophthalmology, I was also a general surgeon at the London Hospital at Whitechapel and I made a study of all forms of surgery,' Mr Lang explained. 'But usually it's not just myself who is operating. For instance, over there just now is a group of my friends who actually worked with me at the hospital, and with them are also a number of Basil's contemporaries. Among them is David Little, Arnold Lawson, Adams, McEwen, and quite a few others.* Each of them is a specialist in his own field and has his own methods and technique, and we all work together as a team assisting each other.

'If I have a patient, say with a grown exostosis,† then I may talk to one of my colleagues and ask him for his opinion. We generally have a consultation and I listen

* Some of the other surgeons in William Lang's team are: W. Pasteur, M.D., F.R.C.P.; Sidney Coupland, M.C., F.R.C.P.; Victor Bonney, M.D., M.S., B.SC., F.R.C.S.; W. Sampson Henley, M.D., M.S., F.R.C.S.; Sir John Bland-Sutton, F.R.C.S.; Sir R. Douglas Powell, Bart., K.C.V.O., M.D.; Sir W. T. Lister, etc. There is also a nursing staff, and the one in charge of it is Sister Ormand.

† The most common benign tumour of the bone, usually seen as a cartilage-capped bony growth protruding from the surface.

to what my colleagues say because they are specialised in particular fields. Now, if a very specialised operation needs to be performed, I prefer one of my colleagues to do it, but I do the talking to the patient and actively assist in the operation because I am the one working through a medium. My son Basil very often operates – he is a fine, a very fine surgeon.'

'When you perform your operations, you frequently flick your fingers. Did you do that as well when you were on earth?'

'Quite, quite. Of course the point was that I worked with trained people they knew what I wanted just by the clicking of my fingers. The same now applies. If I want to start to perform eye surgery, for instance, I say "injection" and click my fingers, but afterwards I just click my fingers. I don't need to say anything, they know exactly what I want because they are all quite as good as – and even better than – I am. We are all equal – surgeons, sisters, and so on – there is no one higher or lower, we are a team.'

'In interviewing a considerable number of your patients, I discovered that some of them had noticed operation scars on their physical bodies – in fact I myself discovered a pink scar-like appearance on my own body,' I said. 'Can you tell me how these phenomena – light pink marks which look like scars and with pink dots which look like stitch marks but which are so smooth that the skin is not affected – come about?'

'I have explained to you that I always attend to the spirit body and that the operations I perform reflect upon the physical body and bring about the desired improvement or cure of the patient. I think this answers your question, because scars are part of operations.'

'But how is it then that some patients do not bear these marks on their bodies?' I asked.

'I think I am justified in saying that scars appear in every case, but the majority are so faint that the human eye cannot discern them. Certain patients, however, possess such very sensitive skins that the marks are clearly visible.'

'Can you enlighten me on the use of ectoplasm* for replacing damaged or diseased parts of the body?'

'Well, ectoplasm is a substance used from the medium's body – it's not from the spirit world – this is why I need a good medium,' Mr Lang answered. 'When a patient, such as yourself, arrives, I make what I call a rod, and this rod joins you to my medium's body. I then draw up a certain amount of ectoplasm which I can mould.

'If a patient, for example, has a growth which is the cause of his ill health, I remove it by an operation and that is the end of it. The patient will in due course be cured. But, if a patient has a piece of diseased intestine, for instance, then I operate to remove it and replace it with ectoplasm, because the part is still vital to the human body. So you see, ectoplasm plays quite an important part in spirit surgery, but it is not something that is of universal and unlimited usage. Sometimes you hear people say that ectoplasm is used for this and that, but that's nonsense, it's just not so.'

'If, for one reason or other, an earthly surgeon cut off too much of an organ during an operation, could you replace that missing part with ectoplasm?' I asked.

'Yes, I attempt to do this, but it's not always successful, it depends on the circumstances and also on the individual patient. But I have had a fair number of patients in whose bodies I rebuilt missing parts in this way quite successfully. In fact, in some cases when patients went to the hospital for X-ray examinations after I had rebuilt a missing part in their bodies with ectoplasm, the X-rays showed that the previously missing parts had indeed "grown again".'

'Would you say that Spiritualists, people who implicitly

* Ectoplasm is a protoplastic substance streaming out of the body of a medium; it is matter, invisible and intangible in the primary state but assuming vaporous liquid or solid condition in various stages of condensation. It often emits a smell. (The word ectoplasm originated from Professor Richet.)

197

believe in spirit healing, benefit more from your operations or treatment than others who have no faith in it but just hope for the best?'

'Not at all, it doesn't make any difference,' Mr Lang stated with emphasis. 'It all depends on the person being "in tune", as I call it.

'Some of those who come to see me have no belief in anything at all, but intrinsically are good persons. I also get some who are, inside themselves, evil. But I am not concerned with this, I am a spirit doctor here to help the sick. So I get them on the healing couch, talk to them and draw their spirit body away a little – as I explained to you earlier on. Even in the most difficult situation I manage to create an atmosphere which is calm and free from emotion, and as and when the patient is mentally and physically relaxed, and in a state to receive the treatment I need to give him, I start attending to his spirit body.

'I cannot stress it often enough that spirit healing has nothing whatsoever to do with faith or faith healing and is consequently available to everyone in need of healing. With spirit healing it is, in this respect, exactly the same as with medical treatment. A patient's personal beliefs or disbeliefs have nothing to do with the effectiveness of the treatment he receives from his own doctor or in hospital, and this applies to spirit healing. The only thing that helps spirit healing to bring about speedier results on the physical body is the patient's will to get better, but this is true of medicine generally.

'I think it is appropriate that I should mention the healing services which are from time to time attended and conducted by persons with strong religious convictions.

'During these services hymns are sung and fervent prayers offered for those members of the congregation in ill health. These proceedings are often carried out until an emotional state is built up and with it a certain amount of magnetic power. This power then passes into the bodies of the patients and, the store-house of energy being thus temporarily revitalised, the aura brightens and the patients feel somewhat better.

'The effect, however, is not lasting, and after a short while the patient relapses into his or her former state of ill health, but with the important difference that his or her mental state is worse than before. They do not understand the reason for their relapse, and if they are deeply religious they tend to become introspective. This leads them to question whether they have shown sufficient faith in God and they begin to ask themselves if they no longer enjoy His favour and have been deprived of His love and understanding. Most of them will doubt now that spiritual healing can restore their health, and in all probability may never seek its assistance again.

'In the circumstances which I have just described no healing has ever, in fact, taken place. The sick have merely been given a spiritual tonic which has had no lasting effect, because the illness has remained untouched. I do not mean to say that those churches, endeavouring to bring about spiritual healing by prayer, should give up trying to help the sick. But if they do not wish merely to scratch the surface of something they do not at present understand, they must seek a new approach to the problem and adopt the methods of spirit healing and train their members to be instruments of the Divine Powers as were Jesus Christ and His disciples.

'There are many people who have the latent gift of healing who could be trained to the services of the church and the medical profession. It is not the prerogative of the few, but many are unaware of such gifts having been bestowed on them. But if these people could enter the realm of spirit healing in the same way that my medium has done, then they could become available to many spirit doctors who are eager to work on earth in the same way as I do, by restoring health to the sick.

'Let me say that spirit healing is a science – a science of the Universe – and to achieve the results of which it is capable you must obey its laws. And, being a science, spirit healing requires no religious ceremony, invocation, or emotion. I wish to make it clear, however, that I pay due respect to those who, in a spirit of thankfulness to

God, turn to hymns and prayers of praise for the benefits and blessings they hope to receive; but these things are not essential.

'If I say that prayers are not necessary for bringing about effective spirit healing, it is not to be assumed for one moment that spirit controls are not of God. We are all of God and I never commence a healing session without giving thanks to God for being allowed to return to earth, and also for the use of my medium.'

I enquired of Mr Lang how he managed to visit the many thousands of patients who have come to him through George Chapman and regularly require distant healing.

'Oh, I just can't be in every place, that's quite impossible,' Mr Lang replied. 'I visit of course a great many patients during their sleeping state, but I only visit those who I feel require my personal attention. Other patients are visited by my colleagues in spirit. It doesn't really matter to the patient whether it is myself, Basil, Lister, or any other spirit doctor who comes to visit him; the important thing is that he receives spirit healing and benefits from it.'

'How do you, or your spirit colleagues, find the patients?'

'It's easy – but it's more correct to say that the patients find *me*. You see, when a patient is ill, he or she thinks of me and thus sends out a thought vibration which is very positive. Now, when it is received into the spirit world it's picked up by someone who then passes it on to me.

'Very often when a person feels very ill and wants me to attend to him as speedily as possible, I may be performing an operation or examining a patient here and cannot, consequently, receive the thought message. So, whoever picks up the vibration goes to help the patient, and then comes to tell me what's happened. As soon as I am free, they take me to wherever the patient is.'

'Would you say that distant healing is as effective as contact healing?'

'Oh, my goodness, no. Contact healing is far more successful. Let me explain. You come to see me here and I

200

know I can help you, so I operate on you. Then I tell you I'm going to visit you during your sleep state and this I do. Now then, when I visit you during your sleep state I can attend to what needs to be done – because I operated on your spirit body during contact healing – and frequently I use healing rays; this is why people often see lights.

'Generally speaking, when a person writes for distant healing only – and is somebody with whom I have not established direct contact before – the results are not nearly as striking.

'Of course distant healing is of considerable importance. In many cases where the patient is very, very ill – maybe a young child or someone who is bedridden – and I know I can really do something, then help is very effective even if the patient has never experienced contact healing. But don't ever get the idea we can do away with contact healing and go over entirely to distant healing. Distant healing is, broadly speaking, just spirit treatment, while with contact healing I can perform *any* necessary operations and, being able to draw so much from the medium, I am able to use almost unlimited power from the spirit world.'

'Having investigated a number of your distant healing cases, I discovered that some of them resulted in truly miraculous cures.'

'Quite. Some patients we visit are very psychic, and when they are really at the lowest degree of consciousness we are able to draw their spirit bodies far enough away – into the spirit world, so to speak. I can then operate and give the patient such treatment as I do in contact healing. On occasions – while the medium is sleeping soundly in his normal rest – I can also use some of his power to supplement the treatment in these particular distant healing cases, and, if there is a strong psychic in the family, I can do much the same. This is why some cases of distant healing are as effective as contact healing. But you must always remember that these special cases are few and far between.'

'You would then advise anyone suffering from a serious illness to come for contact healing whenever possible?'

'Yes – if it is possible.'

'One of your patients told me that you have a secretary in the spirit world who keeps complete records of all your patients for you. Is that correct, and if so, is his name Hunt?'

'Yes, that is so. His name was originally John Hunter but by legal arrangement he changed it to Hunt. He was in fact a friend of mine during my life upon earth, and over here our friendship continues of course. Now, although I've said he's my secretary it's not quite correct because, in the first place, he gives me advice, considerable help, and also keeps my records in order.

'Thanks to dear Hunt, I know what's wrong with a patient as soon as he comes here, because, you see, while I attend to a patient, Hunt records everything that takes place during the consultation. Yesterday for instance, a patient called Clark arrived, but Margaret couldn't remember anything about him because he hadn't been here for years. As soon as they opened the door, I was, however, able to say: "Oh, yes, I know you," and tell him all about his visit some years ago – because of Hunt's invaluable records.'

The conversation returned to spirit healing and Mr Lang confirmed to me that he and his colleagues are able to cure almost any illness – provided it is not too late even for spirit healing. He mentioned his success with several victims of poliomyelitis by removing the deadly virus and preventing paralysis. He also furnished me with proof that he and his colleagues had managed to save victims of leukaemia.

'The word "incurable" which has long been in medical currency – and I suppose I myself have used it on certain occasions – is not always accurate,' Mr Lang concluded. 'If I can judge a patient's life force – the spark, if you wish, the desire to get well – and the patient is determined to fight the illness, then of course I can help.

'It is of no use seeking out the help of a healer or doctor and expecting to play a passive role. A patient, and especially an "incurable" patient, should co-operate by his desire to get better.

'Broadly speaking, nothing is incurable – provided the patient seeks help when his health deteriorates and does not fight the help he is given.'

34

Ever Victorious?

IT WOULD be reasonable to assume that anyone reading this catalogue of success is likely to wonder if it is not inevitable. I asked William Lang if this could be said of his work.

'No. I do not perform miracles and I do not lead patients to believe that I can. When my spirit operations and treatment end in failure – and, unfortunately, this does happen from time to time, though, thank God, only rarely – it is due to the fact that even spirit doctors work within a framework of natural laws. Age must eventually take its toll with every one. Those parts of the body that become worn out with age, cannot be entirely replaced. But in those cases, where I am able to recognise that the earthly life of a patient is approaching its end, I continue to do all I can to relieve suffering. I can still perform operations on their spirit bodies with ectoplasm, but this is only a temporary measure to secure some relief and comfort for them. When the earthly life is nearing its inevitable close we cannot prolong it, but we endeavour to make the passing into the spirit world as easy for the patient as we can.

'Another reason for spirit operations and treatment not being always successful is that some of the patients come to see me too late in the day. In these cases the disease – often caused by a dangerous virus infection – has already secured too devastating a grip on the patient. As a result, nothing that I can do is of any avail, that is in a permanent sense. No, spirit operations and spirit treatment are not *always* successful. But I would again like to emphasise that no disease is incurable, if a patient consults me in time.'

I also spoke with George Chapman on the same subject, and he told me very candidly that some people do not benefit at all from Mr Lang's treatment. He recalled an instance which occurred seven years previously.

'The relatives of a patient who was in a large west country hospital asked me to see him there and to give him spirit healing,' he said. 'They told me that the surgeon in charge of the case had given permission. I was also told that there was an early history of pneumonia and removal of appendix, and that at that time the patient was thought to be suffering from a slipped disc. However, in an operation the surgeon had removed a cancerous abscess; later another operation had been performed in London for the removal of a duodenal ulcer. Just before I'd been asked to visit the hospital a further operation had been carried out to deal with conditions set in the liver and prostate gland. There was a serious concern about the patient's condition and the hospital held out very little hope of recovery. The patient was in severe and constant pain, for which large dosages of morphia were being given.

'When I saw him in a private ward, it looked as if his end was very near. The hospital staff were very kind and co-operative and a nurse remained with the patient while I went into trance and Mr Lang afterwards took over. Well of course he did everything he could to ease the poor man's pain, and he succeeded. The patient became more peaceful and at ease. Mr Lang spoke to the nurse during the treatment, and to the patient's mother telling her what he was doing, and explaining to her that although her son was too far gone, it was possible to alleviate his suffering. The mother was so grateful you know. A few days later the man died peacefully.

'One afternoon, about a year after this incident, my wife received a telephone message to the effect that a child was in a very bad way in a large Midlands general hospital. The surgeon there had said he doubted if the child would last the night. And of course her mother and father were frantic. It upset me, because I love children, so, although the case seemed hopeless, I promised I would drive to the hospital immediately to enable Mr Lang to do what he possibly could for the child. It was a dark night with heavy rain, and conditions were wretched.

'When I arrived at the hospital I learned that the child was suffering from leukaemia and was having a blood transfusion. I had to wait a long time in the depressing atmosphere of a waiting-room, doing my best to comfort the parents who were in despair. Contrary to what I had been given to understand, they had not obtained permission from the hospital authorities for my visit. This resulted in further delay but, when approached, the surgeon in charge readily gave his consent, and in fact watched Mr Lang attending to the child.

'It was one o'clock when I left the hospital, but despite the depressing conditions of the journey home, I felt that even if the child could not be saved, we had done all we could. I wasn't able to get to the hospital again and distant healing was given instead. It was sad that this little child's life couldn't be saved. The call had come too late. The only thing that could be done was to make her last hours on earth as comfortable as possible.

'Both the contact and distant healing had the expected effect. Three weeks after my visit to the hospital the child was able to return home where she spent a few happy months free from pain, before passing peacefully into spirit.'

In a more cheerful vein George Chapman went on to tell me:

'Not all our visits to hospitals ended unhappily. Mr O., for instance, wrote asking for distant healing for his wife, who was in hospital with cancer of the breast. He asked if I would see her there and give her contact healing. Permission for this was granted by the surgeon, so I went. William Lang decided it was necessary to perform some operations on the woman's spirit body, and when he eventually finished his surgery, he stated that she was now clear of cancer, and requested that the surgeon should confirm this.

'The surgeon re-examined the patient and because of doubt decided to obtain another opinion. The woman was seen by another specialist but he too was unable to express a definite opinion. The situation was explained to the husband who was asked if he would permit an exploratory operation to be performed in order that the surgeon could ascertain exactly what had taken place. The husband agreed, and after it had been done, it was stated that "it was a wrong diagnosis in the first place; there must have been just a small cyst which has cleared away".

'The patient was discharged from hospital three days later. This took place in February 1954, and the patient has been fit and well ever since.'

I asked Chapman if he could provide me with an overall percentage of failures.

'I'm afraid I don't know,' he replied. 'It is not easy for me to compile accurate records on the effect of William Lang's treatment, because I depend entirely on information from the patients. Every patient who comes here for contact healing, and those who receive distant healing, are asked to submit health reports regularly. As long as they do this I know to what extent the healing is successful. The trouble is, however, that most of them stop writing to me when they are fully recovered. But I have no means of knowing if the healing is lasting. It is of course true that when a patient experiences any sort of deterioration in health, he or she is quick to write for an appointment with Mr Lang or for distant healing to be resumed; but this is no guarantee that those patients who have *not* communicated again with me since they last reported a complete cure of their complaint, *are* permanently cured.

'You yourself discovered that patients suddenly "fade out" when you examined my files. You saw that a lot of the patients' records are far from up-to-date, and that the last entry in many of them dates back to anything up to ten years, or even longer. I'd like to think that where a patient no longer informs me about his state of health that we've been able to cure him permanently. But how can one be sure? As a matter of fact, the only authentic evidence I have about patients experiencing lasting cures since they stopped writing to me, was furnished by yourself after you had them traced to their homes.

'If I wanted to keep all the case histories up-to-date so that I would know exactly what happened to them I'd have to employ a special clerical staff just for correspondence and filing work. And I, too, would have to give up a lot of time to it. As things stand, there just isn't enough time available for me to enable William Lang to see all the patients who ask for appointments. I have to try to fit them in at dates in the future and arrange that during the waiting time they receive distant healing. I consider it more important to spend what available time is left to me (after dealing with patients' health reports, etc.) by being in trance and enabling William Lang to help the sick, than keeping reliable post-treatment records.'

Under the circumstances, I'm afraid, I cannot provide an answer as to what proportion of failures there is among the enormous number of Mr Lang's successes.

During my investigations I interviewed 153* Lang-Chapman ex-patients, and after the most searching enquiry into all the circumstances found that these men and women had been cured completely and lastingly by Mr Lang – the majority of them many years ago.

Following upon the opinions expressed by Lang and Chapman as to whether spirit healing is always successful,

* Some of these patients objected, for strictly personal reasons, to my publishing their names and addresses, but willingly gave me all the information I required about their medical history and the treatment and cure by Mr Lang. They also allowed me to check and counter-check their tape-recorded statements. Some suggested I should just quote their initials. But as they were unwilling to be interrogated by other researchers if necessary, I decided not to include their cases in this book. I explained earlier that I intended to deal with *named* patients only who were willing to substantiate my enquiry into their cures. Being limited by space, the omission of those patients who wanted to remain anonymous served a two-fold purpose.

I decided to seek the view of a medical man on the subject. The person best qualified to answer this question seemed to me to be Mr S. G. Miron, L.D.S., R.C.S. (Eng.), because he is able to speak with authority both from the orthodox viewpoint and from personal knowledge of William Lang's achievements. I asked him point blank: 'As a researcher of William Lang's work, would you say his spirit operations are always successful?'

'No, I would not agree. I would say they were not more successful than ordinary operations in this phase of existence. The reasons, however, are far deeper and more obscure.

'I have been present at many operations in hospitals where the operation as a technical exercise was completely successful, but the patient died, for one reason or another. In some cases the actual cause of death was never fully established.

'Suffice to say, however, that the majority of cases that come before William Lang are those which have received little benefit from orthodox medical and surgical treatment, and many are very advanced cases. Yet I myself know of a number of cancer sufferers, regarded as hopeless cases, who have recovered and returned to normal health following William Lang's spirit healing.

'The purposes of spirit operations are manifold, but generally they do not differ from the operations performed by ordinary surgeons. Even where William Lang's spirit operations or treatment do not cure a seriously ill patient, I can say without hesitation – speaking from experience and thorough research of Lang's work – that the sufferer is helped tremendously, and greatly eased the passage into the next level of existence.'

During the many interviews I had with William Lang or George Chapman we often talked about the impossibility of giving all but a few new patients an appointment for an early consultation. 'Only if there is a cancellation can a new patient, whose case is urgent, be fitted in. Otherwise it means having to wait your turn, unfortunate as it is,' George Chapman told me.

'The real answer to the problem is the training of more mediums to work with those spirit doctors who are awaiting the day when they too can exercise their skill on earth in the same way as William Lang,' I said.

'This is true in respect to the principles of William Lang's activities as seen in the direct doctor-to-patient approach but it requires long training,' Chapman said. 'Remember how many years it took before the spirit world trained me before I became capable of working with William Lang?'

'Do you happen to know if mediums of your type are being trained now for future work with spirit doctors on this earth?'

'I don't know what sort of training is being given to healing mediums by the spirit people, but I dare say such efforts are being made because of what William Lang has said on various occasions,' Chapman replied. 'The only thing I can tell you for certain is that a trance medium and a non-trance healer are receiving training here at the Tuesday Free Clinic.'

'How is this training of the trance medium being done?'

'Well, I think you'd better ask my control. Anything I could tell you would only be second hand because, as you know, while I am in trance I have no knowledge whatsoever of what is taking place here. William Lang can tell you much better because he is doing the training.'

I broached the question to the spirit doctor, and he gave me the following explanation:

'I have a lady student at the Tuesday Free Clinic, and she's a very promising prospect as a healing-medium. As a matter of fact, she is being trained to become her father's instrument and enable him to work in the same way as George enables me to work. You see, her father was a splendid doctor while he lived on this earth, and he's a dear friend of mine. He is waiting for the day when he'll be able to resume his healing work. He is anxious to set up his own spirit doctor practice with his daughter as medium at Hayes in Middlesex.'

'How is the training carried out?'

'I am only helping with it,' Mr Lang corrected me. 'The actual *mediumistic* training is being done by the spirit people who have the necessary knowledge in this particular field – it's the same process as that employed with George when he was being prepared for becoming my instrument before I took control of his entranced body. However, in order to try to shorten the training period as much as possible, and enable her father to become a spirit doctor more speedily, the daughter receives here what you could call preliminary spirit surgery tuition. And while she is here, developing and getting to know her own healing powers, her father looks in and acquaints himself with our methods of healing, and also takes every opportunity to experiment in taking control of the body of his future instrument.'

'When do you think this lady will be sufficiently trained?'

'It's very difficult to say,' Mr Lang replied diplomatically. 'The training period of a healing-medium – a medium such as George is – is a lengthy affair. But the young lady is making promising progress.'

'As and when the day comes that this new spirit doctor will be able to work through his medium, will it mean that you and George are not as overworked as you are at present?'

'Well, yes. You see, there are many spirit non-trance healers in this country, and some of them are really outstanding with many successes to their credit. But many patients today are not just content with receiving healing and being cured by a healer through the agency of spirit power but who cannot talk to them as a doctor does and explain to them what's wrong with them. They like to speak with the spirit doctor, to ask him questions – as they do with earthly doctors and specialists – and this is why it is so important that as many healing-mediums as possible are trained, so that spirit doctors can work through them.'

'As far as you know, are there many healing-mediums being trained to serve as future instruments for spirit doctors who wish to return to earth?'

'A fair number are being trained but, of course, only *born* mediums can be developed for this special task. But, as time goes on, new healing-mediums will appear on the scene and more and more spirit doctors will be able to perform operations and treat all those sufferers who are in urgent need of help.'

'If the number of spirit doctors increases as time goes by, won't this affect the livelihood of the non-trance healers, many of whom, as you say, achieve remarkable successes with incurable diseases?'

'No, there can never be enough *good* healers. More and more people are turning for help to spirit healing. It is only too obvious that many more healers and spirit doctors are required.'

'If there is eventually a much denser network of spirit doctors and non-trance healers, will it affect the medical profession?'

'Good Lord, no! We are not competing with the medical profession, we are doing all we can to co-operate with them, in so far as they allow us to do so. At present, there are only comparatively few medical men who accept our co-operation; most doctors stubbornly refuse to acknowledge any successes brought about through spirit operations or healing. But when a vast body of spirit doctors and first-class non-trance healers are able to operate all over the country, and irrefutable proof of the efficacy of spirit healing is established beyond contradiction, the medical profession will revise their present hostile attitude and will eventually co-operate. And, then, humanity will benefit as it is entitled to – on the grand scale. Unnecessary suffering and premature deaths will become things of the past.

'Anyone who thinks in terms of competition between spirit healing and the medical profession has got hold of the wrong end of the stick. Let me sum it up this way:

'Spirit healing cures illnesses and brings comfort to the sick, but everyone must always recognise that the medical profession does this too. It is a fine profession and one which humanity could not do without. Surgeons, doctors and nurses give magnificent service to the sick all over the world. No healer should ever discourage a patient from attending a doctor – in fact he should always advise his patient to seek the help of the medical profession. Whenever possible, doctors should be told when their patients are receiving spirit healing. There should be the fullest co-operation between the two professions because each can learn much from the other. After all, modern scientific medicine owes much to its early forbears. And, in the main, spirit doctors who return to do healing work on earth were doctors during their earthly life span. So you see, though, broadly speaking, miles apart at present, spirit doctors and earthly doctors belong to the same profession – the profession whose noble aim is to cure the sick.'

The passionate intensity with which Lang spoke revealed how greatly concerned he was, and is, with human welfare. It also indicated once again how strongly he feels on the subject of the abolition of barriers between orthodox medicine and spirit healing. Surely, these are sufficient reasons for the making of a great attempt to secure a unity that will assuredly benefit mankind.

35

Spirit Healing Cures – Fact or Fiction

WHEN I went to see William Lang on 6 January 1964, I drove to Aylesbury as a sceptic, but at the moment of writing fourteen months later, I am firmly convinced that the seemingly old white-coated gentleman who receives patients at St. Brides is indeed the spirit of the late William Lang, F.R.C.S., acting through his medium's body. I am equally convinced that, in the Aylesbury house, daily cures of a miraculous nature are brought about.

My conviction was bolstered by the stubborn and thorough investigation and research work I engaged in during the past twelve months. Naturally the first stirrings of belief came from my own experience in connection with my eyes, the sight of which is still steadily improving. But, as I pointed out at the beginning of this book, it is not my intention to try to convert anyone to my own way of thinking.

While working on the book, I have frequently talked with doctors and nurses about the cures claimed for William Lang. Many of them had come into contact in one way or another with the remarkable curative changes that occurred after patients sought help at Aylesbury. Some of them openly endorsed the fact that extraordinary cures of incurable diseases had indeed been brought about by the spirit doctor's operations and treatment. Another section, despite confrontation with authenticated evidence of cures, still insisted that the laws of nature could and must have been instrumental –

this despite the overwhelming medical and mathematical odds against the possibility of it happening. And of course there were those who did not wish to commit themselves either way. They just said they were not convinced that the phenomena *had* or *had not* been caused by spirit healing. In all honesty I must confess that this latter group, the non-commital, made up the greatest numbers. It was also distinguished for its *consensus ad idem* on one particular point – all its members said that basically they were not too concerned about how the cures had happened, the main thing was that they had happened.

On frequent occasions I have also spoken with my friend Liam Nolan – a writer and a most critical and down-to-earth man possessing what I consider to be a high degree of intelligence – about the Lang-Chapman partnership, their fabulous successes and, in particular, about the fantastic improvement of my own eyesight. We'd only met and become friends *after* William Lang had saved me from threatened blindness, so Nolan didn't know from personal observation how appallingly poor my vision had been before my visit to St Brides.

I was aware of the fact that Nolan was far from convinced that the spirit doctor could bring about all the miraculous cures I'd told him about, he was too polite in the beginning to press any question or openly challenge anything I'd said. The glint of cynicism in his eyes, however, betrayed that he was far from accepting that the events of which I had spoken could be possible. It struck me that he thought I might have become a victim of self-delusion. As time went by and we continued discussing William Lang and his work, it became more obvious than ever that Nolan could not fathom how the sceptical and cynical journalist and writer he knew me to be could be taken in so completely by what could easily have been pretence or trickery. Of course he never dropped any remark that put it so bluntly, but I had a good idea of how his thoughts were running.

Then, one day when I was telling him about an especially striking example of Lang's skill which I had just investigated, I suggested to my writer friend that he should come with me to Aylesbury to meet the spirit doctor and his medium. He readily agreed. It didn't surprise me. I knew the kind of coldly analytical and perceptive mind he had, and I was fairly sure he'd say yes when I made the suggestion.

Our appointment with William Lang was for four o'clock in the afternoon – after the spirit doctor had attended to his last patient that day.

Liam Nolan sat opposite the doctor, scepticism and alertness written all over his face. I sat on the settee at the far side of the consulting room, watching the two and listening to the interrogation that my friend launched. As the meeting went on, the spirit doctor's polite sincerity began to have some effect on Nolan's semi-hostility. His approach became slightly friendlier, though he continued questioning the spirit doctor over a wide range of subjects. Once or twice his questions led Lang to rise from his chair and walk to a picture on a wall, and to a bookcase.

The interview lasted about an hour.

After, when George Chapman regained consciousness, Nolan talked with him in a nonchalant way about Liverpool, Chapman's youth, work and many other topics. It was quite plain to me that he was keeping the conversation flowing, trying by astute probing and conversational gambits to make Chapman talk as much as possible. He had on occasions said to me that if a person talks long enough and freely enough you will get the key to his character. It seemed to me now that he was trying to pick similarities in speech between Chapman and Lang.

Later, when I was sitting next to Nolan as he drove his car along the A-413 towards London, I enquired what he thought about his meeting with the spirit doctor and his medium.

'I'm sorry to have to say this, Joe, but I am not at all convinced that the man in the white coat is William Lang, the surgeon,' he said.

'What about the marked differences in speech and mannerism between the man in the surgery and Chapman with whom you've just been drinking tea?' I asked.

'That doesn't convince me in the least. Anyone with a flair for acting and some talent could play the two roles quite convincingly. Vocal tricks aren't all that difficult you know.'

'I disagree,' I said, but did not pursue the issue and went on to my next question: 'What about the spirit doctor's vast medical knowledge which you ascertained to a certain extent when questioning him? George Chapman has no medical knowledge at all – he was a garage hand, a butcher, served with the R.A.F. during the war and ended up as a fireman before he became a full-time medium.'

'How do *you* know that Chapman has no medical knowledge?' he fired at me.

'I checked his background and ascertained that he had only an elementary school education. Besides, a number of trained people questioned him during his waking state about medical subjects and confirmed that he has no medical knowledge whatsoever.'

'All this could be a calculated act,' Nolan said. 'Supposing he had no higher school education, that doesn't say he's not intelligent. And it isn't all that difficult for a person with intelligence to pick up an impressive-sounding vocabulary of medical terms from an encyclopaedia, or from the medical reference books in a library. Especially if he wanted to do so badly enough.'

'Aren't you going a bit too far, Liam?'

'I don't think so, Joe. If, for some reason best known to himself, he wanted to create the impression that, in his consulting room, he is the spirit doctor Lang, but in his conscious state he is just an ordinary man, it would be the easiest thing in the world for him to say no, he knows nothing about medicine when he is acting George Chapman again.'

'Very well,' I said, 'let's assume that the claim about the spirit doctor is a fake – fraud if you wish . . .'

'I didn't say that,' Nolan interrupted me.

'I know. But let's assume that the whole thing *is* a fake, fraud, hocus-pocus, trickery, or whatever we wish to call it. What good would it do Chapman?'

'Well, there are two basic reasons why he might be doing it.'

'Namely?'

'Namely: *One*, money. *Two*, could be that he is genuinely interested in conning people into thinking they are getting better. I mean maybe there is the power motive – a sort of medical Will Rogers. Or deep human feeling for people who are sick and who, because of his power to convince them, reckon they're not so bad after all. Some people you know almost revel in the idea that they're not well.'

'Let's put the money motive aside for the moment,' I said, 'because I think I can effectively prove that it's non-existent. Let's take your second reason – that he's interested in, as you say, "conning" people into getting better, how does he do it? How, if there's no spirit doctor working through him?'

'I wouldn't have thought miracles were the sole preserve of spirit doctors,' he replied. 'After all over five million faithful of the Roman Catholic Church have a pretty solid catalogue of miracles running back nearly two thousand years. And their belief is in God, and the saints. What about Lourdes? Even non-Christians and anti-Christians have been on the panels of doctors and investigators who have certified miraculous cures there. And they've done it. Christians might well say that the cures that happen at Aylesbury are acts of God. And could you say they are not?'

'No, but then both William Lang and George Chapman always reiterate that they pray to God for His help and that all healing comes from God. You don't disbelieve that miracles can happen?' I asked.

'As a Catholic, how could I?' he said. 'All I'm saying is that I'm not convinced that, if miracles happen at Aylesbury, they happen because William Lang supposedly controls George Chapman. And, furthermore, I'm still not sure that miracles are accomplished there. A genuine miracle is a pretty phenomenal thing you know, and takes a hell of a lot of proof. There's such a thing as auto-suggestion, and that's powerful in the right hands.'

We left it at that for a while, agreeing to disagree.

Some little time later I asked Nolan if he would help me with the book by editing it and, where necessary, re-writing any parts that needed such treatment. He agreed, and I was pleased for a number of reasons, not the least of which was my awareness that he would bring a balanced and objective mind to the subject. He would not be 'conned'.

As I gathered the material, travelling up and down the country with my tape-recorder, I fed it to my colleague. I refrained from asking him whether he had undergone any change of mind about William Lang. I wanted him to see all the evidence, read what the patients and the doctors had to say. It was some months before I tackled him again, by which time the book was near completion.

'What do you make of the Lang-Chapman healing successes now?' I enquired.

'I am still not a hundred per cent convinced that the man I met at Aylesbury is the spirit doctor he purports to be,' he said in a semi-apologetic tone.

'And what about the unique healing successes? Do you refute them too?'

'No, I don't refute them,' he said. 'The authenticated case histories would make that very hard to do. There seem to have been some astonishing things done, and I can't pretend to understand how. But it is still too much for me to accept that there is such a thing as an unseen spirit body and that Lang, through Chapman, does operations on it and succeeds. It's investing him with the powers of a God, and that I can't accept.'

'But you are prepared to accept that miracles do happen in some inexplicable way after people visit St Brides, and that also George Chapman is in some strange manner involved?'

'I'm very reluctant to commit myself on it, Joe,' he

219

said. 'Something akin to miracles seems to have occurred. Real miracles? I don't know. And what Chapman's part in the whole scheme of things is I'm not sure of either.

'But yes, I do agree that phenomena of a greater or lesser degree have been attendant upon George Chapman's visit to sick people, and their visits to him. I don't accept your explanation. I'm puzzled.'

'As far as I myself am concerned,' I said, 'I am convinced that it *is* William Lang who works through the mediumship of George Chapman, but – everybody is perfectly entitled to his own view and to accept or reject *my* personal belief.

'In my view the only important issue is the question of whether or not these healing results have in fact happened. I think they've been brought about through Lang-Chapman. I am convinced of this, but you and many other people may argue against it. I also happen to believe that the only ones who are qualified to make an authoritative statement about the effectiveness of William Lang's cures and healing successes are the numerous patients of his who experienced both orthodox medical and spirit healing.

'All those patients whose cases are published in this book are living people, and all of them can hardly be wrong. They are able and willing to testify to the great help and benefit they have received through spirit operations and treatment from William Lang, should the need arise. I don't think it entirely reasonable that any one person should dismiss outright all claims of the Lang-Chapman healing successes while there exist such a large body of people – patients and doctors and nurses – who can testify in favour of the "dead" surgeon and his medium.'

Liam Nolan agreed that the bulk of the evidence was impressive and that to dismiss it lightly would be unreasonable.

The number of people from all walks of life – in this

country and many others – who believe that spirit healing can help the sick and who consequently avail themselves of its unique possibilities, is steadily growing. So far as George Chapman and William Lang are concerned, the rapid increase of patients who request early consultations with the spirit doctor is so great that Chapman finds it most difficult to comply with their desire.

Despite this trend, and despite the fact that some doctors, consultant specialists and hospital authorities accept William Lang's successes, the medical profession as a whole will not accept, at the moment, spirit healing in any degree. Indeed, it was not uncommon that when a convincing case of a miraculous cure by William Lang of a so-called incurable was presented for investigation, some of the medical profession just wagged their heads and said in effect: 'No, we cannot accept this. There must have been a mistake in the diagnosis in the first place.'

In their persistence in refusing to accept evidence these ultra-orthodox members of the medical profession are, in a way, enemies of humanity because *without attempting to engage in any research*, they determinedly dismiss any possibility of healing that does not originate from orthodox medicine. Fortunately, however, not every member of the medical profession thinks and behaves on these 'closed shop' lines. But as long as the present 'official' attitude towards spirit healing prevails, most of them dare not openly express their views, nor can they engage in research for fear that they might be accused of 'unprofessional conduct'.

Is it not strange that scientists everywhere are vying with each other to establish links between the earth and the planets, yet no serious scientific investigations are being made into spirit healing – a matter eminently affecting everyone? To establish a link with George Chapman and William Lang might afford a scientific basis for many discoveries for healing the sick, and for assisting the medical profession.

Though neither George Chapman nor William Lang

has ever claimed that the healing of any spectacular case has been the result of a miracle – indeed, both always emphasised very strongly to me, and to countless other people, that Lang does not perform miracles – miracles *do* happen at Aylesbury.

36

Proficient Changes

IN THE original first edition of *Healing Hands* I presented in considerable detail an accurate and honest description of the formidable spirit operations and treatment successes which George Chapman and William Lang achieved at Aylesbury and the Birmingham Spirit Healing Centre – then still in existence.

I had spent well over a year investigating most thoroughly *every* aspect of Chapman's and Lang's unparalleled accomplishments. I began with picking at random a bundle of records containing entries on how spirit operations and treatment lastingly cured a number of different and once 'medically incurable' diseases. My next move was to tape-record my searching interviews with William Lang, while Chapman was in deep trance, to seek his explanation *why* and *how* spirit operations could cure diseases which our present-day highly advanced orthodox medicine could not do. I also extensively interviewed George Chapman – as well as his wife Margaret who, at that time, acted as receptionist and was in direct contact with the countless patients who talked with her about their illnesses, their progress, and even personal matters – to be familiar with all the information which each of the 'spirit healing team' could give me.

Perhaps my most important task was to ascertain whether orthodox medical case histories confirmed that the patients had indeed been victims of the alleged diseases which were 'medically incurable' yet that later clinical examinations and tests established the disease was no longer detectable, the patient was in good health and –

somehow cured. To enable me to obtain *any* information about the former and present state of health from the patient's doctor, the hospital authorities and consultants, I naturally needed the patients' authorisations in writing to allow their doctors and hospitals to disclose the confidential doctor-to-patient information. However, before attempting to obtain medical evidence, I first wanted to see the patients and tape-record their own accounts of their experiences as they interpreted and recalled them.

With my wife Pearl, who had taken on the double function of being my chauffeur and secretary, we drove thousands of miles to interview every patient most searchingly because I was determined to tape-record *every* detail about their illnesses, medical treatment, spirit operations, and their returning to their own doctors and hospital consultants *after* William Lang told them they were now cured, added their cure was the final result of their often very lengthy spirit healing, reiterated the cure would be a lasting one throughout their lives, and eventually proposed they should see their doctors and hospital consultants who would confirm that their once 'incurable' disease was no longer present. I was surprised by the patients' willingness to disclose every detail I needed to know – even when the informal interview sometimes developed into a necessary cross-examination-type of semi-interrogation – and detailed how Lang performed expert spirit operations which eventually brought about lasting cures. They also recalled how they then visited their doctors and hospital consultants who ordered a number of clinical and other tests needed to be performed. The consultants then announced: no trace of the disease could be detected, which amounted to confirming the patient was cured. And when the interview was completed, each patient unhesitatingly agreed to give me a letter in which the doctor, the hospital authorities and consultants were authorised to disclose the patient's confidential medical case history and to give me any additional information I may require.

Although I presented the patients' letters of authorisation, a quite determined effort was necessary to persuade some doctors, and especially hospital authorities, to comply with their patients' letters of authorisation. I succeeded eventually to establish from the medical case histories records that the patients had indeed been classed 'medically incurable', yet the latest records stated: all tests established that no trace of the disease could be detected. I thus obtained official medical confirmation that Lang's spirit operations and treatment had indeed cured the previously medically incurable patients.

While investigating and writing *Healing Hands* I visited William Lang and George Chapman at St Brides regularly and, performing spirit operations on my eyes in three-monthly intervals, Lang achieved the almost impossible. At his suggestion I was eventually examined by an oculist, and the expert vision test established: my sight had improved so drastically that it met the obligatory requirements for the issuing of car driving licences.

Having amassed irrefutable evidence which established that I presented facts – which not only I, but several fully experienced investigators, specialist researchers, and even high-ranking open-minded members of the Medical Profession checked, counter-checked, and confirmed – I considered it my duty to record *every detail* in *Healing Hands*. My motive was a strictly humanitarian one. I reasoned that at least *some* medically incurable sufferers who endured living in agony and utter despair might perhaps be helped, or maybe even cured, if they had the possibility of being acquainted with the details about Lang's and Chapman's spirit operations and treatment. And if, in utter despair, they decided to 'give spirit healing a try', they had nothing to lose; many could be lucky enough to benefit greatly, and some might even be cured, if seeking spirit healing help at St Brides or the Birmingham Spirit Healing Centre.

Almost as if to justify my belief that *Healing Hands* could become a sort of 'saviour' for many a sufferer whose health condition deteriorated steadily and developed to such an extent that life became unbearable when the most powerful drugs failed even to dull the brutal pain, and quite a few of these plagued people prayed intensely to God to put an end to their inhuman ordeals and let them mercifully die – I was unexpectedly provided with additional evidence of how William Lang's spirit operations can sometimes bring about results which normally would be thought of as being impossible.

While *Healing Hands* was in an advanced stage of production and near publication day, I was involved in an accident. The hospital surgeon diagnosed a torn cartilage in my left knee, the X-rays revealed a broken knee-cap and additional injuries. Treatment proved ineffective, my knee resembled more a balloon than part of the body, and considerable swelling spread – not mentioning the increasing severe pain. The orthopaedic surgeon decided my left leg *must* be *amputated*, consoled me it would be just above the knee, and requested me to sign a form which was my authorisation for him to amputate. I hoped William Lang might be able to save me from losing my leg by performing one or more operations on my spirit body and, instead of signing the form I told the surgeon I needed to think about losing my leg and consequently would not sign the form for the time being.

I telephoned George Chapman immediately and reached him just before he went into trance. Having explained the situation, he proposed we should come to St Brides as quickly as possible and promised to stay in trance until our arrival. Pearl drove me to Aylesbury in record time and we arrived while Lang just attended to his last patient that day.

As he eventually examined me on the healing couch, Lang remarked my injury was very serious and considerable skill was required to save my leg. His once famous Scottish orthopaedic surgeon spirit colleague Mr McEwen performed the complex operation, assisted by William Lang, his surgeon son Basil and several other famous surgeons and helpers who were part of William Lang's team. I closely watched Lang using invisible instruments, and although he never once touched my body during the spirit operation, lasting fifty or so minutes, and his hands handled various unseen instruments at least an inch above my knee and leg, I felt considerably painful incisions and other surgery being made.

The operation on my spirit body completed, William sat exhausted on a nearby chair; from his remark I understood, that Mr McEwen, his son Basil, and the rest of the assisting surgeons and helpers, were equally in need of a short rest. It necessitated special skill and techniques to perform the operations for the diverse injuries simultaneously and within the shortest possible time; in addition they had to use special methods to ensure the operations on the spirit body transferred effectively on to the physical body within the next few days to satisfy the hospital orthopaedic surgeon that amputation was no longer essential.

'You won't lose your leg, Joseph,' Lang eventually assured me with great relief. 'The operations were most successful and you won't ever have any trouble with your knee and leg.' He then instructed me to stay the following day in bed to contribute to the immediate transfer on to my physical body. 'When you see the hospital surgeon the day after tomorrow, when he plans to amputate your leg,' Lang concluded, 'watch his face and reactions on finding out that your trouble is over. A pity no one will be there to take a snap-shot of his facial expression. It would be quite a unique photograph.'

Lang's forecast proved correct in every respect. The surgeon's facial expression was indescribable when he ascertained the drastic change in my condition. And when he ordered immediate X-rays of my left knee and compared them with those taken immediately after the accident and showing the fractured knee-cap, he muttered to his assistant: 'It's incredible that anything like this could happen!' During his thirty years as an orthopaedic surgeon he was confronted with various changes of patients' health conditions which, even if considering every medical aspect, remained unsolved puzzles for which even best qualified consultants and medical researchers failed to find a plausible explanation; he had experienced swellings of various nature and dimension suddenly subsiding and vanishing, so he was not perplexed that the balloon-size swelling of my knee – even though it was perhaps the largest and most serious he ever had to attend – was almost no longer noteworthy; but that the first X-ray clearly showed the fractured knee-cap's step-like condition yet the following X-ray established the same knee-cap was in a perfect condition and not the slightest previous damage could be discovered on the perfect film, even when very closely examining it with a strong magnifying glass, made him almost shudder.

Discharging me, the orthopaedic surgeon made it clear that, should there ever be the slightest recurrence, I was to consult him at once. However, over twelve years elapsed since the hurriedly arranged emergency spirit operations were performed; and, as William Lang predicted at the time, my knee and leg remained permanently in perfect condition.

Not very long after the original first edition of *Healing Hands* was published, proficient changes took place and consequently *Healing Hands* gradually became in parts an incorrect and possibly even a misleading book about George Chapman's and William Lang's present day Spirit Healing Establishment and activities. Consequently, the book needs now to be a fully up-to-date version.

One of the changes was the building of the Healing Annexe – a bungalow-type building – which houses a waiting room, William Lang's consulting room, office accommodation, etc. As soon as the Healing Annexe was erected, William Lang's consulting room was moved from the front room in the Chapman residence and the same applied to the rather small waiting room at the far end of the main building. A purpose-built Spirit Healing Annexe with all the necessary amenities provided improved and undisturbed facilities for William Lang's spirit operations and healing and afforded greater comfort for his patients.

Asking Lang to tell me whether the building of the Healing Annexe was his or George's idea, he replied:

'The Annexe was brought about quite simply for the

convenience of the Chapman family. Maybe one of them wanted to listen to music or watch a television programme, but they had to be quiet because if it was too loud it interfered with our work. This meant that they never had their own home. So it was my suggestion that an Annexe should be built in which we would work without being interrupted, and which also afforded the Chapman family their privacy. I said to Margaret one day to tell George to build an Annexe outside for the office staff and for me to work in. It was built for everyone's convenience.'

'In your original healing room at St Brides you had created certain vibrations which were favourable for achieving healing successes.' I said, 'Was it difficult for you to transfer these assisting vibrations from your former consulting room to the newly built Annexe?'

'No, it doesn't matter,' Lang replied. 'I come here to work and have my vibrations created, because it's my team. What I do want quite simply is to work successfully in any room where there is a nice atmosphere, where – as you would say – you feel at home. That is the important thing. But I can work anywhere. People have said to me – people connected with the Press and people connected with psychic work – "You have built up nice conditions here at St Brides, and we were told that other healers won't work anywhere else than in their sanctuary because they feel they won't get any results at any other place than in their sanctuary." Well, that may be so for those healers, but as far as I am concerned I can work successfully anywhere.'

'So there was no interruption at all,' I commented.

'The only thing is that when you have a new building the building is cold,' Lang explained. 'So you have to put light in it but that's quickly done.'

The Annexe became George Chapman's and William Lang's Aylesbury Spirit Healing H.Q. At first George's wife Margaret acted as receptionist, arranging on Lang's instructions future healing appointments and looking after the patients.

Yet, still another change was made later. Michael Chapman, George's son, took over his mother's receptionist duties. It was his first step towards becoming later a member of the spirit surgeon's healing team.

37

The Best of Both Worlds

JOHN LEADBITTER, am ex-miner of Newton Aycliffe, England, was once one of the many sufferers who accepted his doctor's and hospital consultants' shattering diagnosis that he was 'medically incurable' and fated to endure the hopeless existence of living for ever in agony. But, like so many others with similar hopeless diseases, he came across, and read, the original version of *Healing Hands* which induced him to seek William Lang's help, naturally hoping that spirit operations and treatment might be as successful as those described in *Healing Hands*.

I deliberately selected this particular case from a bulky bundle of equally successful case histories because it reveals so clearly that: (1) Lang discovered precisely the grave root-cause of this patient's serious illness, which his own doctor and hospital consultants somehow failed to detect; and (2) adhering to his practice when dealing with particular 'hopeless' cases, he advised Leadbitter to have orthodox medical treatment in addition.

'Combining our spirit operations and treatment with simultaneous medical treatment does not "clash" with one or the other – quite the contrary,' he explained. 'If orthodox medicine is synchronised with our spirit operations, and if all my instructions are fully complied with, the conjoint effort *can* reverse the initial "incurable" verdict. Sometimes prolonged and uninterrupted conjoint treatment is essential to achieve gradual improvement but – sometimes many years later – the once "hopeless, incurable" condition *can finally be cured!'*

I investigated John Leadbitter's case thoroughly; checked his medical records, studied Lang's case-histories, and discussed this case with him while George Chapman was in trance. I also 'grilled' Leadbitter to give me *his own account* about what transpired. He was most cooperative and, to ensure he gave me *undistorted facts only* of his case which had its origins so many years ago, he obligingly checked the elaborate entries he recorded regularly.

John Leadbitter was born in April 1915. He went to the Browney Colliery School which he left at the age of fourteen. He had no alternative but to work in the coal mine – like all the other school-leavers, and like his father had done throughout his life.

'I worked in the mine twenty-six years, until pneumoconiosis – coal dust in the chest and lungs – deteriorated my health so severely that I was unable to continue being a miner,' Leadbitter described the origin of his steadily increasing suffering. 'The *Pneumoconiosis Board* in Newcastle upon Tyne verified my illness, I was invalided out of the mine in 1956 and awarded a pension. I have to be examined at the *Pneumoconiosis Board* every two years, but the diagnosis is always the same: "No improvement." My disability pension was each time reconfirmed and, since I was invalided out in 1956 after my twenty-six years of mining, it remained in force.'

Between 1956 and 1969 John Leadbitter had various jobs which his impaired health enabled him to do efficiently. His pension was insufficient to live on even most frugally but, instead of claiming supplementary benefit to which he was entitled, he decided to increase his pension by doing light work; he could not bear the mere thought of possibly being looked upon as 'a useless idler' or 'work-shy grabber'. But, uninterruptedly working thirteen years – often with very considerable effort – had an adverse effect upon his steadily deteriorating health condition, which finally put a full stop to any hope of ever resuming work.

'I used to go to the newspaper shop every Saturday

morning to get my paper,' Leadbitter described his 'final downfall' in October 1969. 'Then, just as I walked into the shop, my legs began to buckle under me as if they were rubber, my chest and throat felt like being on fire, I was fighting for breath, and I did not know what was happening. I managed with great effort to get back to my car and drive home.

'I had to wait until Monday morning before my doctor came to examine me. He could not diagnose what was wrong and decided to have me examined by a specialist at our local Bishop Auckland Hospital. I was in a shocking condition and my doctor reiterated my case was urgent, but I had to wait two weeks before I could be examined at the hospital. The diagnosis was "Angina" and I was put on tablets which were not doing one pennyworth of good. The specialist then stated I was "incurable" and added that medical skill and treatment could do nothing for me that would improve my health condition.

'I was at my wits' end because I was clearly turning into a vegetable,' he continued. 'I had no energy left and was almost continuously tormented by the burning in my chest and throat, and besides I often had to fight for breath and sometimes feared I was being choked to death. Worse still was the demoralising fact that I could not walk more than some ten yards without having to stop, lean on my stick and wait until my "rubbery" legs regained sufficient strength to let me walk another short distance. My health was so bad that I did not care whether I lived or died.

'In utter despair I went one night in October 1969 to visit my daughter – Mrs Marian Wheeler – who lived six miles from my place. It was an almost superhuman effort to drive there, but when I eventually arrived it turned out to be my salvation,' he recalled the event. 'She had just read your book *Healing Hands* and suggested I should read it. I was in such a desperate condition that I was willing to try *anything* to get better, so I borrowed the book read it, and wrote at once to Aylesbury for an early appointment. Unfortunately for me, George Chapman replied that he was fully booked, but suggested I should write again in 1970. I did so in January and was happy to get an appointment for April 1970 . . .'

While John Leadbitter suffered and waited for his appointment with William Lang, his daughter moved to Nuneaton. Her change of address made it much easier for her father to drive to Aylesbury. He could start his long journey the day before his appointment, stay over night with his daughter, and drive on the following morning.

'Well, the Great Day for my first visit to St Brides arrived,' Leadbitter said with excitement still detectable in his voice, 'when it was my turn to see the man I had been waiting all these months to meet. Mr Lang, a clearly old-ish man, greeted me with the words, "come in, young man, it's nice to see you . . ." I was overjoyed at being called a "young" man as I was fifty-five years of age then.

'Mr Lang then put me on the healing couch, examined me by slightly touching my fully clad body, and said then: The first and most important thing that was imperative to be done was to strengthen the heart muscles on my spirit body and attempt to clear my lungs. I could hear the snap-snap of his fingers and also calling "Basil" – his "dead" spirit surgeon son who assists him when a spirit operation or other special spirit healing is performed. Half an hour or so later, Mr Lang said I should ease myself off the heal-ing couch as my first healing session was completed, and instructed me that during the next four hours I was not to eat more than a couple of biscuits and drink only one cup of tea. At the end of the four hours I had to have a hot bath and afterwards I could have a good meal. I was to make sure to see him again in six months.'

Leadbitter complied with the spirit surgeon's orders to the letter. Driving back to Nuneaton took almost four hours, so on arrival at his daughter's house he was ready to comply with his strict orders and have his hot bath.

'As I stepped out of the bath to dry myself, I smelled a peculiar odour,' Leadbitter described his stunning ex-perience. 'It smelled like ether – as if someone had been in a hospital for an operation. After pulling the plug to let the water out, the smell disappeared. It was uncanny. But to make sure that I had not been imagining I experienced some sort of supernatural phenomenon, I asked my daughter who had run the bath for me if she had put any disinfectant into the water. When she confirmed she had *not added anything*, we both concluded it had probably been some sort of psychic phenomenon which was somehow connected with the spirit operation and perhaps a supernatural indication that the visit to Mr Lang was a success.'

Having returned to his home, John Leadbitter watched for any, even the slightest, progress to occur. But when he satisfied himself that there was only most insignificant improvement, he was not disappointed that his very first visit to Mr Lang did not produce a 'miracle cure'. He realised that his continuously deteriorating health during the past thirty-nine years could not be cured, or significantly improved, by 'just one initial spirit operation for strengthening the heart muscles and part-cleaning his lungs from deep-rooted coal dust layers' – and especially not when, at the time he first visited St Brides, his energy was at its lowest ever, he 'puffed and panted' when attempting to walk even shortest distances, and endured an existence of almost unbearable suffering.

In October 1970, six months after his first visit to Aylesbury, John Leadbitter went to see Mr Lang again. He hoped that additional spirit operations and treatment might result in some more noticeable improvement. His hopes were not in vain, for Lang assured him that the first spirit operation and treatment were successful. The heart muscles were a little strengthened, and some coal dust was removed from the lungs.

While he performed further spirit operations, Lang stated authoritatively: 'The glands in your body are out of balance and until they can be brought back on an even keel your condition cannot improve satisfactorily.' He suggested Leadbitter should consult his doctor and delicately request him to give him orthodox medical gland

235

treatment; he explained that this would bring about much faster results than if treatment was confined to six-monthly spirit operations and treatment only.

'I saw my doctor after my return from St Brides and popped the question "could my glands perhaps be off balance?"' Leadbitter told me. 'The doctor said "they could be" and sent me for a blood test to the Bishop Auckland Hospital. When he received the hospital report, he explained "the thyroid gland, the main gland in the body, is rather under-active." He put me on thyroid tablets, and I started to regain my energy. My doctor said then "I am pleased I found that out." But had Mr Lang not proposed I should tell my doctor that the glands in my body are out of balance, I feel that I would not have made any progress at all and would be "six feet under" long ago or, alternatively, would be sitting here like a Zombie.'

John Leadbitter's treatment was lengthy – he travelled every six months for seven long years to Aylesbury to have regular spirit operations and treatment from William Lang who – at his request assisted by the patient's doctor – eventually succeeded in reverting the original 'medically incurable' verdict and restored Leadbitter's health to such a degree that he can now live an almost normal life.

'Thanks to our Great Friend Mr Lang I never need to use a walking stick now and am able to walk very nicely,' Leadbitter confirmed. 'And were it not for my daughter who got your marvellous book *Healing Hands*, I would never have known of Mr Lang and spirit operations. This once horrible burning in my chest and throat, the alarming fighting for breath, and all the other suffering I had to endure are now past tortures – like some frightening, ugly nightmares.'

He concluded his 'rather happy ending' account, which he told me on 27 November 1977, with a jubilant ring in his voice:

'I last visited George Chapman three weeks ago. I arrived too early at St Brides and had the pleasure of meeting George for the first time ever while he was

George and not yet in trance with his body taken over by Mr Lang. We had coffee together and a little chat. And when the time came for him to turn into deep trance, he led me into Mr Lang's consulting room.

'This gave me the very privileged and unique opportunity to see both George and Mr Lang together. I watched George like a hawk and was astonished how easily and speedily he slipped into trance and emerged as Mr Lang. Within three or so minutes he had transformed himself into exactly the same oldish Mr Lang whom I had met on every visit to St Brides, and who now greeted me with his usual "it's nice to see you, young man." He was so entirely different from George! I shall *never* forget this so incredible-sounding transformation of one man turning into another before my searching eyes that concentratedly watched every single stage, and it will *always* remain *firmly imprinted in my mind throughout my life*, especially as these daily transformations take place to enable Mr Lang by using George's body to change "medically incurable" verdicts into cures, or at least semi-cures, of once hopeless sufferers. I cannot adequately express how deeply I thank God for having bestowed upon me the rare privilege of being destined to experience the true miracle of my once "incurable" condition having been changed into my present and lasting good health condition.'

When I discussed John Leadbitter's case with William Lang, he declared:

'Yes, it was a very difficult case. Thirty-nine years of steadily deteriorating health cannot be cured, or substantially improved, over night, so to say. I warned young Leadbitter right at the start that his condition was exceptionally serious, that he had come to see me only just in time, and that it would require perhaps many years before we might be able to get him on an even keel. He was, and is, very receptive and this helped us quite a bit when we performed the many urgently needed operations on his spirit body, which we supplemented by giving him additional spirit injections and treatment, and not only

237

when he came to see me at St Brides but also on most nights at his home during his sleep state. We were well aware of the fact that, despite our most concentrated efforts, even the most minute improvement would at first be very, very slow; but we also knew that later, when we succeeded in getting the most serious root cause of his continuously worsening condition back on an even keel, considerable and steadily continuing progress would be made, and young Leadbitter would eventually reap the fruit of our lasting success and enjoy living a trouble-free life.'

'Was it imperative to combine spirit operations and healing with orthodox medical treatment?' I slipped in.

'Not imperative, not at all; we could have achieved exactly the same success ourselves and without outside cooperation,' Lang replied. 'But with this particular case, his progress would have been much slower if he had spirit healing only, and this consideration was the reason for my suggestion that young Leadbitter should supplement his healing by also having the right orthodox medical treatment from his doctor to make very much speedier progress. I explained everything to him and he understood and accepted my suggestion. To ensure his doctor gave him the exact supplementary orthodox treatment I stressed he should use a "diplomatic" approach when broaching the possibility that the glands in his body might be out of balance, and so on. As you know, it worked out admirably.'

'Don't you find it somewhat odd that, even though his patient had conveyed to him your diagnosis about his glands being out of balance, his doctor announced proudly: he was glad that *he detected the gland trouble*?'

'Well, it does not really matter,' he said, smiling condescendingly, as he usually does on similar occasions. 'The one and only thing that does matter to me and all of us is: By having listened to, and by having immediately acted upon, his patient's "delicate" reference to his gland trouble possibility, he *proved to be a doctor who cares for the well-being of his patients and who is ready to go out of his way if it could contribute to alleviating suffering*. Remember, Joseph, that quite often even the best qualified doctor, when examining a *physical* body, just cannot detect causes of such a nature as easily as I can when examining the *spirit* body. Boasting that *he detected the gland trouble* was due to suddenly succumbing to *human ego* – one of the most common human failings of insignificant consequence, to which a very considerable number of people who live in *your* world are subject, even though they are ignorant of this being one of your planet's many peculiar influences. But all this does not have the slightest bearing upon *this doctor being a good and caring one.*'

He concluded with considerable emphasis:

'The only two issues that matter to me, my spirit doctor colleagues and helpers, in this particular case are: (1) that young Leadbitter is now a very different man to what he was when I first saw him seven years ago; and (2) that a flesh-and-blood doctor in *your* world actively and to the best of his ability did *everything* he could to restore his patient's health. After all – regardless if we live in *your* world or in *our* spirit world – *we are all doctors whose first consideration and duty is that, with God's help, we succeed in healing our patients.*'

Afterword

WHEN THIS book was first written I was living in Aylesbury, Buckinghamshire, but some twenty or more years ago Dr Lang suggested it was time to move the practice to mid-Wales. During his life on earth, Dr Lang used to visit the Machynlleth area to relax and do a little salmon fishing with his good friend William Morris, who was godfather to his son, Basil, and daughter, Marie Lyndon.

And so the move to Wales took place. I purchased a property called Pant Glas overlooking the Dovey Estuary. Pant Glas was a very small cottage and a lot of hard work took place over the coming years to develop it into my home and healing centre. Patients from all over the world and from all walks of life come here for appointments with the Spirit Surgeon.

Michael, my son (born 1952), works alongside me in our healing practice. We are a partnership, the same as Dr Lang and his son Basil. Michael has been brought up in the healing practice and studied and trained under Dr Lang, who considers him to be a first class healer in his own right. Besides working here at Pant Glas, he also has clinics he visits regularly within the UK and in Europe.

This leads me to the Birmingham Healing Centre. The Christian Spiritualist Church, Silver Street, Kings Heath, no longer exists. Property developers moved in and that put an end to the church. But this did not mean an end to the story, for Mrs Carter gathered her flock together and organised regular coach trips to me in Aylesbury. Nowadays a coach organised by my good friend Mrs Wright visits our healing sanctuary here in Wales two or three times a year, and, as well as this, Michael visits a clinic in Sheldon every two months. So the Birmingham Healing Centre is still being run to this day.

On 4 February 1995 I will be seventy-four years of age. I am lucky to have Michael who will carry on after my passing. I have no intentions to retire and have never been what you could call ill. I am quite healthy, I have never missed a healing session and I expect to carry on for many years yet.

George Chapman 1995